Pathways to Literature

Virginia Evans – Jenny Dooley

Literature adds to reality, it does not simply describe it. It enriches the necessary competencies that daily life requires and provides; and in this respect, it irrigates the deserts that our lives have already become.

***C. S. Lewis** (1898-1963),*
Irish novelist & poet

Express Publishing

Published by Express Publishing

Liberty House, Greenham Business Park, Newbury,
Berkshire RG19 6HW, United Kingdom
Tel.: (0044) 1635 817 363
Fax: (0044) 1635 817 463
email: inquiries@expresspublishing.co.uk
www.expresspublishing.co.uk

First published 2014
Sixth impression 2019

Made in EU

ISBN 978-1-4715-3351-8

Acknowledgements

Authors' Acknowledgements
We would like to thank all the staff at Express Publishing who have contributed their skills to producing this book. Thanks for their support and patience are due in particular to: Megan Lawton (Editor in Chief); Sean Todd (senior editor); Michael Sadler (editorial assistant); Richard White (senior production controller); the Express design team; Warehouse (recording producers); and Kevin Harris, Kimberly Baker, Steven Gibbs and Christine Little. We would also like to thank those institutions and teachers who piloted the manuscript, and whose comments and feedback were invaluable in the production of the book.

Photograph Acknowledgements
Robinson Crusoe: © age/smartmagna.com on p. 50; © corbis/smartmagna.com on pp. 51, 54; **Gulliver's Travels:** © corbis/smartmagna.com on pp. 64, 65; **Pride and Prejudice:** © everett/www.iml.gr on pp. 67, 68, 70, 72; © newscom/www.iml.gr on p. 71; © sipa/www.iml.gr on p. 74; **Wuthering Heights:** © everett/www.iml.gr on pp. 87, 88, 89, 90, 92; **Great Expectations:** © eyevine/www.iml.gr on pp. 107, 108, 112; © everett/www.iml.gr on pp. 107, 109, 110, 112; **Strange Case of Dr Jekyll and Mr Hyde:** © corbis/smartmagna.com on p. 119; **The Picture of Dorian Gray:** © age/smartmagna.com on p. 125; **Romeo and Juliet:** © corbis/smartmagna.com on pp. 163, 166; **Hamlet:** © corbis/smartmagna.com on pp. 174, 175, 176; © everett/www.iml.gr on pp. 164, 169, 170, 174; © akgnewsco/www.iml.gr on pp. 172, 174; **As you Like it:** © corbis/smartmagna.com on pp. 180, 184; **Dr Faustus:** © akgnewsco/www.iml.gr on p. 191; © everett/www.iml.gr on pp. 189, 195; **The Importance of Being Earnest:** © everett/www.iml.gr on pp. 199, 200, 202, 204, 206

Every effort has been made to trace all the copyright holders. If any have been inadvertently overlooked, the publishers will be pleased to make the necessary arrangements at the first opportunity.

Contents

Introduction .... p. 4

Poetry .... p. 11

Unit 1 *Sonnet 18*, William Shakespeare .... p. 12

Unit 2 *She Walks in Beauty*, Lord Byron .... p. 22

Unit 3 *Ulysses*, Alfred, Lord Tennyson .... p. 32

Prose .... p. 45

Unit 1 *Robinson Crusoe*, Daniel Defoe .... p. 46

Unit 2 *Gulliver's Travels*, Jonathan Swift .... p. 56

Unit 3 *Pride and Prejudice*, Jane Austen .... p. 66

Unit 4 *Frankenstein*, Mary Shelley .... p. 76

Unit 5 *Wuthering Heights*, Emily Brontë .... p. 86

Unit 6 *Moby Dick*, Herman Melville .... p. 96

Unit 7 *Great Expectations*, Charles Dickens .... p. 106

Unit 8 *Strange Case of Dr. Jekyll and Mr. Hyde*, Robert Louis Stevenson .... p. 116

Unit 9 *The Picture of Dorian Gray*, Oscar Wilde .... p. 126

Unit 10 *The Time Machine*, H. G. Wells .... p. 136

Unit 11 *The Hound of the Baskervilles*, Sir Arthur Conan Doyle .... p. 146

Drama .... p. 157

Unit 1 *Romeo and Juliet*, William Shakespeare .... p. 158

Unit 2 *Hamlet*, William Shakespeare .... p. 168

Unit 3 *As You Like It*, William Shakespeare .... p. 178

Unit 4 *Doctor Faustus*, Christopher Marlowe .... p. 188

Unit 5 *The Importance of Being Earnest*, Oscar Wilde .... p. 198

Video Activities & Essay Writing .... p. 208

Glossary .... p. 227

Introduction

Types of literature

Poetry

Poetry is any kind of written text that focuses on sound. Poems are written in lines and stanzas (sets of lines). The syllables and words in a poem are put together in a specific way, giving it a particular rhythm called a **meter** – though there are poems that are free of form and may not have a regular meter. *If* by Rudyard Kipling is an example of a poem with a meter; *The Waste Land* by T.S. Eliot an example of one without. Sonnets and epic poems like the *Iliad* by Homer are also types of poems.

Prose

Prose is any kind of written text that isn't poetry. The most common types of prose are novels and short stories, while other types include biographies, memoirs, diaries, and journals. Prose is written in complete sentences and organized in paragraphs and focuses on plot and characters. *Moby Dick* by Herman Melville is an example of prose.

Drama

Drama is literature that is written in order to be performed. A work that is meant to be performed in the theater is called a play. Plays consists mainly of dialogue with some stage directions. *Hamlet* by William Shakespeare is an example of a play.

1 **Label the following extracts** *poetry*, *prose*, **or** *drama*.

a ....

Act 1, Scene 1

Enter SAMPSON and GREGORY, with swords and bucklers, of the house of Capulet.

SAMPSON: Gregory, o' my word, we'll not carry coals.
GREGORY: No, for then we should be colliers.

b ....

CHAPTER 1

The studio was filled with the rich odour of roses, and when the light summer wind stirred amidst the trees of the garden, there came through the open door the heavy scent of the lilac, or the more delicate perfume of the pink-flowering thorn.

c ....

The Raven

Once upon a midnight dreary, while I pondered weak and weary,
Over many a quaint and curious volume of forgotten lore,
While I nodded, nearly napping, suddenly there came a tapping,
As of some one gently rapping, rapping at my chamber door.

Literary elements

Poetry

A **foot** is a group of stressed and unstressed syllables that a line of poetry can be divided into.

- **iamb** – one unstressed syllable followed by one stressed one (gives a natural sound to the poem): relax, unfair, To be ...
- **spondee** – two stressed syllables (often used for emphasis): well-loved, blood boil, There goes ...
- **trochee** – one stressed syllable followed by one unstressed one (gives a sing-song rhythm to the poem): hoping, darkness, Go now ...
- **anapest** – two unstressed syllables followed by one stressed one (often used in longer poems): incomplete, misinformed, On the way ...
- **dactyl** – one stressed syllable followed by two unstressed ones (often used in classical Greek or Latin texts to create a pulse in a poem): marmalade, criminal, Under the ...

2 **What kind of foot is circled in each line of poetry? Write** *iamb*, *spondee*, *trochee*, *anapest*, **or** *dactyl*.

1 ....

There lies the port; the vessel puffs her sail

(*Ulysses* by Alfred Lord Tennyson)

2 ....

Twas the night before Christmas and all through the house

(*Twas the Night Before Christmas* by Clement Clarke Moore)

3 ....

Cannon to right of them,

Cannon to left of them

(*The Charge of the Light Brigade* by Alfred Lord Tennyson)

4 ....

Shall I compare thee to a summer's day?

(*Sonnet 18* by William Shakespeare)

5 ....

And the silken sad uncertain rustling of each purple curtain

(*The Raven* by Edgar Allan Poe)

Figurative language

- **simile** – a comparison of two things, often using the words *like* or *as*: *Oliver ran like the wind.*
- **metaphor** – a strong comparison made by stating one thing *is* another, without using *like* or *as*: *The city is a jungle.*
- **personification** – giving human characteristics to objects and phenomena: *Lightning **attacked** the ground from an **angry** sky.*
- **onomatopoeia** – the use of words that imitate the sounds they describe: *The bees **buzzed** from flower to flower and the birds **chirped** in the trees.*
- **hyperbole** – exaggeration in order to draw attention to something, or for humorous effect: *These books weigh a ton!*
- **irony** – where the true meaning behind a statement is intentionally quite the opposite of its literal meaning: *"Lovely weather," said Kate, looking out of the window at the pouring rain.*
- **alliteration** – the repetition of the same sounds at the beginning of words or in a stressed syllable: *The **s**oldier **s**tood **s**ilent and **s**till.*
- **assonance** – the repetition of vowel sounds in nearby words: *The hunter st**o**pped, c**o**cked his gun, and sh**o**t.*
- **pun** – the humorous or rhetorical effect achieved due to the resemblance in sound between two words: *Broken pencils are pointless.*
- **oxymoron** – a phrase which contains words that seem to contradict one another: *It's an **open secret** that their marriage is in trouble.*
- **imagery** – the use of description to draw the reader into the story. Imagery can be visual (pertaining to sight): *bright sunshine;* **auditory** (pertaining to sound): *a booming voice;* **olfactory** (pertaining to smell): *acrid smoke;* **gustatory** (pertaining to taste): *sweet grapes;* **tactile** (pertaining to touch): *soft skin;* **kinesthetic** (pertaining to movement): *the bobbing boats;* or **organic/subjective** (pertaining to internal bodily sensations, including hunger, thirst, and fatigue): *an exhausted sigh.*

3 **Choose which type of figurative language is being used each time.**

1 **simile/metaphor**

a *All the world's a stage,*
And all the men and women merely players
(*As You Like It* by William Shakespeare) ....

b *Curley was flopping like a fish on a line*
(*Of Mice and Men* by John Steinbeck) ....

2 **personification/onomatopoeia**

a *The earth hath swallowed all my hopes.*
(*Romeo and Juliet* by William Shakespeare) ....

b *... then he heard the clack on stone and the leaping, dropping clicks of a small rock falling.*
(*For Whom the Bell Tolls* by Ernest Hemingway) ....

3 hyperbole/irony

a *I was quaking from head to foot, and could have hung my hat on my eyes, they stuck out so far.*
(*Old Times on the Mississippi* by Mark Twain) ....

b *He looked about as pleasant and relaxed as a coiled rattlesnake.*
(*Breakfast of Champions* by Kurt Vonnegut) ....

4 alliteration/assonance

a *The fair breeze blew, the white foam flew,*
The furrow followed free;
We were the first that ever burst
Into that silent sea.
(*The Rime of the Ancient Mariner* by Samuel Taylor Coleridge) ....

b *Old age should burn and rave at close of day;*
Rage, rage, against the dying of the light.
(*Do Not Go Gentle into that Good Night* by Dylan Thomas) ....

5 pun/oxymoron

a *Not I, believe me: you have dancing shoes*
With nimble soles: I have a soul of lead
So stakes me to the ground I cannot move.
(*Romeo and Juliet* by William Shakespeare) ....

b *Feather of lead, bright smoke, cold fire, sick health!*
(*Romeo and Juliet* by William Shakespeare) ....

6 visual/auditory/olfactory/gustatory/tactile/kinesthetic/organic

a *Tossing their heads in sprightly dance*
(*Daffodils* by William Wordsworth) .... **imagery**

b *So love will take between the hands a face ...*
(*The Moon Compasses* by Robert Frost) .... **imagery**

c *... the yellow brick building, with its tall smokestack ...*
(*My Father on the Verge of Disgrace* by John Updike) .... **imagery**

d *In the daytime ... these motors made a petulant, irritable sound ...*
(*Once More to the Lake* by E.B. White) .... **imagery**

e *The studio was filled with the rich odour of roses ...*
(*The Picture of Dorian Gray* by Oscar Wilde) .... **imagery**

f *I was ready to perish for thirst but so weak I had not strength ...*
(*Robinson Crusoe* by Daniel Defoe) .... **imagery**

g *Mr Leopold Bloom ... liked thick giblet soup, nutty gizzards,*
a stuffed roast heart, liverslices fried with crustcrumbs,
fried hencods' roes.
(*Ulysses* by James Joyce) .... **imagery**

Point of view & narrator

The **point of view** of a story refers to who tells the story or how the story is told. It can sometimes show the author's intentions.

The **narrator** is the person telling the story. The narrator may or may not be a character in the story.

Types of narrator

- **first-person** – the narrator participates in the action, telling it from their point of view, but sometimes has limited knowledge: *When I saw his face I realized that something was wrong.*
- **second-person** – the narrator addresses the reader directly, as though the reader were part of the story: *You walk into your bedroom. You see clutter everywhere and ...*
- **third-person** – the narrator is not known and does not participate in the story, telling it from another person's or other people's point of view.
- **omniscient** – the narrator knows what each character is thinking, feeling, and doing throughout the story. An omniscient narrator has multiple perspectives and may follow one character for a few chapters, and then follow another character for a few chapters, etc.
- **limited** – the narrator knows only part of the whole truth, and may learn as the reader does, make mistakes or draw wrong conclusions that confuse the reader, or even set out to purposely mislead the reader.

4 Choose which kind of narrator is recounting the story in these extracts.

1 a first-person b second-person

You are not the kind of guy who would be at a place like this at this time of the morning. But here you are ...

(*Bright Lights, Big City* by Jay McInerney)

2 a first-person b third-person

Last night I dreamt I went to Manderley again ...

(*Rebecca* by Daphne du Maurier)

3 a second-person b third-person

He was an old man who fished alone in a skiff in the Gulf Stream and he had gone eighty-four days now without taking a fish.

(*The Old Man and the Sea* by Ernest Hemingway)

4 a omniscient b limited

Happy families are all alike; every unhappy family is unhappy in its own way. Everything was in confusion in the Oblonskys' house. The wife had discovered ...

(*Anna Karenina* by Leo Tolstoy)

5 a omniscient b limited

There is something wrong with his appearance; something displeasing, something down-right detestable. I never saw a man I so disliked, and yet I scarce know why.

(*Strange Case of Dr. Jekyll and Mr. Hyde* by Robert Louis Stevenson)

Setting & plot

- The **setting** is the time and place in which the story takes place. For example, the novel *Gone With the Wind* takes place in and around Atlanta, Georgia, during and after the American Civil War.
- The **plot** is what happens in a story. For example, a fisherman's fight with a giant fish is the plot of Ernest Hemingway's allegorical novel *The Old Man and the Sea.* There are many different plots, but they usually follow the same pattern. This is called the **story arc**, and it is depicted in the diagram below.

5 **Match the story arc elements a-e with definitions 1-5.**

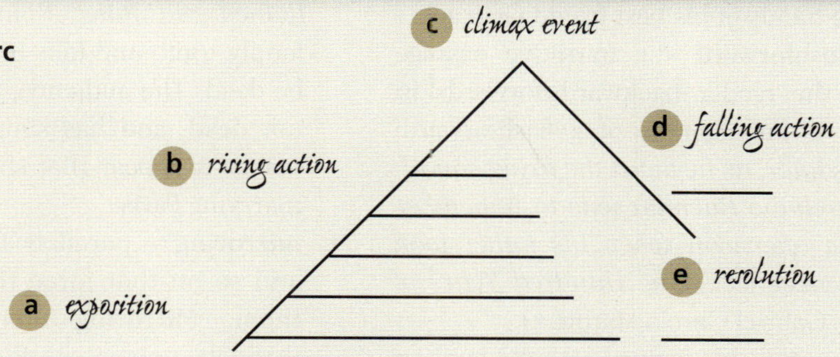

1 ☐	the turning point of the story, where events come to a head
2 ☐	the events that follow and result from the climax
3 ☐	a series of events that build up tension, leading to the climax
4 ☐	the end of the story, where the conflict is resolved
5 ☐	the introduction of the story, giving background on setting, characters, and conflict

Characters

- **protagonist** – the main character in a story
- **antagonist** – the character in conflict with the protagonist
- **major characters** – the important people in a story, complex characters that grow, change, and react
- **foil characters** – characters with opposite traits to a main character, appearing to give emphasis to the main character's traits
- **minor characters** – the flat or one-sided characters in a story, who remain undeveloped

6 **Read the summary of a novel and use the people in bold to complete the table.**

Moby Dick tells the story of **Captain Ahab** and his pursuit of his enemy, a white whale called **Moby Dick.** Moby Dick bit Ahab's leg off on a previous voyage, and Ahab has sworn revenge. The story is told by a young man called **Ishmael,** who has never been on a whaling voyage before. Ishmael, his friend **Queequeg,** and all the other members of the crew are infected by Ahab's bloodlust, with the exception of the chief mate, **Starbuck,** who sees whaling as a way to make a living, and nothing else. His down-to-earth thinking, however, is no match for Ahab's monomania.

protagonist	antagonist	major character	foil character	minor character

Literary techniques

- **foreshadowing** – the use of hints or clues to suggest what will happen later in a story. It is used to create suspense and a sense of the inevitable. A good example of foreshadowing is in John Steinbeck's *Of Mice and Men,* where Candy's ancient dog is shot in the back of the head to prevent its suffering. This foreshadows both the manner of and reason for Lennie's death at the hands of his best friend George.
- **flashback/flashforward** – a narrative passage that takes the reader backwards/forwards in time. Here is an example of a flashforward: *Many years later, as he faced the firing squad, Colonel Aureliano Buendia was to remember that distant afternoon when his father took him to discover ice.* (*One Hundred Years of Solitude* by Gabriel Garcia Marquez)
- **motif** – a recognizable feature within a book or a genre. A key quality of a motif is that it is repeated. The wicked stepmother and sets of three are common motifs in fairy tales.
- **symbolism** – using an object or something else to stand for an idea. This may be a stock symbol such as the dove as a symbol of peace, or it may be something that appears in a story and gains its own significance. For instance, in William Golding's *Lord of the Flies,* the boys use the sound of the conch shell to call meetings. The conch shell comes to symbolize community, and when it is broken, the reader understands that society has completely broken down on the island.
- **allusion** – referencing another literary text or source. For example, when James Joyce named one of the main characters in *Ulysses* Stephen Dedalus, it was an allusion to Daedalus, designer of the Labyrinth and father of Icarus in ancient Greek mythology.
- **situational irony** – when the result of a situation is at odds with the audience's or reader's expectation. A good example is the O. Henry story *The Gift of the Magi,* which depicts a young husband and wife who are very much in love but so poor that they can't afford to buy each other Christmas presents. The woman cuts off her beautiful long hair to sell it to a wig-maker, and uses the money to buy her husband a chain for his pocket watch. On Christmas Day she discovers her husband has sold his watch to buy her combs for her hair.
- **dramatic irony** – when the audience knows more than a character in a story. The character's words and actions have an extra significance that the character is ignorant of. For example, in the final act of Shakespeare's *Romeo and Juliet,* Romeo finds Juliet in her family tomb and kills himself, believing her to be dead. The audience, however, knows she is not dead, and has simply taken a drug that makes it appear that she is, in order to avoid marrying Paris.
- **mirroring** – parallels in characters, events, and so on that force the reader to compare them. Mirroring can also be achieved through opposites. For example, the two main locations in Emily Bronte's *Wuthering Heights* use this technique; Wuthering Heights is a dark forbidding house high in the wild moors, whereas Thrushcross Grange is a bright, spacious mansion set in beautiful grounds in the green valley.
- **conflict** – the disagreement, discord, or contradiction that creates the need for change in a story. Conflict can be internal (within the protagonist) or external (between the protagonist and some other character or entity).

  man versus self (internal) – the struggle between the protagonist and their conscience as, for example, in Christopher Marlowe's *Doctor Faustus.*

  man versus nature (external) – the struggle between the character and some element of nature, such as Captain Ahab's struggle with the whale in *Moby Dick.*

  man versus man (external) – the struggle between two characters in a story, for instance, the fight for leadership between Jack and Ralph in William Golding's *Lord of the Flies.*

  man versus society (external) – the struggle between a character and the rules or laws that govern the society where they live; *1984* by George Orwell is a classic case of this type of conflict.

Poetry

(1609-1842)

Sonnet 18

Objectives

By the end of this unit, you will:

• know about the author and the background information behind the poem • thoroughly understand the poem • be able to identify figurative language in the poem • be able to summarize the poem • be able to put the poem into modern English • be able to analyze the characters, symbols, meter, and themes of the poem • know and be able to describe the structure of a Shakespearean sonnet • be able to use the poem to support your opinions and write a literature essay

VIDEO

Learn About ... William Shakespeare

William Shakespeare (1564-1616) was an English playwright and poet. He is most famous for his plays, but his sonnets are equally important. These short poems are usually love poems addressed to a particular person. Shakespeare wrote at least 154 sonnets. He wrote them when he was already very famous for his plays. Experts place the sonnets into three groups, each addressed to a different person. There are many guesses as to the identity of the three different subjects of the sonnets. Some people think that they know exactly who Shakespeare was writing to. Others, however, don't think that he was writing to any real people at all. The debate will probably not end any time soon, but it doesn't really matter. People can enjoy these poems regardless of who they were written for.

Predict

Step 1

Discuss these questions with a partner.

1 Why is love a popular subject in poetry?

2 Do you think that writing a poem is a good way to tell a person that you love him or her? Why or why not?

Step 2

Look at the key words from *Sonnet 18*. **With a partner, discuss the meaning of the words. Based on the words, predict the main ideas in the poem.**

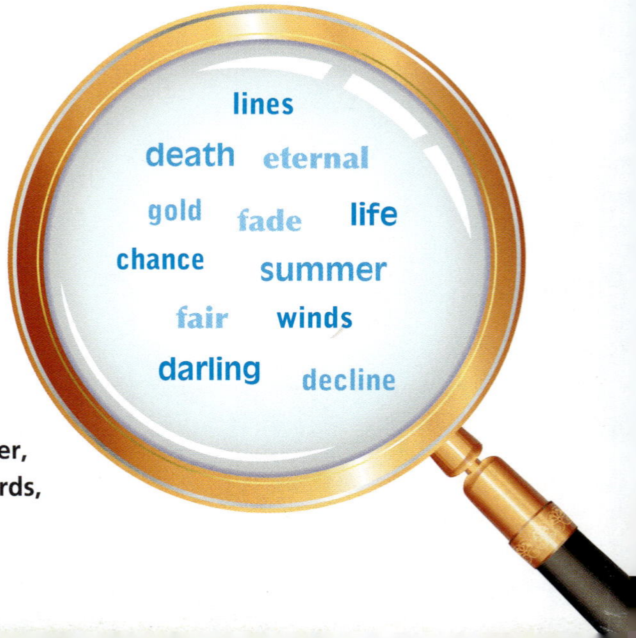

Background information

1 **Read the text and answer the questions.**

1. When was the sonnet published?
2. What type of poem is it?
3. What is the poem about?
4. When and where does it take place?

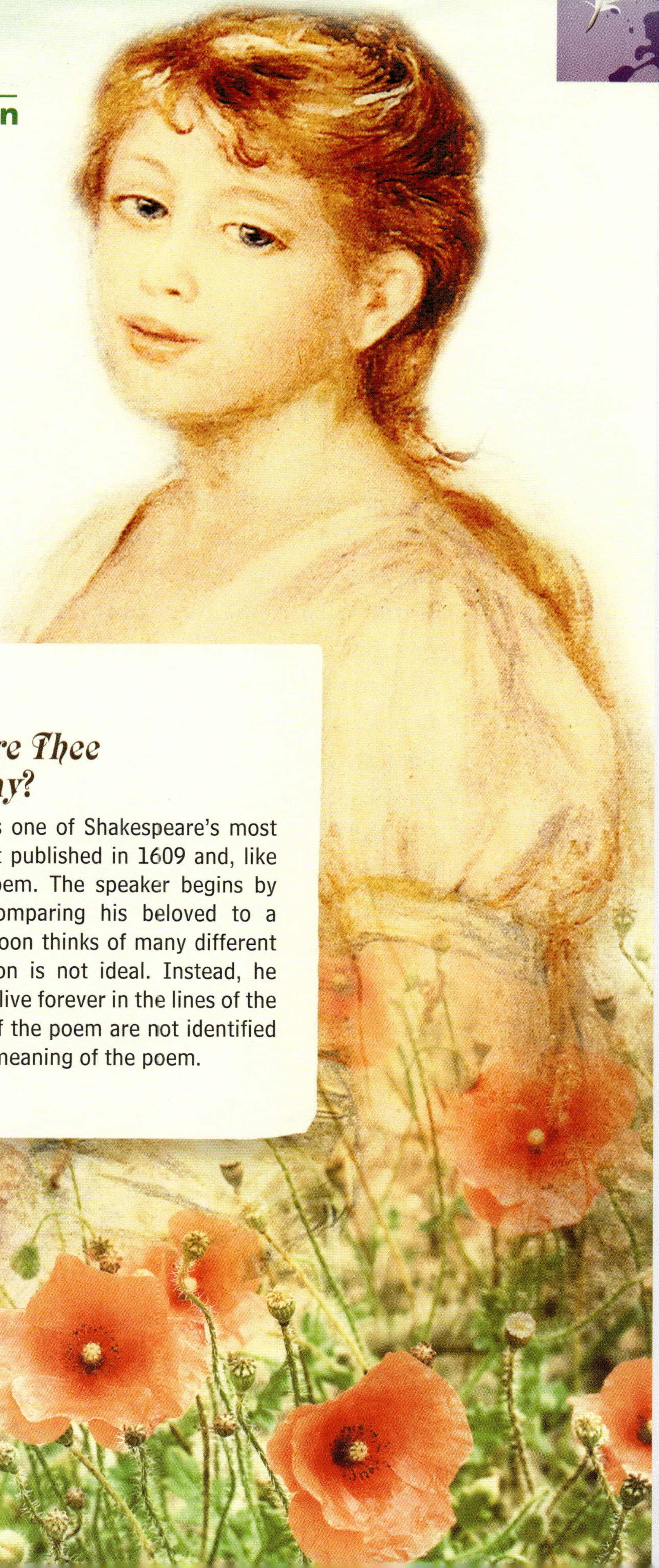

Sonnet 18, or *Shall I Compare Thee to a Summer's Day?*

as it is sometimes called, is one of Shakespeare's most famous sonnets. It was first published in 1609 and, like many sonnets, is a love poem. The speaker begins by considering the idea of comparing his beloved to a summer day. However, he soon thinks of many different reasons why this comparison is not ideal. Instead, he realizes that his beloved will live forever in the lines of the poem. The time and place of the poem are not identified and are unimportant to the meaning of the poem.

1

Listen & Read

2 **Listen to and read *Sonnet 18*. First, read for general understanding. Then, reread the poem. As you read the second time, ask yourself: what imagery does Shakespeare use in the sonnet, and why?**

Sonnet 18

Shall I compare thee to a summer's day?
Thou art more lovely and more temperate:
Rough winds do shake the darling buds of May,
And summer's lease hath all too short a date:
Sometime too hot the eye of heaven shines,
And often is his gold complexion dimm'd;
And every fair from fair sometime declines,
By chance or nature's changing course untrimm'd;
But thy eternal summer shall not fade
Nor losepossession of that fair thou ow'st;
Nor shall Death brag thou wander'st in his shade,
When in eternal lines to time thou grow'st:
So long as men can breathe or eyes can see,
So long lives this and this gives life to thee.

Respond

3 **Respond to the poem by answering these questions with a partner.**

1. Was your prediction about the main ideas of the poem correct? Explain.
2. How did the author communicate the main ideas? Pick one (or more) and explain.

   a with images **b** with dialogue **c** by presenting them directly
3. Which of the words in the phrase bank do you think best describe how the speaker feels in the poem? Explain.

Phrase Bank

- sad
- joyful
- in love
- thoughtful
- proud
- excited
- nervous

Understand

4 **Read the questions and choose the correct answers.**

1. What does the speaker say about a summer day?

   a It is not as lovely as his beloved.

   b It is normally very hot.

   c It is calm and temperate.

   d It is usually windy.

2. Beautiful things become less beautiful because of chance and ....

   a death

   b nature

   c fate

   d time

3. What will allow the beloved to live forever?

   a the summer day

   b the poem

   c the beloved's beauty

   d the speaker's feelings

4. What does "this" refer to in the last line of the poem?

   a the beloved's beauty

   b the summer

   c nature

   d the poem itself

Figurative Language

5 **Work with a partner. Find two examples of personification and one example of a pun in the poem.**

Summarize

6 **First, fill in the graphic organizer based on the poem you read.**

Character(s)	Main Idea(s)

7 **Now, use your graphic organizer to summarize the poem with a partner.**

Listen

8 **Listen to a tutorial about** *Sonnet 18*. **Then, answer the questions.**

1 What is the tutorial mostly about?
- **a** a comparison of two symbols
- **b** an analysis of a symbol
- **c** reasons why authors use symbols
- **d** ways that symbols change

2 What makes the sun imperfect?
- **a** It is always too hot.
- **b** It is not usually bright enough.
- **c** It is only fully lovely in summer.
- **d** It is always covered in clouds.

3 What does the sun symbolize in the poem?
- **a** true love
- **b** lost childhood
- **c** past summers
- **d** natural beauty

4 What does NOT symbolize the imperfection of natural beauty in the poem?
- **a** the poem itself
- **b** flowers
- **c** a summer's day
- **d** the season of summer

Translate

9 **Shakespeare wrote** *Sonnet 18* **sometime after 1600. The language that he used is very different from the English that people use today. Look at the example below. Use it as a guide to translate the rest of the poem into modern English with a partner.**

Original	**Modern**
Shall I compare thee to a summer's day?	*Can I compare you to a summer day?*
Thou art more lovely and more temperate:	*You are much lovelier than a summer day.*
Rough winds do shake the darling buds of May,	
And summer's lease hath all too short a date:	
Sometime too hot the eye of heaven shines,	
And often is his gold complexion dimm'd;	
And every fair from fair sometime declines,	
By chance or nature's changing course untrimm'd;	
But thy eternal summer shall not fade	
Nor lose possession of that fair thou ow'st;	
Nor shall Death brag thou wander'st in his shade,	
When in eternal lines to time thou grow'st:	
So long as men can breathe or eyes can see,	
So long lives this and this gives life to thee.	

About the Title

10 **Shakespeare did not give his sonnets formal titles – at least not that we know of. Instead, we use numbers to refer to the sonnets (informally, many people also use the first line of the sonnet). The numbers show the order in which the sonnets were originally published. This order may or may not be arbitrary. It's uncertain whether or not Shakespeare was actually involved in the publication of the sonnets. Many believe that someone published them without his permission. As such, the title of** *Sonnet 18* **does not carry much – if any – special significance.**

What title would you give the poem? Why? Discuss your answer with a partner.

Analyze the Characters

11 Fill It In.

First, listen to the tutorial. Then, use words from the phrase bank to complete the graphic organizer.

Phrase Bank

- lovely
- a writer
- loves someone
- young
- temperate
- high self-esteem

The Speaker	The Beloved

12 Think About It.

Use the graphic organizer to answer the following questions.

- What do you know about the speaker?
- What do you know about the beloved?
- Which character do you know more about, the speaker or the beloved?

13 Talk It Over.

With a partner, discuss your answers to the previous questions. Then, discuss the following questions together.

- This poem is supposed to be about the speaker's beloved. Why do you think that the speaker doesn't spend more time describing the person that he loves?
- Who is the main character of the poem, the speaker or the beloved?
- If you were the beloved, how would you feel about reading this poem?

Analyze the Symbols

14 Match It.

A symbol is something that stands for something else. For example, a rose can symbolize love. Match the symbols from the poem to their meanings.

	Symbols		Meanings
1	summer	A	beauty
2	darling buds of May	B	chance or fate
3	unpredictable weather	C	youth

15 Think About It.

With a partner, discuss your answers to the previous step. Why did you choose those answers?

16 Talk It Over.

In groups of four, talk about which symbol you think is most important to the poem and why. Agree on a symbol in your group and choose one group member to report to the rest of the class.

Analyze the Meter

17 Mark It Up.

Reread the poem. Underline the syllables that are emphasized. Then listen to the poem again to check your work. The first line is given here as an example.

Shall I compare thee to a summer's day?

Iambic pentameter is a special kind of rhythm, or meter. An iamb is a pattern of an unstressed syllable followed by a stressed syllable. The prefix penta- means five. So lines of iambic pentameter have five iambs – five sets of one unstressed and one stressed syllable. Most Shakespearean sonnets use this rhythm.

18 Think About It.

Answer the following questions with a partner.

- Is every unstressed syllable followed by a stressed one?
- How many syllables are in each line?
- Does the poem follow the rules of iambic pentameter strictly?

19 Talk It Over.

As a class, discuss the importance of meter in a poem. Why did Shakespeare choose iambic pentameter for most of his sonnets?

Analyze the Themes

20 Fill It In.

The most obvious theme in *Sonnet 18* is the speaker's love for the beloved. Another important theme, however, is immortality (eternal life) and how to achieve that. Fill in the graphic organizer with lines from the poem that relate to the two different themes.

Theme	Lines from Poem
love	
immortality	

21 Think About It.

Which theme do you think is most important to the poem and why?

22 Talk It Over.

With a partner, discuss your answer to the previous question.

In-Depth Analysis: Sonnets

A sonnet is a specific kind of poem. It follows a particular rhyme scheme and has a set number of lines. Sonnets originated in Italy in the thirteenth century. They became very popular and eventually spread to other countries, including England. In England, the form of the sonnet changed slightly, and it is in this tradition that Shakespeare wrote his famous sonnets.

English sonnets (sometimes called Shakespearean sonnets) are structured in very particular ways. For one thing, they all have fourteen lines. These lines are broken into four groups: three quatrains and one couplet at the end. A quatrain is a group of four lines; a couplet is a group of two lines. The quatrains have an alternating rhyme scheme. That is, the first quatrain's rhyme scheme is ABAB, the second's is CDCD, and the third's EFEF. The couplet comes at the very end of the sonnet. In Shakespearean sonnets, the couplet's rhyme scheme is GG. In sum, the sonnet's structure is: ABAB CDCD EFEF GG.

A sonnet is more than just its form, however. The content of a sonnet is equally as important. Many sonnets are love poems. Traditionally, the first half of a sonnet presents a problem, or a question. The second half presents an answer or resolution. One line in the poem (usually the ninth) functions as the turning point in the poem. It signifies the shift from "problem" to "resolution." This is called the "volta," which means "turn" in Italian. Shakespearean sonnets don't follow this exact pattern. That is, there is not always a strict problem or question. However, the *volta* is still present and it does represent a shift in tone or mood. In most Shakespearean sonnets, the ninth line of the poem usually marks the *volta*. In addition to the *volta*, the couplet at the end also has special significance. It usually serves to sum up the main idea or dominant feeling of the poem.

23 **Read the In-Depth Analysis and answer the following questions individually.**

- Based on the In-Depth Analysis, what do you expect the rhyme scheme of *Sonnet 18* will be?
- Reread the poem. Mark the rhyme scheme. For each new rhyme, use a new letter. When a rhyme repeats, repeat that letter. The first quatrain is given below as an example.

Shall I compare thee to a summer's day?	*A*
Thou art more lovely and more temperate:*	*B*
Rough winds do shake the darling buds of May,	*A*
And summer's lease hath all too short a date:	*B*

* In Shakespeare's time, the word "temperate" would have been pronounced [ˈtɛmpərˌeɪt], making it rhyme with the word "date." Today, however, we pronounce the word [ˈtɛmprɪt].

- How closely does *Sonnet 18* maintain the rhyme scheme of a typical sonnet? Can you identify the quatrains and the couplet?

24 **Reread the poem with a partner. Pay close attention to line 9. Then, with a partner, answer the following questions.**

- What is the poem about BEFORE line 9?
- What does the speaker say in line 9?
- What is the poem about AFTER line 9?
- What is the shift or change that you see in this line?

25 **Now, focus on the last two lines of the poem, the couplet. Discuss the following questions with a partner.**

- What does the couplet mean?
- How does the message of the couplet relate to the poem as a whole?

Write

26 **In** *Sonnet 18*, **the speaker tells his beloved that the poem will allow the beloved to live forever. This theme of immortality is one of the most important in the poem. In a 250- to 300-word essay, explain how the speaker communicates the theme of immortality. Include lines from the poem and explain their significance to the theme of immortality and the idea that beauty will live forever in the poem.**

VIDEO See p. 208 for video activities & essay writing

2 She Walks in Beauty

Objectives

By the end of this unit, you will:

• know about the author and the background information behind the poem • thoroughly understand the poem • be able to identify figurative language in the poem • be able to summarize the poem • be able to analyze the title, characters, symbols, meter and rhyme, and themes of the poem • know about Romanticism in some depth • be able to use the poem to support your opinions and write a literature essay

VIDEO

Learn About ... Lord Byron

Lord Byron (1788-1824) was an English poet, and one of the most important and well-known figures of the Romantic movement. Romanticism was a reaction against the cold, logical thinking of the eighteenth century. Romantic writers focused on the natural world, emotions, and passion. These last two words also characterize the life of Lord Byron. He was one of the first literary celebrities – and he was always in the middle of a scandal. He left Britain for good in 1816 when his wife divorced him. His many illicit love affairs were causing too much unnecessary attention and gossip. He moved around a lot in Europe, and in 1823 he decided to go to Greece and help the Greeks fight for their independence from the Ottoman Empire. While he was helping the Greek soldiers, he got sick. His doctors could not cure him, and he died.

Today, Lord Byron is remembered as a passionate and talented poet. Though his life was cut short, his achievements and poetry continue to inspire people to this day.

Predict

Step 1

Discuss these questions with a partner.

1 Why do you think beauty is a common topic in poetry?

2 How can words communicate the idea of visual beauty?

Step 2

Look at the key words from *She Walks in Beauty*. With a partner, discuss the meaning of the words. Based on the words, predict the main ideas in the poem.

Background information

1 Read the text and answer the questions.

1. What is the poem about?
2. How does Byron perceive a woman's beauty in the poem?
3. Is it a new approach to praising a woman's beauty?
4. What does Byron admire in the woman?

She Walks in Beauty

is one of Lord Byron's most famous poems. It describes a beautiful woman – but it's not necessarily a love poem. Byron admires the woman's beauty, but he doesn't talk about his feelings toward her. Instead, she's more like an object or a piece of art. She's admired for her appearance and otherwise given little thought. The poem continues the long tradition of praising a woman for her beauty. In addition, Byron admires the woman's innocence and purity of thought. *She Walks in Beauty* is a very famous and beautiful poem and has an important place in the Romantic movement.

2

Listen & Read

2 🎧 **Listen to and read** *She Walks in Beauty*. **First, read for general understanding. Then, reread the poem. As you read the second time, make a note of the imagery used in the poem.**

She Walks in Beauty

She walks in beauty, like the night
Of cloudless climes and starry skies;
And all that's best of dark and bright
Meet in her aspect and her eyes;
Thus mellowed to that tender light
Which heaven to gaudy day denies.

One shade the more, one ray the less,
Had half impaired the nameless grace
Which waves in every raven tress,
Or softly lightens o'er her face;
Where thoughts serenely sweet express,
How pure, how dear their dwelling-place.

And on that cheek, and o'er that brow,
So soft, so calm, yet eloquent,
The smiles that win, the tints that glow,
But tell of days in goodness spent,
A mind at peace with all below,
A heart whose love is innocent!

Respond

3 Respond to the poem by answering these questions with a partner.

1. Was your prediction about the main ideas of the poem correct? Explain.
2. How does the author communicate the main ideas? Pick one (or more) and explain.

   a with images b with dialogue c by presenting them directly
3. Who is the speaker in the poem?
4. Which of the words in the phrase bank do you think best describe how the speaker feels in the poem? Explain.

Phrase Bank

- in awe
- surprised
- sad
- happy
- amazed
- nervous
- angry

Understand

4 Read the questions and choose the correct answers.

1. What meets in the woman's eyes?

   a cloudless climes

   b starry skies

   c all that's best of dark and light

   d her aspect
2. What color is the woman's hair?

   a brown

   b black

   c blond

   d red
3. What do the woman's thoughts show?

   a how special her mind is

   b what she's thinking about

   c how beautiful her face is

   d why she's feeling happy
4. What is true of the woman?

   a She is worried about something.

   b She is in love with someone.

   c She does not know the speaker.

   d She feels calm and at peace.

Figurative Language

5 Work with a partner. Find two examples of alliteration and one example of assonance in the poem.

2

Summarize

6 **First, fill in the graphic organizer based on the poem you read.**

Character(s)	Main Idea(s)

7 **Now, use your graphic organizer to summarize the poem with a partner.**

Listen

8 **Listen to a tutorial about** *She Walks in Beauty*. **Then, answer the questions.**

1 What is the tutorial mostly about?

- **a** a comparison of two poems
- **b** the mood of two poems
- **c** reasons authors pick different images
- **d** ways that point of view changes poems

2 In what way are the two poems similar?

- **a** They both talk about the light of the sun.
- **b** They have a similar subject.
- **c** They use identical images.
- **d** They both avoid scientific comparisons.

3 Why did Romantic literature favor the night over the day?

- **a** They knew little about the day.
- **b** Images of the day had been used before.
- **c** They associated the day with science.
- **d** The night was as lovely as the day to them.

4 Who is the speaker in *She Walks in Beauty* addressing?

- **a** the audience
- **b** the woman
- **c** Shakespeare
- **d** nobody specific

Analyze the Title

9 **The title of the poem is the first half of the first line of the poem. This seems at first glance to mean little, but it is worth bearing in mind that the convention (one that Byron followed for other poems) was to use the entire first line as a title. Here, Byron uses just the first half, and poets rarely do things without reason. The first half of the first line, therefore, leaves us with certain expectations. Fill in the gaps below with three suggestions you might expect to complete the line.**

10 **Compare your ideas with Byron's version. Discuss with a partner the effect produced by ending the line with "like the night."**

She walks in beauty, like the night

11 **With this line, and indeed throughout the poem, Byron uses a technique called "enjambment." This means that one line is not a complete sentence or clause on its own, but is completed by the line that follows. What enjambment does is play with the expectations of the reader, and provides a sense of both suspense and surprise. Look at how Byron completes the first line with the second line of the poem and answer the questions with a partner.**

She walks in beauty, like the night
Of cloudless climes and starry skies;

- What kind of night is she compared to? Where are "cloudless climes"?
- What effect does this have on the effect of the "night" comparison?
- In what way is her beauty like this kind of night? Find examples from the rest of the poem.

Analyze the Characters

12 Fill It In.

First, listen to the tutorial. Then, use words from the phrase bank to complete the graphic organizer.

Phrase Bank

- male
- dark hair
- white skin
- pure
- has a peaceful mind
- innocent

The Speaker	The Woman

13 Think About It.

Use the graphic organizer to answer the following questions.

- What do you know about the speaker?
- What do you know about the woman?
- Which character do you know more about, the speaker or the woman?

14 Talk It Over.

With a partner, discuss your answers to the previous questions. Then, discuss the following question.

- Why do you think the speaker doesn't speak more about himself or about his feelings?

Analyze the Symbols

15 Match It.

Symbols are quite commonly used in poems. Authors use symbols to stand for something else. Look at the following list of symbols and their meanings from *She Walks in Beauty*. Match each symbol to its meaning.

Symbols		Meanings
1	night/darkness	A purity
2	brightness/light	B inner beauty
3	physical beauty	C mystery

16 Think About It.

With a partner, discuss your answers to Ex. 15. Why did you choose those answers?

17 Talk It Over.

In groups of four, talk about which symbol you think is most important to the poem and why. Agree on a symbol in your group and choose one group member to report to the rest of the class.

Analyze the Meter and Rhyme

18 Mark It Up.

Reread the poem. Underline the syllables that are stressed. The first line is given here as an example. Then, go back through the poem and mark the rhyme scheme. Use a new letter for each new rhyme and repeat letters for repeated rhymes. Finally, listen to the poem again to check your work.

She walks in beauty like the night *A*

This poem is written in **iambic tetrameter**. This means that there are four iambs in every line. An iamb is a group of one unstressed and one stressed syllable. So, in total, each line has eight syllables. This rhythm is one of the most common in English poetry and was especially popular in religious music and poems. *She Walks in Beauty* was originally intended to be set to music, which partially explains Byron's choice of meter.

19 Think About It.

Answer the following questions with a partner.

- What is the pattern of stressed and unstressed syllables in the poem?
- How many syllables are in each line?
- What is the meter of the poem?
- Do all the lines of the poem match the rhythm perfectly? Explain.
- What is the rhyme scheme of the poem?

20 Talk It Over.

As a class, discuss your answers to the previous questions.

Analyze the Themes

21 Fill It In.

She Walks in Beauty **is concerned with the beauty of a woman; therefore, it's no surprise that beauty is an important theme in the poem. The poem doesn't simply praise the woman's physical appearance, however. Her virtue – or goodness – is also important. Fill in the graphic organizer with lines from the poem that support the themes of the poem.**

Theme	Lines from Poem
beauty	
virtue	

22 Think About It.

Which theme do you think is most important to the poem and why?

23 Talk It Over.

With a partner, discuss your answer to the previous question.

In-Depth Analysis: Romanticism

Romanticism is a movement that began in the eighteenth century and continued on into the nineteenth century. It first started in Europe, but spread throughout much of the Western world to varying degrees. The movement started as a reaction to the scientific and rational Age of Enlightenment. Romantics were dissatisfied with cold descriptions of the natural world. They wanted to bring back some passion to the popular consciousness. The Romantic movement produced masterpieces of music, visual art, and, of course, literature.

Romantic literature is characterized by several different things. One of the most important is the idea of emotion. During the Age of Enlightenment, people believed that reason and science were the only ways to know truth. Romantics, however, elevated the importance of human emotion. As such, much romantic writing is passionate and unrestrained.

Another characteristic of Romanticism was a deep love for the natural world. Romantics saw nature as the purest, most perfect example of beauty. They idealized nature and believed that the natural world was the most appropriate setting for humans. Society, they believed, was the cause of all human problems. For this reason, many Romantic poems and novels use the natural world to represent purity and beauty.

A final important characteristic of Romanticism was the idea of introspection, mystery, and melancholy. Romantic characters often experience some kind of unexplainable sadness. They spend much time thinking about themselves and their feelings. To the Romantics, this was a sign that a person was a deep and passionate being. Experiencing negative emotions like sadness was a sign that a person was capable of feeling deeply.

Romanticism was a very important movement in the literary world. It also was important to the world of painting and music. There continue to be echoes of Romanticism in many of the literary works of today.

24 **Read the In-Depth Analysis and answer the following questions individually.**

- What is Romanticism?
- What are three important characteristics of Romanticism?

25 **Reread the poem with a partner. Then, with your partner, answer the following questions.**

- How does *She Walks in Beauty* embody characteristics of Romanticism?
- For each of the characteristics you identified above, find lines from the poem that illustrate it.

26 **Now, answer the following questions as a class.**

- Is *She Walks in Beauty* a Romantic poem? Explain.
- What characteristics of Romanticism are more prominent in the poem?

Write

27 *She Walks in Beauty* **is a good example of a Romantic poem. It clearly illustrates some of the most important ideas of Romanticism. Write a 250- to 300-word essay about how** *She Walks in Beauty* **represents the ideals of Romanticism.**

VIDEO See p. 209 for video activities & essay writing

3 *Ulysses*

Objectives

By the end of this unit, you will:

• know about the author and the background information behind the poem • thoroughly understand the poem • be able to identify figurative language in the poem • be able to summarize the poem • be able to analyze the title, characters, symbols, setting, meter, and themes of the poem • know about dramatic monologues in some depth • be able to use the poem to support your opinions and write a literature essay

VIDEO

Learn About ... Alfred, Lord Tennyson

Alfred, Lord Tennyson (1809-1892) is one of the best-known and best-loved English poets. He started writing at a very young age. In fact, at the age of twelve, he wrote a poem with over 6,000 lines. As a boy, his home life was difficult. Attending college at the University of Cambridge was a much-needed break from the turmoil of his unstable family. There, he joined a literary club and became more confident in his writing. Still, bad reviews of his first serious published works (in 1830 and 1833) discouraged him so greatly that he didn't publish again for nine years. In 1842, he released two volumes of poetry, both of which were very well received. Later, in 1850, he was named Poet Laureate – a position that made him the official poet of the British state. After that, he lived comfortably and spent much of his time writing in the country. Today, he is still one of Britain's favorite poets.

Predict

Step 1

Discuss these questions with a partner.

1 Do you prefer a life of excitement or stability? Explain.

2 Which is more important, fulfilling your duty or following your heart? Explain.

Step 2

Look at the key words from *Ulysses*. With a partner, discuss the meaning of the words. Based on the words, predict the main ideas of the poem.

pg 37 – 39 - in class
pg 40 - 41 HW
pg 42 - 43 in class / HW

Background information

1 Read the text and answer the questions.

1. Who is Ulysses?
2. What is the *Iliad* about?
3. Who was Ulysses in relation to Achilles?
4. How long did Ulysses take to go back to Ithaca?
5. Was the journey back home easy? Why (not)?
6. What is Tennyson's poem about?

Ulysses is about a character from the *Odyssey*, a work by the great Greek poet Homer. Ulysses was a Greek king of Ithaca. He left his home and his infant son, Telemachus, to fight in the Trojan War (this story is the subject of Homer's the *Iliad*). The war went on a long time and many of Ulysses' friends died, including the great warrior, Achilles. When the war was over, Ulysses and his men began their long journey home. It wasn't easy. In fact, it took them ten years to get from Troy back to Ithaca. The war itself was ten years long, so by the time he got home, Ulysses had been gone for two decades. During this time, Ulysses encountered problems, met many interesting creatures, and had fantastic adventures. He eventually returned home to his kingdom and family and retook his rightful place as king, husband, and father. Tennyson's poem picks up where the Odyssey leaves off. It tells of how Ulysses feels once he has returned to Ithaca and expresses his longing for the adventures of his past.

Listen & Read

2 **Listen to and read *Ulysses*. First, read for general understanding. Then, reread the poem. As you read the second time, ask yourself: what is the rhyme scheme of this poem?**

ULYSSES

It little profits that an idle king,
By this still hearth, among these barren crags,
Match'd with an aged wife, I mete and dole
Unequal laws unto a savage race,
That hoard, and sleep, and feed, and know not me.
I cannot rest from travel: I will drink
Life to the lees: All times I have enjoy'd
Greatly, have suffer'd greatly, both with those
That loved me, and alone, on shore, and when
Thro' scudding drifts the rainy Hyades
Vext the dim sea: I am become a name;
For always roaming with a hungry heart
Much have I seen and known; cities of men
And manners, climates, councils, governments,
Myself not least, but honour'd of them all;
And drunk delight of battle with my peers,
Far on the ringing plains of windy Troy.
I am a part of all that I have met;
Yet all experience is an arch wherethro'
Gleams that untravell'd world whose margin fades
For ever and forever when I move.
How dull it is to pause, to make an end,
To rust unburnish'd, not to shine in use!
As tho' to breathe were life! Life piled on life
Were all too little, and of one to me
Little remains: but every hour is saved
From that eternal silence, something more,
A bringer of new things; and vile it were
For some three suns to store and hoard myself,
And this gray spirit yearning in desire
To follow knowledge like a sinking star,
Beyond the utmost bound of human thought.
This is my son, mine own Telemachus,
To whom I leave the sceptre and the isle,—
Well-loved of me, discerning to fulfil
This labour, by slow prudence to make mild
A rugged people, and thro' soft degrees
Subdue them to the useful and the good.
Most blameless is he, centred in the sphere
Of common duties, decent not to fail
In offices of tenderness, and pay
Meet adoration to my household gods,
When I am gone. He works his work, I mine.
There lies the port; the vessel puffs her sail:
There gloom the dark, broad seas. My mariners,
Souls that have toil'd, and wrought, and thought with me—
That ever with a frolic welcome took
The thunder and the sunshine, and opposed
Free hearts, free foreheads —you and I are old;
Old age hath yet his honour and his toil;
Death closes all: but something ere the end,
Some work of noble note, may yet be done,
Not unbecoming men that strove with Gods.
The lights begin to twinkle from the rocks:
The long day wanes: the slow moon climbs: the deep
Moans round with many voices. Come, my friends,
'Tis not too late to seek a newer world.
Push off, and sitting well in order smite
The sounding furrows; for my purpose holds
To sail beyond the sunset, and the baths
Of all the western stars, until I die.
It may be that the gulfs will wash us down:
It may be we shall touch the Happy Isles,
And see the great Achilles, whom we knew.
Tho' much is taken, much abides; and tho'
We are not now that strength which in old days
Moved earth and heaven, that which we are, we are;
One equal temper of heroic hearts,
Made weak by time and fate, but strong in will
To strive, to seek, to find, and not to yield.

Respond

3 **Respond to the poem by answering these questions with a partner.**

1. Was your prediction about the main ideas of the poem correct? Explain.
2. How does the author communicate the main ideas? Pick one (or more) and explain.
   - a with images
   - b with dialogue
   - c by presenting them directly
3. Who is the speaker in the poem?
4. Which of the words in the phrase bank do you think best describe how the speaker feels in the poem? Explain.

Phrase Bank

- thoughtful
- regretful
- ashamed
- excited
- nostalgic
- restless

Understand

4 **Read the questions and choose the correct answers.**

1. What does Ulysses say he has become?
   - a a hero
   - b a legend
   - c a name
   - d a father
2. What will Ulysses look for on his journeys?
   - a adventure
   - b excitement
   - c fame
   - d knowledge
3. Who is Telemachus?
   - a Ulysses' son
   - b a Greek hero
   - c Ulysses' friend
   - d a great ruler
4. Where might Ulysses meet Achilles?
   - a beyond the sunset
   - b in the Happy Isles
   - c in Ithaca
   - d in Troy

Figurative Language

5 **Work with a partner. Find one example of a simile, one example of a metaphor, and one example of auditory imagery in the poem.**

Summarize

6 **First, fill in the graphic organizer based on the poem you read. The conflict is the difference between what a character wants and the reality of his or her situation.**

Character(s)	Setting

Main Idea(s)	Conflict

7 **Now, use your graphic organizer to summarize the poem with a partner.**

Listen

8 **Listen to a lecture about *Ulysses*. Then, answer the questions.**

1 What is the lecture mostly about?

- **a** the sources of Tennyson's poem
- **b** a comparison of the poem to other epics
- **c** the reason Tennyson wrote the poem
- **d** different literary depictions of Ulysses

2 What contributes most to Ulysses' successes?

- **a** his perseverance
- **b** his loyalty
- **c** his intelligence
- **d** his strength

Analyze the Title

9 Find It.

Ulysses is the main character and speaker of the poem. We learn about him through his own words. We also know things about him because of the role he plays in Greek mythology. For example, Ulysses is well-known for being an intelligent person. He uses his brains to get out of (and sometimes to get into!) many difficult situations. In order to defeat the Trojans, for instance, Ulysses devised a clever plan. The Greeks hid inside of a large hollow horse and left the horse outside of Troy. The Trojans thought that the horse was a gift, so they took it inside the city. Later that night, the Greek soldiers crept out of the horse and opened the gates to allow the rest of the Greek army inside the city, which they then destroyed. Reread the poem and think about what Ulysses says about himself. As you read, underline every time Ulysses describes himself.

10 Think About It.

Using the underlined portions of the passage, write a short paragraph explaining what Ulysses says about himself. Include as many details as possible.

11 Talk It Over.

Share your paragraph with a partner. Then, read your partner's paragraph. Compare and contrast your two descriptions. Add additional information to your description as needed. Then, as a class, discuss why you think Tennyson decided to name the poem after Ulysses.

3

Analyze the Characters

12 Fill It In.

First, listen to the lecture. Then, use the phrase bank to complete the Venn diagram.

Phrase Bank

- intelligent • crafty • a hero
- loves to explore • proud
- desires knowledge • selfish
- leaves his family

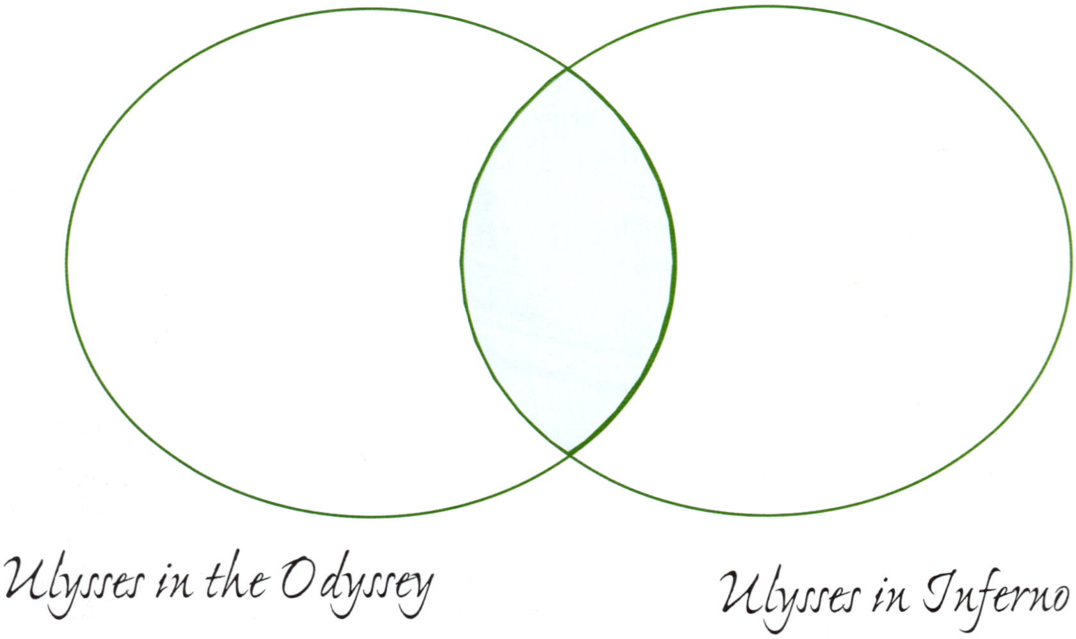

13 Think About It.

Use the Venn diagram to answer the following questions individually.

- How is the depiction of Ulysses in the *Odyssey* different from his depiction in *Inferno*?
- How are the two depictions of Ulysses the same?
- Which depiction is closest to the depiction of Ulysses in Tennyson's poem?

14 Talk It Over.

With a partner, discuss your answers to the previous questions. Then, discuss the following question.

- Why do you think that Tennyson chose to characterize Ulysses in the way that he did?

Analyze the Symbols

15 Match It.

Like many poems, *Ulysses* contains symbols. Look at the following list of symbols and their meanings from *Ulysses*. Match each symbol to its meaning.

Symbols		Meanings
1	the sea	A death
2	beyond the sunset	B freedom
3	eternal silence	C unknown places

16 Think About It.

With a partner, discuss your answers to the previous step. Why did you choose those answers?

17 Talk It Over.

In groups of four, talk about which symbol you think is the most important to the poem and why. Agree on a symbol in your group and choose one group member to report to the rest of the class.

Analyze the Setting

Tennyson does not explicitly state the setting of *Ulysses*, but the reader is expected to know the original story of Ulysses. Knowing this story also informs us of where and when the poem most likely takes place. We can assume that Ulysses is at home, in his kingdom of Ithaca, sometime after he returned from his 20-year absence. The setting is important because it helps explain Ulysses' feelings. He's recently visited many different places, all of which had interesting people and sights. Ithaca, however, is familiar and likely boring. It doesn't fill him with wonder or excitement. Similarly, after being gone for twenty years, things have changed in Ithaca. His son, who was a baby when Ulysses left, is now an adult. Ulysses' wife is twenty years older, and he hasn't had time to gradually get used to this, as most people would have. The setting of the poem directly contributes to Ulysses' feelings of dissatisfaction in the poem.

18 Fill It In.

Use information from the poem and the paragraph to fill in the graphic organizer.

Aspect of Setting	Importance in *Ulysses*
time	
place	

19 Think About It.

Answer the following questions with a partner.

- How is the time period in which the poem takes place important to the ideas in the poem?
- How is the place in which the poem takes place important to the ideas in the poem?
- How would the poem be different if it took place today, in the 21st century?

20 Talk It Over.

As a class, discuss your answers to the previous questions.

Analyze the Meter

21 Mark It Up.

Read the following lines from the poem. Underline the stressed syllables. Listen to a recording of the lines to check your work.

A It little profits that an idle king

B Made weak by time and fate, but strong in will

C Myself not least, but honored of them all

D There lies the port; the vessel puffs her sail

E Life to the lees. All times I have enjoyed

The poem is written in unrhymed iambic pentameter, the most common form of meter in English poetry. To review, each line of iambic pentameter consists of five groups, called iambs. An iamb is one unstressed syllable followed by one stressed syllable. Thus, each line is ten syllables long. Tennyson mostly sticks to this rhythm because it very closely matches the natural rhythm of spoken English. The rhythm isn't always perfect iambic pentameter, however. This makes the poem seem more realistic because, even though iambic pentameter is the closest to speech, no one speaks entirely in iambic pentameter all of the time.

22 Think About It.

Answer the following questions with a partner.

- Which lines are in perfect iambic pentameter?
- What is the pattern of stressed and unstressed syllables in the lines that are NOT iambic pentameter?
- Why do you think that Tennyson added lines that don't perfectly match iambic pentameter?

23 Talk It Over.

As a class, discuss your answers to the previous questions.

Analyze the Themes

24 Fill It In.

Ulysses **is about the desire of one man to explore, see new things, and learn. It also expresses an acknowledgement and acceptance of death. Finally, it expresses the futility of a life lived without taking risks. Use lines from the poem to fill in the graphic organizer.**

Theme	Lines from Poem
exploration	
death	
futility of a conventional life	

25 Think About It.

Which theme do you think is most important to the poem and why?

26 Talk It Over.

With a partner, discuss your answer to the previous question.

In-Depth Analysis: Dramatic Monologue

Ulysses is a classic example of a dramatic monologue. A dramatic monologue is a kind of poem in which the poet takes on the persona of some character or imaginary person. For this reason, these poems are also known as persona poems. The speaker in these poems is never the poet – it's always someone different. There are three important characteristics of dramatic monologues.

The first is that the reader only hears one voice throughout the poem. That is, only one person – the speaker – says everything in the poem. A dramatic monologue, then, is basically a long speech given by one person. In this speech, the reader learns things about the speaker, including his or her background, history, and feelings. In *Ulysses*, Tennyson speaks in the voice of the character of Ulysses.

Secondly, the speaker talks to another person or people, but this is never stated directly. We are led to understand by changes in the speaker's words, tone, and other subtle cues. The audience members (whoever they may be) do NOT speak. There is no dialogue. In *Ulysses*, we know that Ulysses is talking to someone – and not just himself – because he says things like, "This is my son…" and "Come, my friends…" In this way, a dramatic monologue is more than just the private thoughts of the speaker. They are the speaker's words directed at someone else.

Finally, the poet records this conversation with the sole intention of revealing things about the speaker, such as his or her personality, ideas, and feelings. This means that every line of a dramatic monologue should tell the reader something that he or she needs to know to understand the speaker. For an example, consider the first line of *Ulysses*. The speaker states, "It little profits that an idle king." In this line, we learn that Ulysses feels he is being idle. Though he later describes his work as king ("I mete and dole/Unequal laws unto a savage race"), he clearly does not think that it's actually worthwhile. Every subsequent line is similar – it reveals things about the speaker and his thoughts, feelings, and history.

Dramatic monologues became especially popular during the Victorian Era (1837-1901). This is the time period during which Tennyson wrote. As such, *Ulysses* is one of the prime examples of this poetic form.

27 **Read the In-Depth Analysis and answer the following questions individually.**

- What is a dramatic monologue?
- What are three important characteristics of dramatic monologues?

28 **Reread the poem with a partner. Then, with a partner, answer the following questions.**

- How does *Ulysses* embody characteristics of a dramatic monologue?
- For each of the characteristics you identified above, find lines from the poem that illustrate it.

29 **Now, answer the following questions as a class.**

- How would the poem be different if the speaker were Penelope (Ulysses' wife)? What if the speaker were Telemachus (Ulysses' son)?
- With the above questions in mind, what is one potential disadvantage of telling a story with a dramatic monologue?

Write

30 **Three important themes in *Ulysses* are exploration, death, and the futility of living a conventional life.**

Choose one of these three themes and explore how it is addressed in the poem. Include at least three examples from the poem to support your points. Write a 250- to 300-word essay exploring Tennyson's treatment of one of the three important themes in *Ulysses*.

VIDEO See p. 210 for video activities & essay writing

Words of Wisdom

We know what we are, but know not what we may be.
William Shakespeare

Neither a borrower nor a lender be.
William Shakespeare

Love all, trust a few, do wrong to none.
William Shakespeare

A friend should bear his friend's infirmities.
William Shakespeare

It is a wise father that knows his child.
William Shakespeare

Wisely and slowly; they stumble who run fast.
William Shakespeare

I love not Man the less, but Nature more.
Lord Byron

Be thou the rainbow in the storms of life.
Lord Byron

Tis strange – but true; for truth is strange; Stranger than fiction.
Lord Byron

Always laugh when you can. It is cheap medicine.
Lord Byron

Every moment dies a man, Every moment one is born.
Alfred, Lord Tennyson

Knowledge comes, but wisdom lingers.
Alfred, Lord Tennyson

My strength is as the strength of ten, because my heart is pure.
Alfred, Lord Tennyson

No man ever got high by pulling other people down.
Alfred, Lord Tennyson

A lie which is half a truth is ever the blackest of lies.
Alfred, Lord Tennyson

Prose
(1719-1901)

1 Robinson Crusoe

Objectives

By the end of this unit, you will:

• know about the author and the background information behind the novel • thoroughly understand the passage from the novel • be able to identify figurative language in the passage • be able to summarize the passage • be able to analyze the title, characters, setting, symbols, and themes of the novel • know about diction in some depth • be able to use the passage to support your opinions and write a literature essay

VIDEO

Learn About ... Daniel Defoe

Daniel Defoe (c. 1660-1731) was a very important English writer. Along with another man, Samuel Richardson, he helped bring the modern novel to English audiences. Defoe didn't simply write fiction, however. In fact, there is very little that Defoe didn't write about. His political writings, for example, got him into trouble on more than one occasion. Some people consider him to be one of the founders of modern journalism and political commentary. Conservative estimates attribute over 275 individual works to Defoe, though others are as high as 550. Either way, he was indeed a prolific writer and has had an incredible influence on English literature throughout the ages. *Robinson Crusoe*, for example, is one of the first examples of the novel in the English language. The rest of his work deals with an incredibly diverse range of topics, including religion, history, and the supernatural. Though people do not know much about Defoe's personal life, his mark on English literature is common knowledge.

Predict

Step 1

Discuss these questions with a partner.

1. Do you enjoy being alone, or do you prefer being around other people? Why?
2. How would you feel if you were stranded on a desert island?

Step 2

Look at the key words from the passage from *Robinson Crusoe*. **With a partner, discuss the meaning of the words. Based on the words, predict the main ideas of the passage.**

Background Information

1 Read the text and answer the questions.

1. What is Robinson Crusoe like, based on the information in the first paragraph?
2. Where was Crusoe going when his ship was wrecked, and why?
3. How many people survived the shipwreck?
4. How does Crusoe adapt to life on the desert island?
5. Who is Friday?

Robinson Crusoe is one of the earliest examples of a realistic novel in the English language. It tells the story of a young man, Robinson Crusoe, who gets stranded on a desert island. Crusoe leaves his home as a young man to go to sea, against his family's wishes. After several smaller misadventures, he ends up in Brazil with a sugar plantation. Soon, he decides to sail to Africa to buy some slaves for his plantation. This is when he runs into trouble.

His ship encounters a storm, and the ship crashes into the rocks near an island. Everyone jumps overboard to try to save themselves. Crusoe, however, is the only one to survive. He makes it to the island, where he begins to build a new home. He is able to return to the ship several times and bring back supplies to the island. Soon, he has a very comfortable place to live – complete with livestock and crops.

One day, Crusoe encounters people on the island. He discovers that they are cannibals with some prisoners. He helps one of the prisoners escape, a man he names Friday. Soon, he and Friday are close friends. After some time, a ship of Europeans comes to the island. Crusoe and Friday make a deal with the captain of the ship and he takes them back to Europe. Crusoe had lived on the island for 28 years.

1

Listen & Read

2 **Listen to and read the passage from *Robinson Crusoe*. First, read for general understanding. Then, reread the passage. As you read the second time, underline the specific words that Defoe uses to describe Crusoe's reactions to seeing the footprint.**

The original edition of Robinson Crusoe did not contain chapter breaks. Later editions added them in, but they vary from edition to edition. This following passage takes place when Robinson Crusoe has been stranded on the island for about fifteen years. By this time, Crusoe has made the island into a very comfortable place to live. He has pet dogs, cats, goats, and even parrots. He's learned how to grow barley and rice and he even knows how to bake bread. His life on the island is pleasant, if a bit lonely. Everything changes one day when he makes a strange discovery.

Respond

3 **Respond to the passage by answering these questions with a partner.**

1. Was your prediction about the mood of the passage correct? Explain.
2. How did the author create the mood? Think about the words he uses.
3. How does Robinson Crusoe feel in this passage?

It happened one day, about noon, going towards my boat, I was exceedingly surprised with the print of a man's naked foot on the shore, which was very plain to be seen on the sand. I stood like one thunderstruck, or as if I had seen an apparition. I listened, I looked round me, but I could hear nothing, nor see anything; I went up to a rising ground to look farther; I went up the shore and down the shore, but it was all one; I could see no other impression but that one. I went to it again to see if there were any more, and to observe if it might not be my fancy; but there was no room for that, for there was exactly the print of a foot – toes, heel, and every part of a foot. How it came thither I knew not, nor could I in the least imagine; but after innumerable fluttering thoughts, like a man perfectly confused and out of myself, I came home to my fortification, not feeling, as we say, the ground I went on, but terrified to the last degree, looking behind me at every two or three steps, mistaking every bush and tree, and fancying every stump at a distance to be a man. Nor is it possible to describe how many various shapes my affrighted imagination represented things to me in, how many wild ideas were found every moment in my fancy, and what strange, unaccountable whimsies came into my thoughts by the way.

When I came to my castle (for so I think I called it ever after this), I fled into it like one pursued. Whether I went over by the ladder, as first contrived, or went in at the hole in the rock, which I had called a door, I cannot remember; no, nor could I remember the next morning, for never frightened hare fled to cover, or fox to earth, with more terror of mind than I to this retreat.

I slept none that night; the farther I was from the occasion of my fright, the greater my apprehensions were, which is something contrary to the nature of such things, and especially to the usual practice of all creatures in fear; but I was so embarrassed with my own frightful ideas of the thing, that I formed nothing but dismal imaginations to myself, even though I was now a great way off. ... While these reflections were rolling in my mind, I was very thankful in my thoughts that I was so happy as not to be thereabouts at that time, or that they did not see my boat, by which they would have concluded that some inhabitants had been in the place, and perhaps have searched farther for me. Then terrible thoughts racked my imagination about their having found out my boat, and that there were people here; and that, if so, I should certainly have them come again in greater numbers and devour me; that if it should happen that they should not find me, yet they would find my enclosure, destroy all my corn, and carry away all my flock of tame goats, and I should perish at last for mere want.

Understand

4 Read the questions and choose the correct answers.

1 What scares Crusoe?
- a a footprint
- b a person
- c a boat
- d a ghost

2 What does Crusoe do when he gets scared?
- a hurries home
- b looks for a stranger
- c tries to attack
- d calls for help

3 Which of the following is Crusoe NOT afraid that people will do?
- a ruin his crops
- b steal his animals
- c find his house
- d steal his boat

4 Why did Crusoe have trouble sleeping?
- a He was afraid.
- b People were nearby.
- c He was watching for danger.
- d He was uncomfortable.

Figurative Language

5 Work with a partner. Find two examples of similes in the passage.

Summarize

6 **First, fill in the graphic organizer based on the passage you read.**

7 **Now, use your graphic organizer to summarize the passage with a partner.**

Listen

8 **Listen to a lecture about** *Robinson Crusoe*. **Then, answer the questions.**

1 What is the speaker mostly talking about?

- a the influence of the book
- b the important characters of the book
- c the source material of the book
- d the popularity of the book

2 What did Crusoe and Selkirk have in common?

- a They were both gone for over twenty years.
- b They both had goats for meat and milk.
- c They both had pet dogs and cats.
- d They were both left behind on purpose.

Analyze the Title

The original title of *Robinson Crusoe* was *The Life and Strange Surprising Adventures of Robinson Crusoe, of York, Mariner: Who lived Eight and Twenty Years, all alone in an un-inhabited Island on the Coast of America, near the Mouth of the Great River of Oroonoque; Having been cast on Shore by Shipwreck, wherein all the Men perished but himself. With An Account how he was at last as strangely delivered by Pirates.* After several editions, Defoe's publishers shortened the name to simply *Robinson Crusoe*.

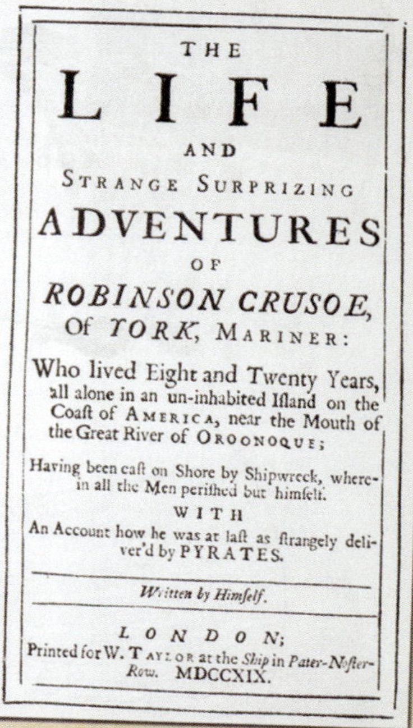

THE
LIFE
AND
STRANGE SURPRIZING
ADVENTURES
OF
ROBINSON CRUSOE,
Of *YORK*, MARINER:
Who lived Eight and Twenty Years, all alone in an un-inhabited Ifland on the Coaft of AMERICA, near the Mouth of the Great River of OROONOQUE;
Having been caft on Shore by Shipwreck, wherein all the Men perifhed but himfelf.
WITH
An Account how he was at laft as ftrangely deliver'd by PYRATES.

Written by Himfelf.

LONDON;
Printed for W. TAYLOR at the *Ship* in *Pater-Nofter-Row.* MDCCXIX.

9 **With a partner, answer the following questions.**

- Why do you think that the title of the book was changed?
- What is good about having a longer title? What is bad about it? Explain.

10 **Look at four other possible titles that the publishers could have chosen from the original. Why aren't they suitable titles for the book?**

1 *An Uninhabited Island*
2 *The Great River of Oroonoque*
3 *Shipwreck!*
4 *Delivered by Pirates*

11 **Why do you think Daniel Defoe didn't just call his book** *Alexander Selkirk*, **and write a book describing Selkirk's adventure? Discuss with your partner, then with the class as a whole.**

Analyze the Characters

12 Fill It In.

First, listen to the lecture. Then, use words from the phrase bank to complete the Venn diagram.

Phrase Bank

- naive • arrogant • pure
- open • laughs at others
- feels superior • shipwrecked
- separated from friends and family • loyal

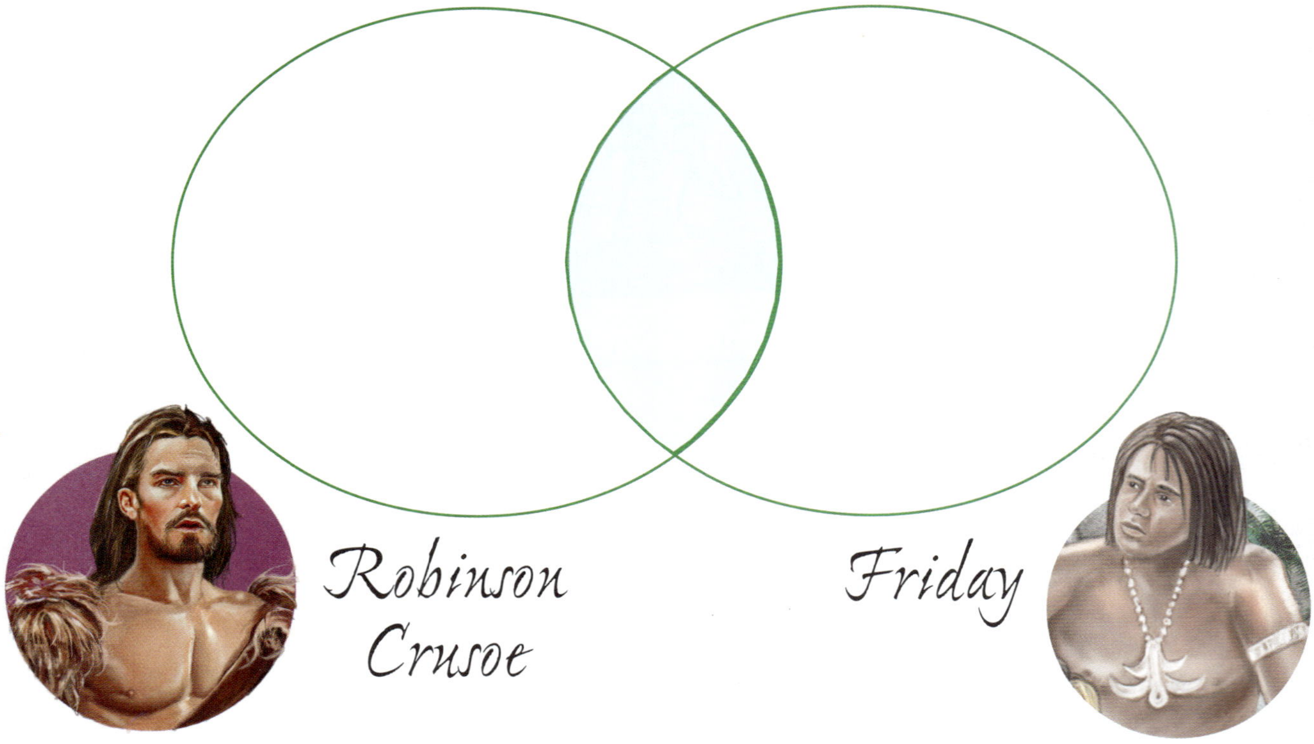

13 Think About It.

Use the Venn diagram to answer the following questions individually.

- What do the characters have in common?
- How are the men different?

14 Talk It Over.

Discuss the answers to the previous questions with a partner. As a class, discuss the following question.

What do the attitudes of the two characters represent?

Analyze the Setting

15 Fill It In.

Listen to a lecture about the setting in *Robinson Crusoe*. Then, use information from the lecture to fill in the graphic organizer.

Setting	Description
the island	

16 Think About It.

With a partner answer the following questions.

Why do you think Defoe chose to set the story on this island? Could the story take place in a different setting?

17 Talk It Over.

As a class, discuss your answers to the previous question.

1

Analyze the Symbols

18 Fill It In.

First, listen to the following lecture about the symbolism of the footprint in *Robinson Crusoe*. Then, use information from the lecture to fill in the second column of the graphic organizer.

Symbol	Meaning	Example
the footprint		*"When I came to my castle… I fled into it like one pursued"*

19 Think About It.

Can you find any examples from the passage that help you understand the meaning of the footprint? Fill in the third column of the graphic organizer with as many examples as you can find. One has been included for you.

20 Talk It Over.

With a partner, discuss the following questions.

- Do you think that Crusoe wants to meet another person? Why or why not?
- Why do you think that Crusoe is nervous about the footprint?

Analyze the Themes

21 Fill It In.

Use lines from the passage to fill in the graphic organizer.

Theme	Lines from Passage
view of outsiders	
fear	

22 Think About It.

Which theme do you think is most important in this passage and why?

23 Talk It Over.

Discuss your answer to the previous question in groups of four. Select one group member to report the group's answer to the class.

In-Depth Analysis: Diction

In literature, the word "diction" refers to word choice. Authors use different diction for different purposes. For example, consider the subtle difference between "asked" and "requested." Writers choose different words depending on the mood, the tone, and their own style. Careful readers pay attention to the individual words that an author uses. Often, writers use diction to help communicate ideas or feelings that are not immediately obvious.

In Robinson Crusoe, Defoe's diction represents the thoughts of Robinson Crusoe himself. The story is told from Crusoe's point of view. When examining the diction in Robinson Crusoe, then, readers should remember that the word choice reflects Crusoe's hidden thoughts or ideas.

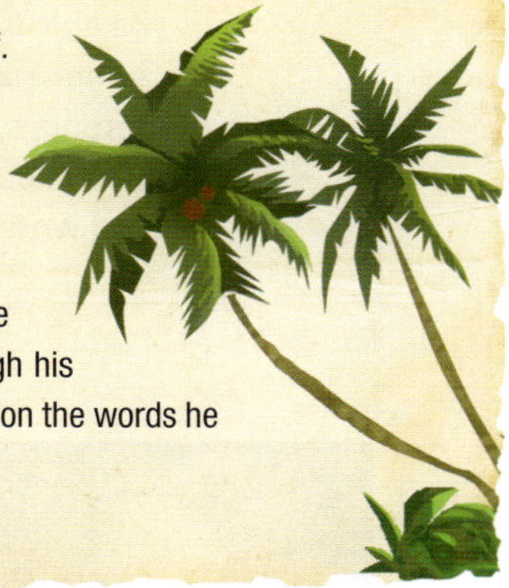

The passage from Robinson Crusoe tells us how Crusoe feels when he encounters a footprint on the beach. This is a very emotional scene. Crusoe is very frightened. As he describes his actions upon seeing the footprint, he reveals his feelings of unease through his choice of words. In particular, we learn that Crusoe feels safest inside of his house based on the words he uses to talk about the house.

24 **Read the In-Depth Analysis and then fill in the graphic organizer. In the left column are all the different words that Crusoe uses to describe his home in the passage. Use a dictionary to fill in the right column with the definitions of the words.**

Word	Definition
fortification	
castle	
retreat	

25 **With a partner, discuss the following questions.**

- What do the words in the graphic organizer have in common?
- How do the words in the graphic organizer differ from words like *house* or *home*?
- What feelings do the words in the graphic organizer seem related to?

26 **As a class, discuss your answers to the previous questions. In addition, answer this question: What does Defoe's diction reveal about Crusoe?**

Write

27 **Daniel Defoe uses particular diction to communicate the thoughts and feelings of Robinson Crusoe. In the passage you have read, Crusoe describes his house with some interesting words. In a 250- to 300-word essay, discuss Defoe's use of diction in the passage. Include examples of interesting word choices, what those words mean, and what they reveal about Crusoe.**

VIDEO
See p. 211
for video activities & essay writing

2 Gulliver's Travels

Objectives

By the end of this unit, you will:

• know about the author and the background information behind the novel • thoroughly understand the passage from the novel • be able to identify figurative language in the passage • be able to summarize the passage • be able to analyze the characters, setting, symbols, and themes of the novel • know about satire in some depth • be able to use the passage to support your opinions and write a literature essay

VIDEO

Learn About ... Jonathan Swift

Jonathan Swift (1667-1745) was an important Irish writer. His personal beliefs influenced his writing a great deal, and much of what he wrote had political or religious meaning behind it. At an early age, he started a career in politics. He moved to London and began spending time with other prominent politicians and writers. In his forties, however, he found himself out of favor with the government and the Queen, and he decided to return to Ireland, where he became the dean of Saint Patrick's Cathedral. As the dean, Swift was in charge of the daily operations of the church, including keeping records of finances and making sure that all priests were performing the duties of their station. Although he missed the busy life of London, Swift soon began writing many different kinds of political pamphlets and essays. It was during this period of his life that Swift wrote *Gulliver's Travels*, his most famous and successful book. In the last years of his life, Swift suffered greatly. He lost most of his mental capacity and his friends were compelled to take over his finances and daily care. He died on October 19, 1745, at the age of 77 and was buried in St. Patrick's Cathedral. His contribution to literature continues to be recognized today.

Predict

Step 1

Discuss these questions with a partner.

1 Do you think that people should use science only to solve problems? Or is it acceptable to use science just to learn something new? Explain.

2 What are some interesting scientific discoveries from your life?

Step 2

Look at the key words from the passage from *Gulliver's Travels*. With a partner, discuss the meaning of the words. Based on the words, predict main ideas of the passage.

method
ingenuity
begging
cucumbers
sunshine
gunpowder
ice
project
treatise
fire
academy

Background Information

1 Read the text and answer the questions.

1. Was Lemuel Gulliver a real man? How do we know?
2. Where did Gulliver find a king that dominates a country from the air?
3. How did Gulliver feel by the end of his travels?
4. What did Swift dislike about the Age of Enlightenment?
5. In what way did Swift disagree with Defoe?

Gulliver's Travels is about the fictional journeys of a man called Lemuel Gulliver. The book is divided into four parts, each describing a journey. The first part tells about Gulliver's visit to a land called Lilliput, full of tiny people with a dangerous and aggressive nature, considering their size. He makes it home from this land, but on his next trip, he is shipwrecked in another strange place: Brobdingnag. The people here are giants, though their nature is quite peaceful and their country ruled fairly and rationally. Part three relates Gulliver's visits to the flying island of Laputa (where people pursue the most abstract art and knowledge imaginable), Balnibarbi (the land below Laputa, which the king controls from Laputa by blocking sunshine and rain or dropping down rocks), and other lands. Part four is the last part, and it tells about Gulliver's time in the country of the Houyhnhnms – intelligent talking horses who rule a race of filthy greedy human-like creatures called Yahoos. When Gulliver finally returns home, he is so disgusted by humanity that he refuses to speak with anyone, preferring to spend his time in his stables, talking to his horses.

The book is a satire. That is, it pokes fun at certain people, places, and ideas by presenting similar people, places, or ideas in a ridiculous way. Jonathan Swift used this book to point to the flaws he saw in many of the ideas of the Age of Enlightenment, where science was seen as a new god, as well as the growing power of the British Empire and other topical issues. It is also, broadly, a satire of the travel books popular at the time, and particularly of Daniel Defoe's *Robinson Crusoe*, which had been published seven years before and extolled the virtues of the individual man and his capabilities. Gulliver encounters only inhabited islands and established societies, and even at the end, when he tries to find a desert island to live on alone, he is brought back home by sympathetic captains. Swift seems to be implying that humans are stuck with society, for better or worse.

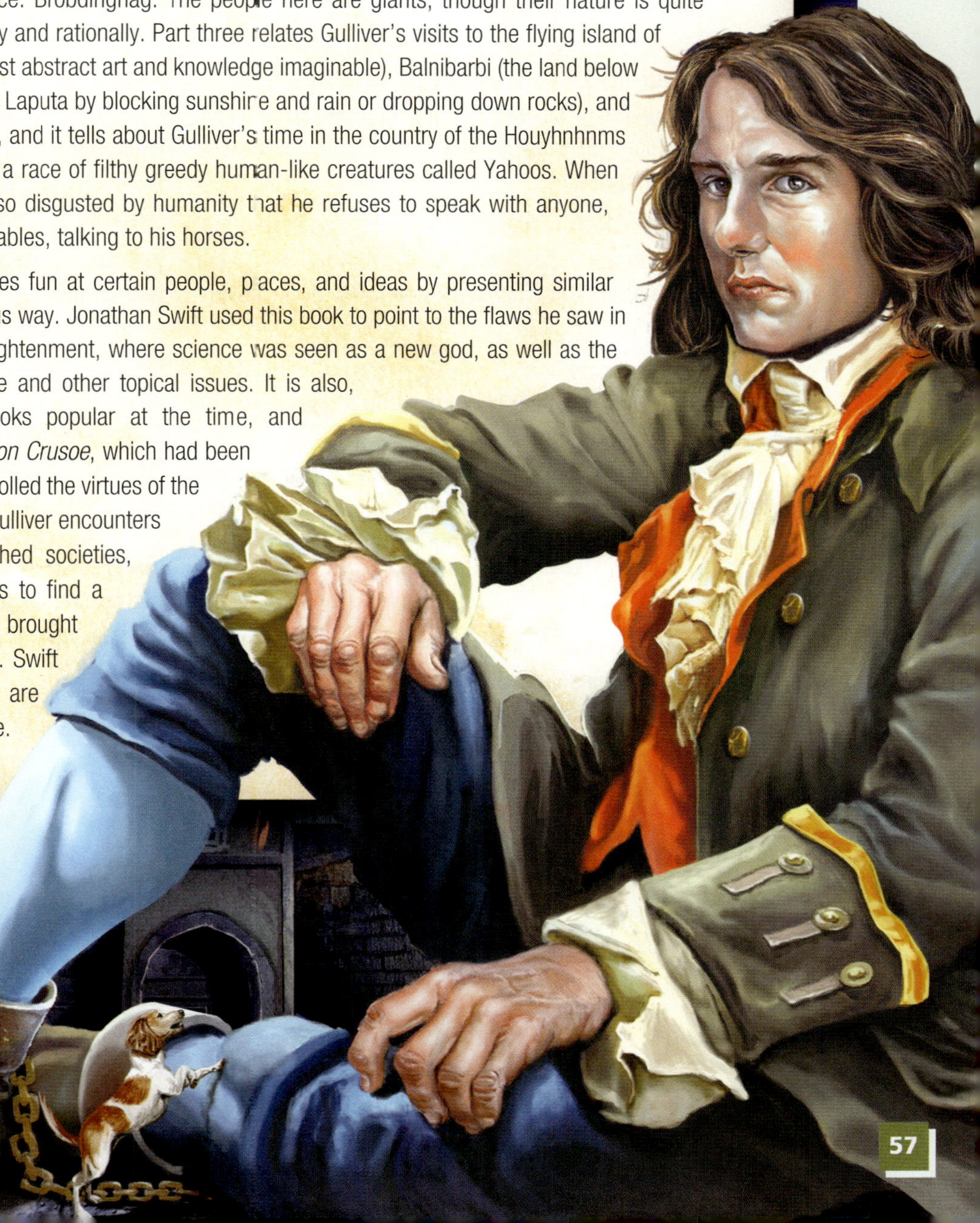

Listen & Read

2 🎧 **Listen to and read the passage from** *Gulliver's Travels*. **First, read for general understanding. Then, reread the passage. As you read the second time, decide what kind of person or group Swift is making fun of.**

In this passage from Gulliver's Travels (Part 3, Chapter 5), Gulliver is taking a tour of an academy – a place where scientists come together to invent things – in Lagado. Lagado is the capital city of Balnibarbi, ruled over by a king who lives on the flying island of Laputa. The people from Balnibarbi and Laputa are very preoccupied with science and invention – but many of their scientific ideas are very impractical, as Gulliver soon finds out.

This academy is not an entire single building, but a continuation of several houses on both sides of a street, which growing waste, was purchased and applied to that use.

I was received very kindly by the warden, and went for many days to the academy. Every room in it has one or more projectors; and I believe I could not be in fewer than five hundred rooms.

The first man I saw was of a meagre aspect, with sooty hands and face, his hair and beard long, ragged, and singed in several places. His clothes, shirt, and skin, were all of the same colour. He has been eight years upon a project for extracting sunbeams out of cucumbers, which were to be put in phials hermetically sealed, and let out to warm the air in raw inclement summers. He told me, he did not doubt, that, in eight years more, he should be able to supply the governor's gardens with sunshine, at a reasonable rate: but he complained that his stock was low, and entreated me "to give him something as an encouragement to ingenuity, especially since this had been a very dear season for cucumbers." I made him a small present, for my lord had furnished me with money on purpose, because he knew their practice of begging from all who go to see them.

I saw another at work to calcine ice into gunpowder; who likewise showed me a treatise he had written concerning the malleability of fire, which he intended to publish.

There was a most ingenious architect, who had contrived a new method for building houses, by beginning at the roof, and working downward to the foundation; which he justified to me, by the like practice of those two prudent insects, the bee and the spider.

Respond

3 Respond to the passage by answering these questions with a partner.

1. Was your prediction about the main idea of the passage correct? Explain.
2. How did the author communicate the main ideas? Pick one (or more) and explain.
   a with images **b** with dialogue **c** by explaining them directly
3. Who are the important people in this passage?
4. Which of the words in the phrase bank do you think best describe how Gulliver feels in the passage? Explain.
5. Imagine you were Gulliver. Describe the scene. How do you feel?

Phrase Bank

- surprised
- amazed
- shocked
- amused
- bored
- interested

Understand

4 Read the questions and choose the correct answers.

1. What was the first projector working with?
   a cucumbers
   b soot
   c airtight bottles
   d clothing
2. Why does the first projector ask for money?
   a He is hungry.
   b He needs supplies.
   c He is in debt.
   d He needs new clothes.
3. What did one projector write a paper about?
   a ice
   b gunpowder
   c fire
   d architecture
4. What kind of animal inspired one projector?
   a a fish
   b a mammal
   c an insect
   d a bird

Figurative Language

5 Work with a partner. Find one example of visual imagery and one example of irony in the passage.

Summarize

6 **First, fill in the graphic organizer based on the passage you read.**

7 **Now, use your graphic organizer to summarize the passage with a partner.**

Listen

8 **Listen to a lecture about** *Gulliver's Travels*. **Then, answer the questions.**

1 What is the speaker mostly talking about?

- **a** why Swift was prosecuted for *Gulliver's Travels*
- **b** how Swift thought of the idea for *Gulliver's Travels*
- **c** how Swift tried to hide authorship of *Gulliver's Travels*
- **d** when Swift first published *Gulliver's Travels*

2 Why did Swift ask someone to copy his book?

- **a** so the handwriting couldn't be traced to him
- **b** because he needed help getting published
- **c** so he could pretend he'd written the whole thing
- **d** because he needed multiple copies of the book

About the Title

The original title of *Gulliver's Travels* was *Travels into Several Remote Nations of the World, in Four Parts.* By *Lemuel Gulliver, First a Surgeon, and then a Captain of Several Ships*. Today, though, most people just call it by the shorter name.

9 **Answer the following questions with a partner.**

- How is the original title similar to the original title of *Robinson Crusoe*?
- Which title do you think is better, the longer one or the shorter one? Explain.

Analyze the Characters

10 Fill It In.

First, listen to the lecture. Then, use words from the phrase bank to fill in the table.

Phrase Bank

• curious • one-dimensional • intelligent • impractical • observant • think about • complex, abstract ideas • middle class • represent(s) the everyman • represent(s) the ivory tower • represent(s) the Royal Society • practical • resourceful • dynamic • doesn't change

Gulliver	Projectors

11 Think About It.

Use the graphic organizer to answer the following questions individually.

- How is the character of Gulliver different than the projectors?
- What do those differences make you think about the projectors? What do they make you think about Gulliver?

12 Talk it Over.

Discuss the answers to the previous questions with a partner. Share your ideas with the class.

Analyze the Setting

13 Fill It In.

Listen to the following lecture about the setting in *Gulliver's Travels*. Then, use information from the lecture to fill in the graphic organizer.

Place	Inhabitants	Meaning
Lilliput & Blefuscu		
Brobdingnag		
Laputa & Balnibarbi		
country of the Houyhnhnms		

14 Think About It.

With a partner, answer the following question.

Think about the projectors and what you know about them. What do you think the academy could represent?

15 Talk It Over.

As a class, discuss your answers to the previous question.

Analyze the Symbols

16 Fill It In.

In *Gulliver's Travels*, most things are symbols. The characters, places, and action all stand for some idea. Based on what you've learned so far, write down four symbols and their meanings in the table.

Symbol	Meaning

17 Think About It.

Answer the following questions.

- Why does Jonathan Swift use symbols instead of just saying what he means?
- Can someone enjoy the story of *Gulliver's Travels* without understanding the symbolism of it?

18 Talk It Over.

Discuss your answers to the previous questions with a partner.

Analyze the Themes

Two of the important themes in *Gulliver's Travels* are science and power. In the book, Gulliver sees examples of science put to good use and science put to poor use. Gulliver's observations lead the reader to believe that science is best when put to practical use – not when pursued for abstract reasons. Power is another important idea in *Gulliver's Travels*. Gulliver has lots of power when he's in Lilliput and no power in Brobdingnag. His experiences show us how arbitrary power really is. The passage from *Gulliver's Travels* clearly relates to science. But it also alludes to ideas of power, particularly in the relationship between Gulliver and the projectors.

19 Fill It In.

Use lines from the passage to fill in the graphic organizer.

Theme	Examples from Passage
science	
power	

20 Think About It.

Which theme do you think is most important in this passage and why?

21 Talk It Over.

Discuss your answer to the previous question with a partner.

2

In-Depth Analysis: Satire

Satire is a kind of literary genre which pokes fun at society by illuminating its shortcomings, vices, and injustices. Satire makes an ideal, behavior, or belief seem ridiculous. This is usually done in a playful and even humorous way, but is still intended to make people think about their own behavior.

There are two kinds of satire: Horatian and Juvenalian. These get their names from two of the earliest satirists, Horace and Juvenal, who were Roman poets. Horatian satire is more playful, witty, and general. Juvenalian satire, on the other hand, is often more angry, abrasive, and personal. In *Gulliver's Travels*, the satire is mostly Juvenalian. Swift attacks specific people, governments, and practices. Though the book is definitely funny, the criticisms of the British state and European self-importance are often scathing.

For example, when Gulliver visits Lilliput, he spends a lot of time explaining conflicts in the Lilliputian court and parliament. These conflicts seem petty and foolish to Gulliver – and, of course, to the reader. Yet they directly correspond to contemporary political conflicts in Britain. In pointing out the absurdity of the Lilliputian conflicts, Swift implies that their British counterparts are no less foolish. Their constant wars with their similarly tiny neighbors from the island of Blefuscu remind readers of the unending conflicts between Britain and France at the time.

The entire book is full of examples like this. When Gulliver visits the academy, his descriptions of the projectors' ridiculous experiments make us laugh. These projectors, however, are similar to the members of the Royal Society in Britain. So by indirectly comparing the projectors to the Royal Society, Swift suggests that the Royal Society is just as useless as the academy in Balnibarbi. Both pursue knowledge that has no useful purpose for humanity, and both are completely cut off from the society that supports them.

Some people have treated *Gulliver's Travels* as a children's book, but this could not be further from the truth. In reality, it's a harsh criticism of life in the eighteenth century. It was for this reason that Swift published the book anonymously, pretending it was written by Gulliver himself; it was designed to upset some very powerful people, and it did. It was also, however, enormously popular, and has never been out of print since.

22 **Read the In-Depth Analysis and answer the following questions with a partner.**

- What is satire?
- Read the quotations below and, based on the information in the text, decide which is from Horace's satires and which is from Juvenal's satires.

1 .... **2**.................. ....

"O fortunate tradesman!' the ageing soldier cries.
Body shattered by harsh service, bowed by the years.
The merchant however, ship tossed by a southern gale,
Says: 'Soldiering's better. And why? You charge and then:
It's a quick death in a moment, or a joyful victory won."

"What could I do at Rome? I don't know how to cheat;
If a book is bad, I am unable to praise it and ask for one;
...
nobody is going to be a thief with me as his accomplice,
and that right there is why I'm going in no governor's entourage..."

- What kind of satire does Swift use in *Gulliver's Travels*?
- What is Swift satirizing in *Gulliver's Travels*?

23 **Reread the passage from** *Gulliver's Travels*. **With a partner, answer the following questions.**

- What is the main subject of this section?
- What is Swift satirizing in this section?
- How does Swift make the subject of his satire seem ridiculous?

24 **Discuss the following questions as a class.**

- Do you think that people were offended by *Gulliver's Travels*? If so, who? Explain.
- Does satire still exist as a literary form today? Does it exist in any other forms? Explain.
- Do you think satire is an effective or an ineffective form of social criticism? Explain.

Write

25 **Symbols are incredibly important to** *Gulliver's Travels*. **Using your answers from the sections above, write a 250- to 300-word essay about three of the symbols in the story and what they represent.**

VIDEO See p. 212 for video activities & essay writing

3 Pride and Prejudice

Objectives

By the end of this unit, you will:

• know about the author and the background information behind the novel • thoroughly understand the passage from the novel • be able to identify the point of view in the passage • be able to summarize the passage • be able to analyze the title, characters, setting, and themes of the novel • know about character in some depth • be able to use the passage to support your opinions and write a literature essay

VIDEO

Learn About ... Jane Austen

Jane Austen (1775-1817) was an English writer whose novels of romance and society are still very popular with readers today. Austen came from a very large family. She had six brothers and one sister. She and her sister attended school for a few years, but had to stop when Austen was around eleven years old because her family could no longer afford the expense. This was only the end of Austen's formal education, however. She continued to read and study while living at home with her family. Her father encouraged this, and he also encouraged Austen to write – something which was somewhat scandalous for women to do at the time. She continued to write as she grew older and eventually published several books – though she published them anonymously. Some of the most important themes in Austen's books are related to women, their independence, and marriage. She was an important commentator on the social inequalities of her lifetime. She died young, in 1817, and so only published six novels. Still, she continues to be well-loved and one of the most-adapted of English authors to screen and stage.

Predict

Step 1

Discuss these questions with a partner.

1 When you meet someone new, how do you decide whether or not you like them?

2 What is more important when making a new friend: their appearance or their actions? Explain.

Step 2

Look at the key words from the passage from *Pride and Prejudice***. With a partner, discuss the meaning of the words. Based on the words, predict main ideas of the passage.**

Background Information

1 Read the text and answer the questions.

1. Which of the Bennet daughters are main characters?
2. Why is it important for the Bennet daughters to marry well?
3. How is Mr. Bingley important for Mrs. Bennet?
4. What kind of novel is *Pride and Prejudice*, on the most basic level?
5. What criticism does Jane Austen give of her society in the novel?

Pride and Prejudice is about the Bennet family. Mr. and Mrs. Bennet have five daughters. Jane is the oldest, and she is beautiful, kind, and good. Elizabeth is the next oldest. She, too, is pretty, but not as beautiful as Jane. She's free-spirited, outspoken, and intelligent. She's also the main character. The other three daughters are not as important to the story. They are Mary, the foolish intellectual, and Lydia and Kitty, the silly flirts. Because of the laws and customs in England at the time, none of these daughters will inherit the family home when Mr. Bennet passes away. In addition, Mr. Bennet is not a wealthy man. Therefore, his daughters will be left with nothing when he is gone. For this reason, both Mr. and Mrs. Bennet are very concerned with finding husbands for their daughters. Marriage is the only means by which the Bennet girls can avoid becoming destitute. At the beginning of the book, a new man named Mr. Bingley moves to town. He is rich, so Mrs. Bennet immediately wants to introduce him to her daughters. The ball described in the following passage is the first chance the Bennet women have to meet Mr. Bingley and their impressions of him and his friend Mr. Darcy are given.

On the surface, *Pride and Prejudice* is a romance, where Elizabeth and Mr Darcy slowly move from dislike of one another to falling in love. However, under the surface is Jane Austen's keen and often biting humor, as she lays open the hypocrisy and materialism of her society, where every woman by necessity must find a man – and one with means. On each level – as a romance, a comedy of manners, and a social critique – the novel works exquisitely well, earning it a place alongside the other classics of English literature.

3

Listen & Read

2 Listen to and read the passage from ***Pride and Prejudice***. First, read for general understanding. Then, reread the passage. As you read the second time, underline the words and phrases used to describe the positive side of the men.

In this passage, from Chapter 3, we meet Mr. Bingley and Mr. Darcy. Both men are new to the area and have caused great excitement with the young women of the area due to their being in secure financial positions. This section describes the two men and explains how people react to them. The setting is a ball, or a dance, given in the town. It was the first time that many of the people in town had seen or met Mr. Bingley.

Mr. Bingley was good looking and gentlemanlike; he had a pleasant countenance, and easy, unaffected manners. His brother-in-law, Mr. Hurst, merely looked the gentleman; but his friend Mr. Darcy soon drew the attention of the room by his fine, tall person, handsome features, noble mien; and the report which was in general circulation within five minutes after his entrance, of his having ten thousand a year. The gentlemen pronounced him to be a fine figure of a man, the ladies declared he was much handsomer than Mr. Bingley, and he was looked at with great admiration for about half the evening, till his manners gave a disgust which turned the tide of his popularity; for he was discovered to be proud, to be above his company, and above being pleased; and not all his large estate in Derbyshire could then save him from having a most forbidding, disagreeable countenance, and being unworthy to be compared with his friend.

Mr. Bingley had soon made himself acquainted with all the principal people in the room; he was lively and unreserved, danced every dance, was angry that the ball closed so early, and talked of giving one himself at Netherfield. Such amiable qualities must speak for themselves. What a contrast between him and his friend! Mr. Darcy danced only once with Mrs. Hurst and once with Miss Bingley, declined being introduced to any other lady, and spent the rest of the evening in walking about the room, speaking occasionally to one of his own party. His character was decided. He was the proudest, most disagreeable man in the world, and every body hoped that he would never come there again. Amongst the most violent against him was Mrs. Bennet, whose dislike of his general behaviour was sharpened into particular resentment by his having slighted one of her daughters.

Respond

3 Respond to the passage by answering these questions with a partner.

1 Was your prediction about the main idea of the passage correct? Explain.

2 How did the author communicate the main ideas? Pick one (or more) and explain.

a with images   b with dialogue   c by explaining them directly

3 Who are the important people in this passage?

4 Which of the words from the phrase bank do you think best describe how Mr. Bingley feels in the passage? Which might describe Mr. Darcy's feelings? Explain.

Phrase Bank

- excited
- bored
- tired
- unimpressed
- happy
- upset
- interested

5 Imagine that you are at that ball. What are you wearing? What do you see, feel, hear, taste? How do you feel? How does this scene differ from a similar modern one?

Understand

4 Read the questions and choose the correct answers.

1 Which of the following is NOT attractive about Mr. Darcy?

a his appearance

b his income

c his home

d his attitude

2 How does Mr. Darcy compare to Mr. Bingley?

a He is better-looking.

b He is more of a gentleman.

c He has more money.

d He is friendlier.

3 Why do people stop liking Mr. Darcy?

a He thinks he's better than them.

b He talks too much and too loudly.

c He dances with too many women.

d He insults people to their faces.

4 Who particularly dislikes Mr. Darcy?

a Miss Bingley

b Mr. Bingley

c Mrs. Bennet

d Mrs. Hurst

Point of View

5 Work with a partner. Does a first-person narrator or a third-person narrator tell the story? Is the narrator omniscient or limited? How do you know?

Summarize

6 **First, fill in the graphic organizer based on the passage you read.**

Character(s)

Main Idea(s)

Main Event(s)

Conflict

7 **Now, use your graphic organizer to summarize the passage with a partner.**

Listen

8 **Listen to a lecture about** *Pride and Prejudice*. **Then, answer the questions.**

1 What is the speaker mostly talking about?
   a the historical and social setting of *Pride and Prejudice*
   b the differences between the upper and middle classes in *Pride and Prejudice*
   c the discrimination faced by women during the time *Pride and Prejudice* took place
   d the problems that poor people faced in *Pride and Prejudice*

2 Which people were members of the landed gentry?
   a Mr. Bingley
   b Mr. Darcy
   c the Bennet sisters
   d the Bingley sisters

3

Analyze the Title

9 Fill It In.

Look up the definitions of the words in the graphic organizer. Fill in the empty column.

Word	Definition
pride	
prejudice	

10 Think About It.

With a partner, discuss the meanings of the two words. Then, answer the following questions.

- Which character in the passage best shows the meaning of the word "pride"? Explain.
- Are there any characters that exhibit "prejudice"? Explain.

11 Talk It Over.

As a class, discuss your answers to the previous question. Then, answer the following question as a group.

Based on the passage, does *Pride and Prejudice* seem like a good name for the book? Why or why not?

Analyze the Characters

12 Fill It In.

a. 🎧 **Listen to the first half of the lecture. Then, use words from the phrase bank to fill in the first Venn diagram.**

Phrase Bank

• rich • friendly • dances • ignores others
• quiet • a gentleman • excellent manners
• talkative • insulting • single
• upper class • rude • hospitable • proud

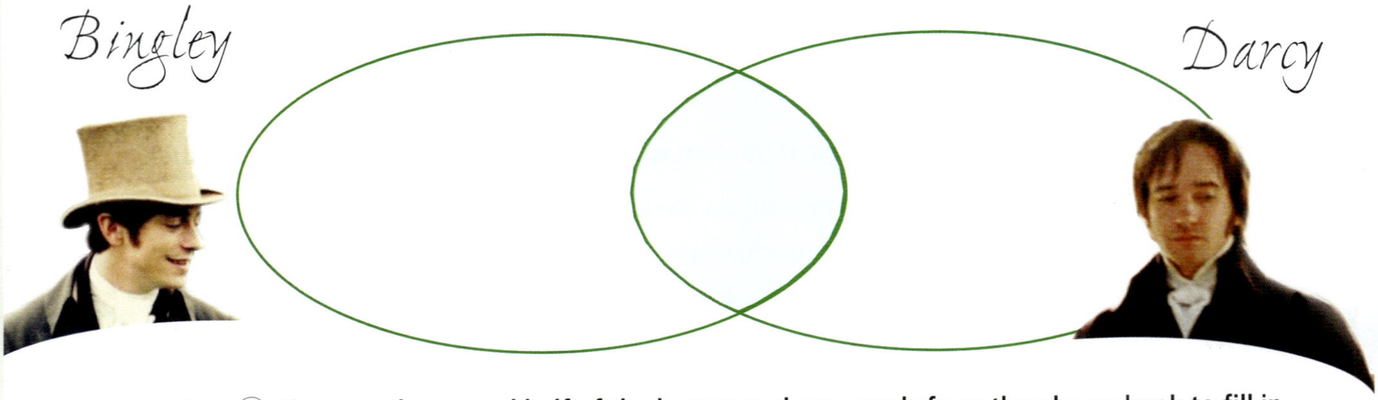

b. 🎧 **Listen to the second half of the lecture and use words from the phrase bank to fill in the second Venn diagram.**

Phrase Bank

• oldest sister • finds true love • outspoken
• virtuous • honest • clever • good-natured
• complex character • beautiful • quick to judge
• second oldest sister • gentle • dull

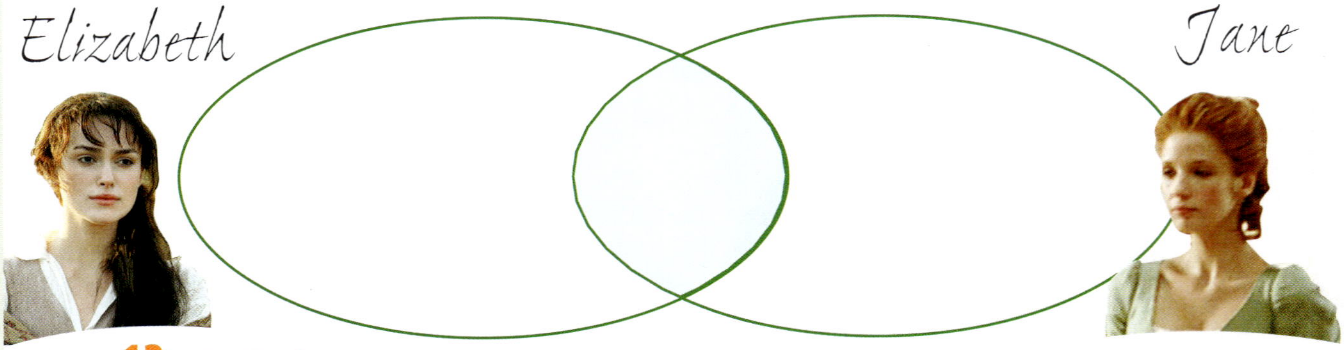

13 Think About It.

Use the Venn diagrams to answer the following questions individually.

- Are Bingley and Darcy more similar than different? What about Jane and Elizabeth?
- Are Bingley and Jane suited? What about Darcy and Elizabeth?

14 Talk It Over.

Discuss the answers to the previous questions with a partner. Share your ideas with the class.

Analyze the Setting

15 Fill It In.

Listen to the following lecture about the setting in *Pride and Prejudice*. Then, use information from the lecture to fill in the graphic organizer.

Aspect of Setting	Importance
time	
place	

16 Think About It.

Answer the following questions with a partner.

- How is the time period in which the story takes place important to the ideas in the novel?
- How is the place in which the story takes place important to the ideas in the novel?
- How would the story be different if the time or place changed?

17 Talk It Over.

As a class, discuss your answers to the previous questions.

Analyze the Themes

18 Fill It In.

Social class and pride are two of the most important themes in *Pride and Prejudice*. Use lines from the passage to fill in the graphic organizer.

Theme	Lines from Passage
social class	
pride	

19 Think About It.

Which theme do you think is most important in this passage and why?

20 Talk It Over.

Discuss your answer to the previous question with a partner.

3

In-Depth Analysis: Character

Characters are the people that the reader meets in a novel. They are important to literary works because it is through the characters that the reader experiences the action in the story. Characters are what keep the action going, drive the plot, and encounter and resolve conflicts. Without characters, it would be very hard to have a story.

Writers reveal things about characters in many different ways. It would be boring, for example, if a writer simply told you everything about a character the first time you saw that character on the page. It's much more interesting for the information to be revealed piece by piece. Writers can reveal things about characters by telling the reader directly, describing how the character looks, letting us hear the character speak, sharing the character's private thoughts and feelings, showing how the character affects other people, and making the character act. All of these things come together to paint the picture of a complete character.

These different means of characterization are all important. And, in some cases, they may conflict with one another. For example, a character may say that he is a kind and gentle person. Later, however, the character might get into a fist fight with someone else. At this point, the reader has to decide which version of the character to believe in: the character who says he's kind and gentle, or the character who beats people up. Good writers know that people are complicated, so there will often be conflicts between who a person seems to be at first, and how he or she acts later on.

Another important point about characters is that they often change throughout a story. For example, in *Pride and Prejudice*, Mr. Darcy has a very bad attitude at the beginning. By the end of the story, however, he has overcome much of his pride. He realizes that he's been acting poorly and makes an effort to change. By the end of the novel, he is a far different person from how he is when the reader first meets him.

Not all characters grow and change. This isn't the mark of bad writing. It simply reflects what the author wants to emphasize. Mr. Bingley, for instance, doesn't change throughout the course of the novel. At the beginning, he is kind, gentlemanly, handsome, and rich. He stays this way throughout the story. This is because the story is not really about him. He's involved and he's important, but his character is not the one being scrutinized. Mr. Bingley as a character is most important as a device for moving the plot forward. His own personal development is not important to the story.

21 Read the In-Depth Analysis and reread the passage from *Pride and Prejudice* to fill in the graphic organizer.

Method of Characterization	Examples from the Passage: Mr. Bingley	Mr. Darcy
telling the reader directly		
describing appearance		
the characters' words		
the characters' effect on others		
the characters' actions		

22 With a partner, answer the following questions.

- Which method of characterization is most prevalent in the passage? Why do you think that is?
- Which method of characterization do you think is most effective? Why?
- Does Austen reveal things about Mr. Bingley and Mr. Darcy in different ways? Explain.

23 Based on the In-Depth Analysis, it is clear that Mr. Darcy will change. As a class, discuss how you think he might change over the course of the novel and why.

Write

24 In the passage from *Pride and Prejudice*, the reader meets two different characters, Mr. Bingley and Mr. Darcy. Although these men have some things in common and are friends, they are also quite different. Using your answers to the sections above, write a 250- to 300-word essay comparing and contrasting Mr. Darcy and Mr. Bingley.

VIDEO See p. 213 for video activities & essay writing

4 Frankenstein

Objectives

By the end of this unit, you will:

• know about the author and the background information behind the novel • thoroughly understand the passage from the novel • be able to identify figurative language in the passage • be able to summarize the passage • be able to analyze the title, characters, setting, symbols, and themes of the novel • know about allusion in some depth • be able to use the passage to support your opinions and write a literature essay

VIDEO

Learn About ... Mary Shelley

Mary Shelley (1797-1851) was an English writer. She is most famous for her novel, *Frankenstein: or, The Modern Prometheus*. She also wrote poetry and worked tirelessly to get her husband, Percy Shelley, published. Her mother, Mary Wollstonecraft, was an early proponent of women's rights and a writer as well. She died when her daughter was just ten days old. Mary Shelley was raised by her father, the political philosopher William Godwin. He encouraged her to learn and study, which she did. In 1816, she married Percy Shelley, whom she had met two years earlier. The two traveled around Europe together, and in 1816, spent the summer in Geneva, Switzerland, with some of their friends, including Lord Byron. The friends sat in front of the fire one evening, reading ghost stories aloud. Lord Byron suggested that they all write their own horror story. Soon afterward, Mary Shelley thought of the idea for *Frankenstein*. She finished and published her novel, something that was exceedingly uncommon for a woman to do in this time period. Today, this is one of the most popular and well-known stories in English and has been adapted for stage and screen many times.

Predict

Step 1

Discuss these questions with a partner.

1 Do you think scientists ever regret their discoveries? Why or why not?

2 Are there moral boundaries which scientists should not cross, even in the pursuit of progress? Explain and give examples.

Step 2

Look at the key words from the passage from *Frankenstein*. With a partner, discuss the meaning of the words. Based on the words, predict the mood of the passage.

Background Information

1 Read the text and answer the questions.

1 Why does Victor Frankenstein tell Captain Walton his story?
2 What was Frankenstein's reaction to his creation?
3 How many people did the creature kill?
4 What was Frankenstein doing near the North Pole?
5 What did 18th century scientists think electricity was doing to the frog?

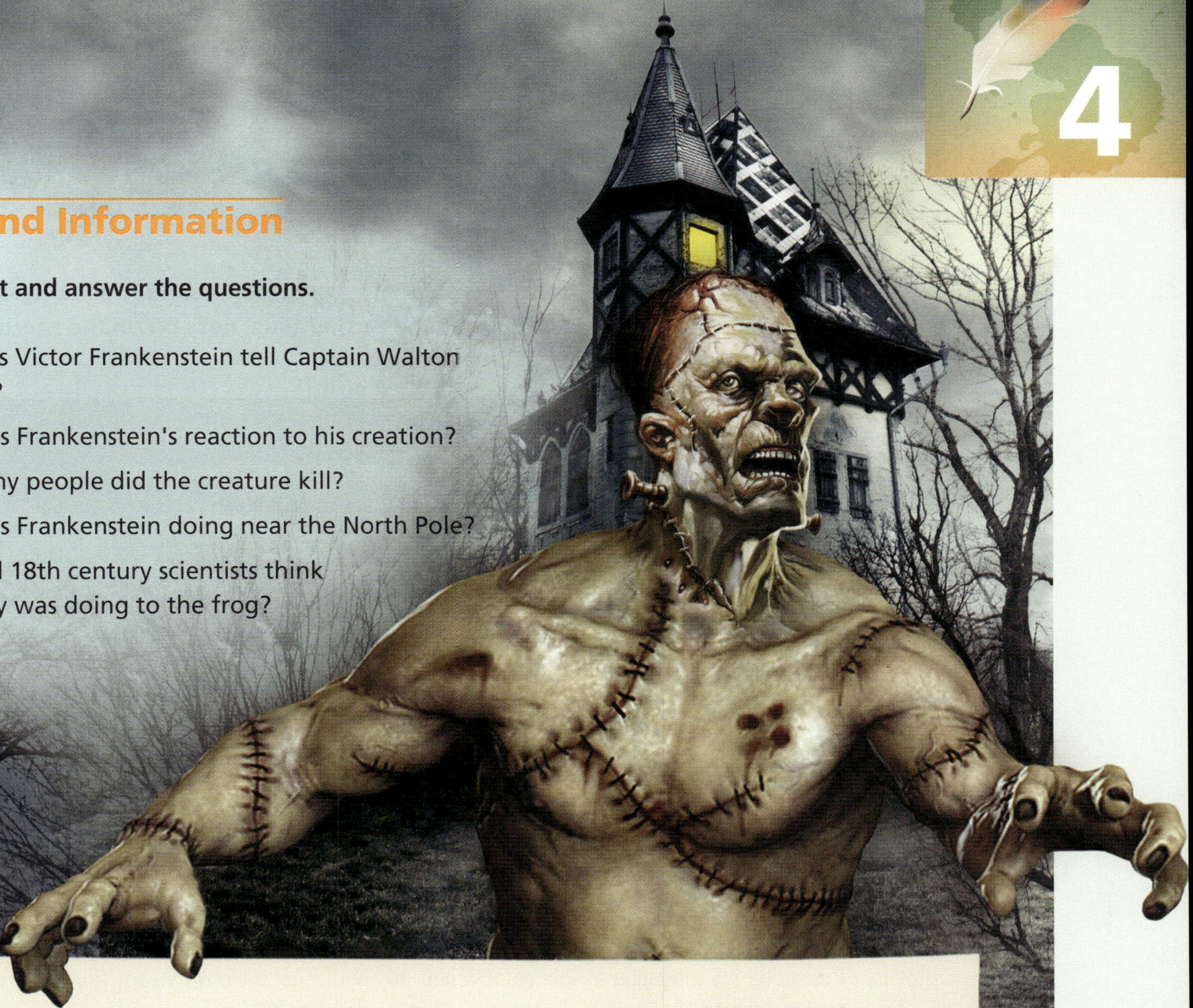

Frankenstein takes place in the late 1700s. It begins on board a ship bound for the North Pole. The ship's captain, Robert Walton, sees a solitary figure moving across the ice. Later, he sees another man and brings the man onto the ship. This man is Victor Frankenstein. In Walton's expedition towards the North Pole (which had not even been attempted at the time of the novel's publication), Frankenstein recognizes his own obsessive pursuit of knowledge, and he decides to tell Walton his life story as a cautionary tale.

When Frankenstein was a student he became obsessed with the creation of life. In fact, he became so obsessed that he decided to create a human being. He studied very hard and began building a person out of stolen body parts. Using electricity, he brought the body to life. However, when Victor saw what he had created, he was immediately disgusted. He couldn't even bear to be in the same room as it and he fled. The creature subsequently disappeared.

Victor was so upset that he got sick. He went home once he was well, only to find out that his younger brother had been murdered. Victor knew that it was the creature. Feeling guilty, he took a trip to the mountains to relax. There, he met the creature face to face. The creature could speak and was intelligent. He told Victor about his life and what he'd been through. He'd learned to speak and read, but every time someone saw him, they ran away or tried to hurt him. The creature was very lonely and asked Victor to make him a friend.

At first, Victor agreed. But as he got closer and closer to finishing the new creature, he became more and more afraid of the consequences, so he destroyed all of his progress and said that he'd never make another. The creature became very upset and killed first Victor's friend, and then his wife, and Victor began chasing it further and further north to kill it. Shortly after he finishes telling his story, Victor dies. The creature comes aboard the ship shortly afterward, and is very sad to hear of Victor's death. It decides it has nothing now left to live for, and says it will build a funeral pyre to burn itself on.

The novel is important because it shows the scientific concerns of the time. For example, scientists in the 1790s noticed that when electrical currents were applied to the muscles of a dead frog, the legs twitched. People now understand that electricity caused the muscle fibers to contract, but in the past, they believed that electricity held some vital life force. Shelley drew on this principle in her novel. In addition, the novel references new understanding about electromagnetism and other scientific pursuits. Indeed, *Frankenstein* would not have seemed implausible to people in Shelley's time period.

4

Listen & Read

2 **Listen to and read the passage from** ***Frankenstein*****. First, read for general understanding. Then, reread the passage. As you read the second time, note down the specific ways in which Victor describes his creation's appearance.**

This passage comes from Chapter 5 of the novel. Here, Victor tells of what happened on the fateful night when he first brought the creature to life.

It was on a dreary night of November that I beheld the accomplishment of my toils. With an anxiety that almost amounted to agony, I collected the instruments of life around me, that I might infuse a spark of being into the lifeless thing that lay at my feet. It was already one in the morning; the rain pattered dismally against the panes, and my candle was nearly burnt out, when, by the glimmer of the half-extinguished light, I saw the dull yellow eye of the creature open; it breathed hard, and a convulsive motion agitated its limbs.

How can I describe my emotions at this catastrophe, or how delineate the wretch whom with such infinite pains and care I had endeavoured to form? His limbs were in proportion, and I had selected his features as beautiful. Beautiful!–Great God! His yellow skin scarcely covered the work of muscles and arteries beneath; his hair was of a lustrous black, and flowing; his teeth of a pearly whiteness; but these luxuriances only formed a more horrid contrast with his watery eyes, that seemed almost of the same colour as the dun white sockets in which they were set, his shrivelled complexion and straight black lips.

The different accidents of life are not so changeable as the feelings of human nature. I had worked hard for nearly two years, for the sole purpose of infusing life into an inanimate body. For this I had deprived myself of rest and health. I had desired it with an ardour that far exceeded moderation; but now that I had finished, the beauty of the dream vanished, and breathless horror and disgust filled my heart. Unable to endure the aspect of the being I had created, I rushed out of the room, and continued a long time traversing my bedchamber, unable to compose my mind to sleep. At length lassitude succeeded to the tumult I had before endured; and I threw myself on the bed in my clothes, endeavouring to seek a few moments of forgetfulness.

Respond

3 Respond to the passage by answering these questions with a partner.

1. Was your prediction about the mood of the passage correct? Explain.
2. How did the author create the mood? Pick one (or more) and explain.
   a with images   b with dialogue   c by explaining it directly
3. Who are the important people in this passage?
4. Which of the words in the phrase bank do you think best describe how Victor feels in the passage? Explain.

Phrase Bank

- happy • excited
- disgusted • afraid
- shocked • angry
- indifferent

5. Imagine you were Victor. How would you feel?

Understand

4 Read the questions and choose the correct answers.

1. Which of the following colors does Victor NOT use to describe the creature?
   a black
   b yellow
   c white
   d red
2. What does Victor use to bring the creature to life?
   a an invented tool
   b a magical chant
   c an electric shock
   d a mixture of chemicals
3. What does Victor do when he sees the creature?
   a He leaves.
   b He screams.
   c He hides.
   d He paces.
4. What bothers Victor most about the creature?
   a its voice
   b its appearance
   c its movements
   d its strength

Figurative Language

5 Find one example of onomatopoeia and one example of kinesthetic imagery in the text.

4

Summarize

6 First, fill in the graphic organizer based on the passage you read.

Character(s)	Setting

Main Event(s)	Conflict

7 Now, use your graphic organizer to summarize the passage with a partner.

Listen

8 Listen to a lecture about *Frankenstein*. Then, answer the questions.

1 What is the speaker mostly talking about?

- a different popular genres of fiction
- b how *Frankenstein* fits into a fiction genre
- c the difficulty in classifying *Frankenstein*
- d a comparison of science fiction to fantasy

2 What element do science fiction and fantasy share?

- a Both could be possible in the future.
- b Both use magic as a plot device.
- c Neither are set in the real world.
- d Neither are concerned with technology.

Analyze the Title

9 Find It.

Listen to the lecture. Then, use words from the phrase bank to complete the Venn diagram.

Phrase Bank

- Greek hero
- steals fire
- creates people
- creates one person
- oversteps boundaries
- goes against nature
- punished
- European scientist
- ashamed of his creation
- tries to help his creation

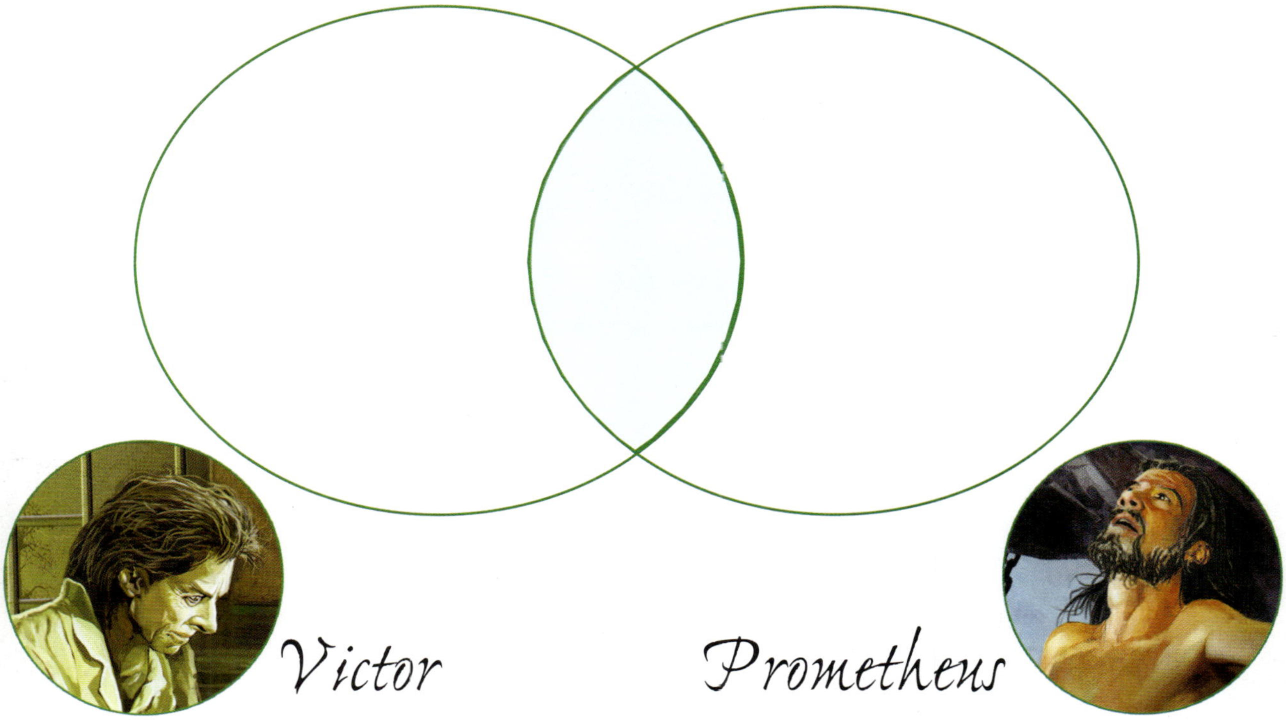

10 Think About It.

How are the stories of Victor Frankenstein and Prometheus similar? How are they different?

11 Talk It Over.

With a partner, discuss your answers to the previous questions. Then, talk about why you think Mary Shelley included the alternate title, *The Modern Prometheus*.

4

Analyze the Characters

12 Fill It In.

First, listen to the lecture. Then complete the graphic organizer with examples of each character trait in Victor and the creature.

Character Trait	Victor	Creature
self-pity		
overly emotional		
self-importance		

13 Think About It.

Use the graphic organizer to answer the following questions individually.

- How are the two characters the same?
- How are they different?

14 Talk It Over.

Discuss the answers to the previous questions with a partner. Share your ideas with the class.

Analyze the Setting

15 Fill It In.

Listen to the following lecture about the setting in *Frankenstein*. Then, use information from the lecture to fill in the graphic organizer.

Aspect of Setting	Importance in *Frankenstein*
time	
place	

16 Think About It.

With a partner, answer the following questions.

- Why do you think Shelley chose to set the novel in this time and place? Could the story take place in a different setting?

17 Talk It Over.

As a class, discuss your answers to the previous questions.

Analyze the Symbols

18 Match It.

Some important symbols in the novel are the monster himself, light and fire, and exploration. Match the symbols to their meanings.

Symbol		Meaning
1	the monster	A the duality of knowledge (it can both help and harm)
2	light/fire	B the negative consequences of going against nature
3	exploration	C the dangers of overstepping the boundaries of human knowledge

19 Think About It.

With a partner, discuss your answers to the previous section. Explain why you chose the answers that you did.

20 Talk It Over.

As a class, discuss the following questions.

- Based on what you know about the book, which symbol do you think is the most important? Why?

4

Analyze the Themes

21 Fill It In.

Two important themes from *Frankenstein* are listed below. Fill in the graphic organizer with words or lines from the passage that relate to these themes.

Theme	Lines from Passage
the consequences of going against nature	
the natural limits of human knowledge	

22 Think About It.

Which theme do you think is most important in this passage and why?

23 Talk It Over.

Discuss your answer to the previous question with a partner.

In-Depth Analysis: Allusion

In literature, an allusion is a reference to another work, such as a work of art, a piece of music, or another literary work. Authors use allusions to draw parallels between two characters or situations without going into great detail. If, for example, an author compared two of his characters to Romeo and Juliet, the reader might assume that the characters are doomed and will never be together, since that's what happens in Shakespeare's play.

In *Frankenstein*, Mary Shelley draws a parallel between Victor Frankenstein and Prometheus. The story of Prometheus comes from ancient Greece. According to some legends, Prometheus created the first humans. He taught them how to talk, read, and hunt. Then he stole fire from the Greek gods and gave it to the humans of the Earth. This angered the gods greatly, since by doing this, he was showing disrespect to them. As a punishment, the leader of the Greek gods, Zeus, chained Prometheus to a rock. Every day, a bird came and ate part of Prometheus' liver. Every night, the liver grew back. So Prometheus lived in agony for the rest of his life.

Mary Shelley's audience would have been aware of this story. They would have seen the similarities between the characters, as well as the differences. For example, Prometheus did everything out of love for humans, but Frankenstein has no love for his creation – quite the opposite. In addition, as a modern Prometheus from Enlightenment Europe, Frankenstein represents humans' quest for knowledge – especially scientific knowledge.

By comparing Victor to Prometheus, Mary Shelley places him in this long tradition of figures whose willingness to go against natural law and insatiable desire for knowledge lead to their ruin.

24 **Read the In-Depth Analysis and answer the following questions individually.**

- What do Victor and Prometheus have in common?
- What are some differences between Victor and Prometheus?

25 **With a partner, answer the following questions.**

- Based on the similarities and differences listed above, do you think that the characters of Victor and Prometheus are more alike than they are different, or vice versa? Explain.
- Which are more important to understanding the story of *Frankenstein*, the similarities between the two characters or their differences?

26 **In groups of four, discuss your answers to the previous questions. Then, as a group, write a short paragraph answering the following question. Use evidence from the In-Depth Analysis to back up your answers.**

- Authors use allusions to draw parallels between two characters or situations. Why do you think Mary Shelley chose to allude to Prometheus in *Frankenstein*?

Write

27 **Victor Frankenstein is a modern Prometheus, reminding us of the dangers of going against nature. Write a 250- to 300-word essay about the importance this theme has in the story of** *Frankenstein*, **and its consequences.**

VIDEO See p. 214 for video activities & essay writing

5

Wuthering Heights

Objectives

By the end of this unit, you will:

• know about the author and the background information behind the novel • thoroughly understand the passage from the novel • be able to recognize the use of dramatic irony in the passage • be able to summarize the passage • be able to analyze the title, characters, setting, symbols, and themes of the novel • know about conflict in some depth • be able to use the passage to support your opinions and write a literature essay

VIDEO

Learn About ... Emily Brontë

Emily Brontë (1818-1848) was an English writer and one of the famous Brontë sisters. Her older sister, Charlotte, and her younger sister, Anne, were also writers. Their mother died when Emily was only two years old. Soon, the family experienced more tragedy when Emily's two older sisters both caught tuberculosis at a boarding school and subsequently died. For most of her life, Emily did not attend school. Instead, she educated herself by reading books from her father's library. Charlotte, Emily, and Anne wrote stories and poems together, and in fact jointly published a volume of poetry in 1846 under the pseudonyms Currer, Ellis, and Acton Bell respectively. In 1847, Emily published *Wuthering Heights*, once more using the name Ellis Bell. Earlier that same year, Charlotte Brontë had published *Jane Eyre* to great success, and Anne Brontë's *Agnes Grey* appeared at the same time as *Wuthering Heights*. Charlotte and Anne went on to publish more novels, but *Wuthering Heights* was to be Emily's only full-length work. She died of tuberculosis only a year after its publication.

Predict

Step 1

Discuss these questions with a partner.

1 Is it possible to feel romantic love for two different people at the same time? Explain.

2 What are some reasons that people marry one another? Are some reasons better than others? Explain.

Step 2

Look at the key words from the passage from *Wuthering Heights*. With a partner, discuss the meaning of the words. Based on the words, predict the main ideas of the passage.

Background Information

1 **Read the text and answer the questions.**

1. Which character is related to Heathcliff by blood?
2. Which characters have the same name?
3. Why wouldn't Catherine Earnshaw marry Heathcliff?
4. List the deaths mentioned in the order that they happened.
5. How did readers react to the novel?

Wuthering Heights takes place between the 1770s and 1800. The story begins with a man called Lockwood. He's renting a house called Thrushcross Grange from Heathcliff. After a strange encounter with Heathcliff and the other residents of his house, and a dream of the ghost of a young woman called Catherine, Lockwood asks the housekeeper, Nelly, what's going on. Nelly then proceeds to tell Lockwood the entire tale.

Heathcliff came to live at Wuthering Heights long ago, when he was a child. He was adopted by Catherine's father, Mr. Earnshaw. Her brother Hindley hated Heathcliff and, when Mr. Earnshaw died, treated Heathcliff very poorly. Catherine met her neighbors, the Lintons, who then lived at Thrushcross Grange. Edgar Linton was her age, and she eventually agreed to marry him, although she was in love with Heathcliff. Despite her love for him, Catherine didn't not want to marry Heathcliff because he was beneath her in social class and had no money. Heathcliff was devastated at being overlooked by Catherine and disappeared from the area for a long time.

When he came back, he was rich, but Catherine was married to Edgar. Heathcliff spent all of his time taking revenge on Hindley, who had treated him so badly in the past. Hindley had become a depressed alcoholic with a young son, Hareton. Hindley drank and gambled all day long, and Heathcliff won Wuthering Heights from him in a card game. Heathcliff also decided to marry Edgar's sister, Isabella, in order to punish Edgar for marrying Catherine. He seduced Isabella and soon they were married. This made Catherine ill, and she soon died after giving birth to a baby girl, whom Edgar named Catherine too. Soon, Hindley also died, leaving his son to live with Heathcliff at Wuthering Heights. Isabella left Heathcliff because of his violence towards her, and soon after gave birth to their son, Linton. She died, however, and Heathcliff got his son back. Next to die was Edgar, but just before he did, Heathcliff forced a marriage between Linton and Catherine. In this way, his son took possession of Edgar's old house, Thrushcross Grange. Linton, though, had always been weak and died just a month after the wedding. The novel ends with Heathcliff's death, and Hareton and Catherine planning to marry.

The novel caused quite a storm. Although it contains no explicit content, it was shocking to readers at the time for its passionate nature and dark subject matter. Like her sisters, and like many female authors of the age, Emily Brontë had chosen a male pseudonym, and a number of critics said that only a man could have come up with such a black tale, with violence and death in nearly every chapter. The characters were amoral and, in many cases, unlovable. Despite many people's initial horror, however, it was a success, and has since become a classic of English literature.

Listen & Read

2 **Listen to and read the passage from *Wuthering Heights*. First, read for general understanding. Then, reread the passage. As you read the second time, note down how you think Heathcliff must feel, hearing Catherine speak.**

In this passage, from Chapter 9, Catherine speaks with Nelly about her plans for marriage, her feelings for Edgar Linton, and her love for Heathcliff. They are in the kitchen at Wuthering Heights. The time is sometime in the 1770s. Unbeknownst to Catherine, Heathcliff is nearby and overhears everything.

'Nelly, will you keep a secret for me?' she pursued, kneeling down by me, and lifting her winsome eyes to my face with that sort of look which turns off bad temper, even when one has all the right in the world to indulge it.

'Is it worth keeping?' I inquired, less sulkily.

'Yes, and it worries me, and I must let it out! I want to know what I should do. Today, Edgar Linton has asked me to marry him, and I've given him an answer. Now, before I tell you whether it was a consent or denial, you tell me which it ought to have been.'

...

'Your brother will be pleased; the old lady and gentleman will not object, I think; you will escape from a disorderly, comfortless home into a wealthy, respectable one; and you love Edgar, and Edgar loves you. All seems smooth and easy: where is the obstacle?'

'*Here!* and *here!*' replied Catherine, striking one hand on her forehead, and the other on her breast: 'in whichever place the soul lives. In my soul and in my heart, I'm convinced I'm wrong!'

'That's very strange! I cannot make it out .'

'It's my secret. But if you will not mock at me, I'll explain it: I can't do it distinctly; but I'll give you a feeling of how I feel… I've no more business to marry Edgar Linton than I have to be in heaven; and if the wicked man in there had not brought Heathcliff so low, I shouldn't have thought of it. It would degrade me to marry Heathcliff now; so he shall never know how I love him: and that, not because he's handsome, Nelly, but because he's more myself than I am. Whatever our souls are made of, his and mine are the same; and Linton's is as different as a moonbeam from lightning, or frost from fire… If all else perished, and he remained, I should still continue to be; and if all else remained, and he were annihilated, the universe would turn to a mighty stranger: I should not seem a part of it. My love for Linton is like the foliage in the woods: time will change it, I'm well aware, as winter changes the trees. My love for Heathcliff resembles the eternal rocks beneath: a source of little visible delight, but necessary. Nelly, I am Heathcliff! He's always, always in my mind: not as a pleasure, any more than I am always a pleasure to myself, but as my own being.'

Respond

3 Respond to the passage by answering these questions with a partner.

1 Was your prediction about the main ideas of the passage correct? Explain.

2 How did the author communicate the main ideas? Pick one (or more) and explain.

a with images b with dialogue c by explaining it directly

3 Who are the important people in this passage?

4 Which of the words in the phrase bank do you think best describe how Catherine feels in the passage? Explain.

Phrase Bank

• upset • confused
• happy • scared
• ashamed • sad
• indifferent

Understand

4 Read the questions and choose the correct answers.

1 What does Catherine ask Nelly?

a if she should tell everybody about Edgar

b if she should marry Heathcliff

c if she should have accepted Edgar's proposal

d what Nelly thinks about Heathcliff

2 Which is NOT a reason that Nelly gives for being in favor of marrying Edgar?

a Catherine's parents will be happy.

b She will have a happier home.

c Edgar's parents will be happy.

d She and Edgar love each other.

3 Why doesn't Catherine want to marry Heathcliff?

a He's not handsome enough.

b His social class is not high enough.

c She loves Edgar more than him.

d She thinks of him as a brother.

4 What does Catherine say about Heathcliff?

a He will not be happy with her.

b He does not love her.

c He is better than Edgar.

d He is the same as her.

Literary Techniques

5 Why is this passage an example of dramatic irony? How does it make the reader feel? Share your ideas with the class.

Summarize

6 **First, fill in the graphic organizer based on the passage you read.**

Character(s)

Setting

Main Event(s)

Conflict

7 **Now, use your graphic organizer to summarize the passage with a partner.**

Listen

8 **Listen to a lecture about** *Wuthering Heights*. **Then, answer the questions.**

1 What is the speaker mostly talking about?

- a the narrator of *Wuthering Heights*
- b the main characters in *Wuthering Heights*
- c the setting of *Wuthering Heights*
- d the time frame of *Wuthering Heights*

2 What is Lockwood's importance in the story?

- a His actions set the story in motion.
- b He narrates the action of the story.
- c He is a substitute for the reader.
- d He provides commentary on the story.

Analyze the Title

9 Find It.

Listen to the lecture and fill in the second column of the graphic organizer. Then complete the third column with your own ideas.

Word	Definition	How it makes you feel ...
wuthering		
heights		

10 Think About It.

Wuthering Heights is a novel in the Gothic genre, which was extremely popular in the late 18th and 19th centuries. Gothic stories were tales of horror, often involving supernatural elements such as vampires and ghosts. It was a common practice to give Gothic works the name of a house, castle, or other residence as a title. This is because the general setting in a Gothic novel is enormously important, and all the more so the specific place where the main characters live. The building is generally old, imposing, and isolated from the outside world, with memories and secrets of its own, falling slowly to pieces through neglect. It is usually set in dark and forbidding surroundings, and all of this creates an atmosphere of fear, dread, and suspense.

Read the extract below from *Wuthering Heights* describing the house. How does it fit with Gothic conventions outlined in the box above?

"Wuthering Heights is the name of Mr. Heathcliff's dwelling. 'Wuthering' being a significant provincial adjective, descriptive of the atmospheric tumult to which its station is exposed in stormy weather. Pure, bracing ventilation they must have up there at all times, indeed: one may guess the power of the north wind blowing over the edge, by the excessive slant of a few stunted firs at the end of the house; and by a range of gaunt thorns all stretching their limbs one way, as if craving alms of the sun. Happily, the architect had foresight to build it strong: the narrow windows are deeply set in the wall, and the corners defended with large jutting stones.

Before passing the threshold, I paused to admire a quantity of grotesque carving lavished over the front, and especially about the principal door; above which, among a wilderness of crumbling griffins and shameless little boys, I detected the date '1500', and the name 'Hareton Earnshaw'."

11 Talk It Over.

With a partner, discuss the meanings of the two words and how they make you feel. Then answer the following question.

- Why do you think Emily Brontë named the house and the novel *Wuthering Heights*?

5

Analyze the Characters

12 Fill It In.

a. Listen to the first half of the lecture. Then, use words from the phrase bank to fill in the first Venn diagram.

Phrase Bank

• weak • blond hair • sadistic • handsome
• dark skin • blue eyes • rich • a gentleman
• cowardly • obsessive • of high social status
• cries about a puppy • nearly kills a dog
• an outsider • vengeful • patient • driven • kind

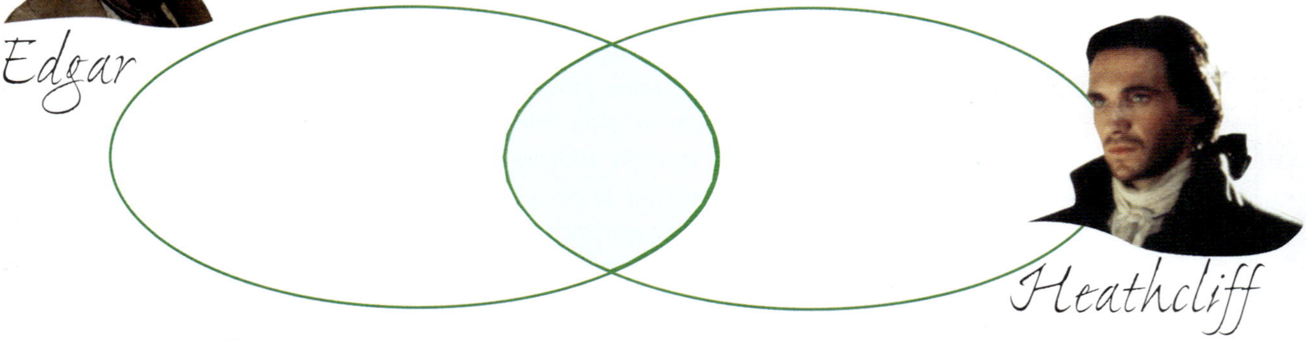

b. Listen to the second half of the lecture and use words from the phrase bank to fill in the second Venn diagram.

Phrase Bank

• wild • refined • attracted to Heathcliff
• spoiled • free-spirited • dark hair • shallow
• blonde hair • strong • abused • fragile
• dark eyes • blue eyes • sturdy • cruel

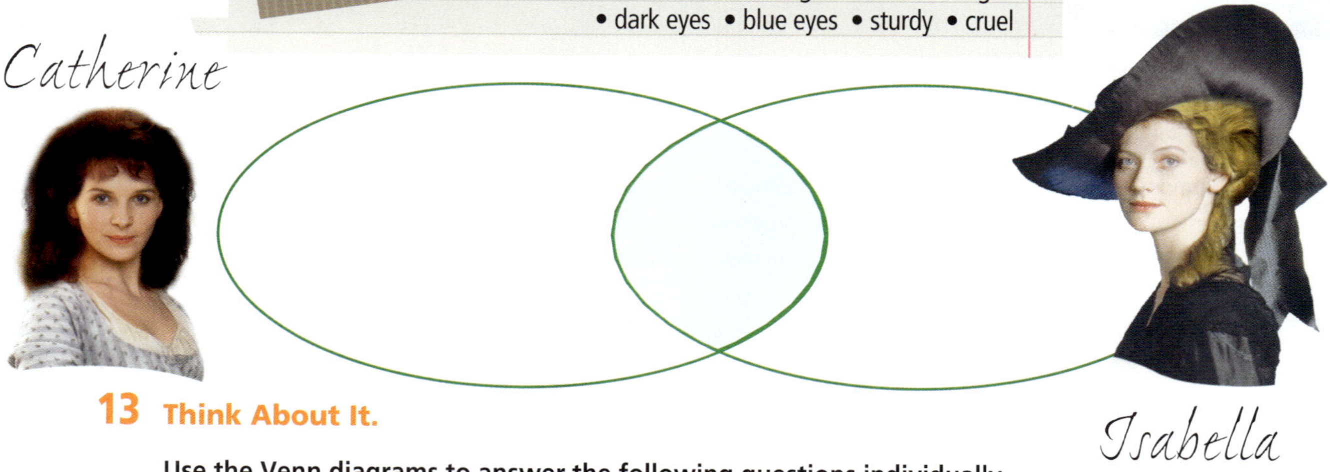

13 Think About It.

Use the Venn diagrams to answer the following questions individually.

- Are Edgar and Heathcliff more similar than different? What about Catherine and Isabella?
- Are Edgar and Catherine suited? What about Heathcliff and Isabella?

14 Talk It Over.

Discuss the previous questions with a partner. As a class, discuss the following question.

- Why did Catherine choose to marry Edgar and not Heathcliff?

Analyze the Setting

15 Fill It In.

Listen to the following lecture about the setting in *Wuthering Heights*. Then, use information from the lecture to fill in the graphic organizer.

Aspect of Setting	Importance in *Wuthering Heights*
time	
place	

16 Think About It.

With a partner, answer the following questions.

- Why do you think Brontë chose to set the novel in this time and place? Could the story take place in a different setting?

17 Talk It Over.

As a class, discuss your answers to the previous questions.

Analyze the Symbols

18 Match It.

Some important symbols in the novel are Wuthering Heights, the moors, and Thrushcross Grange. Match the symbols to their meanings.

Symbol

1 [ ] Wuthering Heights
2 [ ] the moor
3 [ ] Thrushcross Grange

Meaning

A comfort, luxury, warmth, civilization
B discomfort, cold, rudeness, unhappiness
C passion, wildness, danger

19 Think About It.

With a partner, discuss your answers to the previous section. Explain why you chose the answers that you did.

20 Talk It Over.

As a class, discuss the following questions.

- Which symbol do you think is the most important? Why?

Analyze the Themes

21 Fill It In.

Three important themes from *Wuthering Heights* are listed below. Fill in the graphic organizer with words or lines from the passage that relate to these themes.

Theme	Lines from Passage
love	
obsession	
social class	

22 Think About It.

Which theme do you think is most important and why?

23 Talk It Over.

Discuss your answer to the previous question with a partner.

In-Depth Analysis: Conflict

In a novel, a conflict occurs when one or more characters or entities want opposite or incompatible things. For example, perhaps one man has something that another man wants. The rest of the story could be about the resolution of this conflict. Will the first man steal from the second? Will he try to barter or trade with him? Maybe the second man will give him the object, but only if he performs some task. These possibilities are what make a good story. Without conflict, there would be no story to tell. If one man wanted something from another and the second man simply gave it up willingly, it would make for a very short story, and not a particularly interesting one.

There are several different kinds of conflict in literature. The most obvious one – used in the example above – is called "man versus man." (Note that here the word "man" here means any character, not just a male.) In this kind of conflict, two people have opposite or incompatible goals. Think, for example, of Edgar and Heathcliff. They both love Catherine, but they can't both be with her. This means that the two are in conflict.

A second kind of conflict is "man versus society." This conflict occurs when a person wants something that goes against the norms of their society. That is, they want to do something that most people think is wrong or improper. This conflict is also evident in *Wuthering Heights*. Heathcliff is an outsider in his society because of his appearance and social status. He wants to be with Catherine, but she is considered above him, so society does not allow it.

Characters can also feel a conflict called "man versus nature." Stories of people who are shipwrecked and must survive against all odds are good examples of this conflict. In *Wuthering Heights*, the weather often causes conflicts. For instance, Lockwood must spend a night at Wuthering Heights against his will when a blizzard prevents him from walking home.

Finally, characters may experience an internal conflict: "man versus self." In this kind of conflict, a character experiences two separate, but incompatible desires. Catherine has such a conflict when she must choose between Heathcliff and Edgar. She must somehow come to terms with both of her desires.

24 **Read the In-Depth Analysis. What are the four kinds of conflict? Give an example from the novel of each kind.**

25 **In groups of four, discuss your answers to the previous question. Then, as a group, write a short paragraph answering the following question. Use evidence from the In-Depth Analysis to back up your answers.**

- Authors use conflicts to move along the action in a novel. Based on the passage and what you know about *Wuthering Heights*, which conflict is the most important to the story and why?

Write

26 **Heathcliff and Edgar are two of the main characters in the novel. Write a 250- to 300-word essay comparing and contrasting the two men, and commenting on the significance of their differences in light of the choice Catherine is forced to make between them. When you can, quote the passage directly.**

VIDEO See p. 215 for video activities & essay writing

6

Moby Dick

Objectives

By the end of this unit, you will:

• know about the author and the background information behind the novel • thoroughly understand the passage from the novel • be able to identify figurative language in the passage • be able to summarize the passage • be able to analyze the title, characters, setting, symbols, and themes of the novel • know about foils in some depth • be able to use the passage to support your opinions and write a literature essay

VIDEO

Learn About ... Herman Melville

Herman Melville (1819-1891) was an American author. He was born in New York City and lived there for most of his childhood. When he finished school, he decided to get work at sea. Over the next few years, Melville worked on various ships and wrote about his experiences. These travel accounts sold fairly well. Encouraged by this, Melville set to writing what he considered to be his masterpiece: *Moby Dick*. Unfortunately, it sold extremely poorly. Critics hated it and Melville became less and less popular. Indeed, he struggled financially for most of his life. When he died in 1891, he was not considered by anyone to be a major name in American literature. This all changed, however, in the 1920s. People rediscovered his writing, including *Moby Dick*. Now, he is one of the most important figures in American literature, and *Moby Dick* is widely considered to be his masterpiece.

Predict

Step 1

Discuss these questions with a partner.

1 Why can the desire for revenge be so strong?

2 Can revenge ever be a healthy action? Why or why not?

Step 2

Look at the key words from the passage from *Moby Dick*. **With a partner, discuss the meaning of the words. Based on the words, predict the mood of the passage.**

Background Information

1 Read the text and answer the questions.

1 What is "whaling"?
2 Who or what is Moby Dick?
3 Who tells the story in *Moby Dick*?
4 What are the names of the main characters, and what are their positions on the Pequod?
5 Why is Moby Dick important to the story?

Moby Dick takes place sometime in the late 1830s or early 1840s (no exact year is given in the text) and tells the story of a whaling ship, the Pequod. In the past, large ships went out to hunt whales. The people sold the whales for their blubber, or fat, their meat, and, in the case of sperm whales, a substance called spermaceti. This liquid was important for making perfume, among other things. Whaling was a dangerous but exciting job. The narrator of *Moby Dick* is a young man called Ishmael. He comes aboard the ship looking for work and an adventure. What he doesn't realize is that the ship's captain, Ahab, is unhealthily obsessed with a white whale called Moby Dick. Although the whalers catch whales throughout their trip, Ahab remains fixated on the prospect of finding and killing Moby Dick. Eventually the men do encounter the whale. They pursue him for three days, and are attacked several times. On the third day, the whale sinks the boat and everyone dies except for Ishmael.

Throughout the book, Ishmael meets many other interesting characters aboard the ship. His best friend is Queequeg, a harpooner from somewhere in the South Seas. Ishmael distrusts him at first because of his strange appearance and religious customs. The men soon become close friends, however. Other crew members include Starbuck, the thoughtful chief mate, who is alone in opposing the captain's strange quest for revenge; Stubb, the always-cheerful second mate; and Flask, the third mate, who believes that nothing is sacred.

Ishmael tells the story from his point of view for most of the novel. At times, however, his narrative voice disappears and a more omniscient (all-knowing) narrator appears. This gives a unique flavor to this American classic.

6

Listen & Read

2 **Listen to and read the passage from** *Moby Dick*. **First, read for general understanding. Then, reread the passage. As you read the second time, note down what the characters say about Moby Dick.**

In this passage, from Chapter 36, Captain Ahab has just told the men on the ship that he will give a piece of gold to the first person to spot Moby Dick, the white whale.

"Captain Ahab," said Starbuck, who, with Stubb and Flask, had thus far been eyeing his superior with increasing surprise, but at last seemed struck with a thought which somewhat explained all the wonder. "Captain Ahab, I have heard of Moby Dick—but it was not Moby Dick that took off thy leg?"

"Who told thee that?" cried Ahab; then pausing, "Aye, Starbuck; aye, my hearties all round; it was Moby Dick that dismasted me; Moby Dick that brought me to this dead stump I stand on now. Aye, aye," he shouted with a terrific, loud, animal sob, like that of a heart-stricken moose; "Aye, aye! it was that accursed white whale that razeed me; made a poor pegging lubber of me for ever and a day!" Then tossing both arms, with measureless imprecations he shouted out: "Aye, aye! and I'll chase him round Good Hope, and round the Horn, and round the Norway Maelstrom, and round perdition's flames before I give him up. And this is what ye have shipped for, men! to chase that white whale on both sides of land, and over all sides of earth, till he spouts black blood and rolls fin out. What say ye, men, will ye splice hands on it, now? I think ye do look brave."

"Aye, aye!" shouted the harpooneers and seamen, running closer to the excited old man: "A sharp eye for the white whale; a sharp lance for Moby Dick!"

"God bless ye," he seemed to half sob and half shout. "God bless ye, men. Steward! go draw the great measure of grog. But what's this long face about, Mr. Starbuck; wilt thou not chase the white whale? art not game for Moby Dick?"

"I am game for his crooked jaw, and for the jaws of Death too, Captain Ahab, if it fairly comes in the way of the business we follow; but I came here to hunt whales, not my commander's vengeance. How many barrels will thy vengeance yield thee even if thou gettest it, Captain Ahab? it will not fetch thee much in our Nantucket market."

"Nantucket market! Hoot! But come closer, Starbuck; thou requirest a little lower layer. If money's to be the measurer, man, and the accountants have computed their great counting-house the globe, by girdling it with guineas, one to every three parts of an inch; then, let me tell thee, that my vengeance will fetch a great premium HERE!"

"He smites his chest," whispered Stubb, "what's that for? methinks it rings most vast, but hollow."

"Vengeance on a dumb brute!" cried Starbuck, "that simply smote thee from blindest instinct! Madness! To be enraged with a dumb thing, Captain Ahab, seems blasphemous."

Respond

3 Respond to the passage by answering these questions with a partner.

1. Was your prediction about the mood of the passage correct? Explain.
2. How did the author create the mood? Think about the words of the characters.
3. Who are the important people in this passage?
4. How do you think Captain Ahab feels in the passage?

Understand

4 Read the questions and choose the correct answers.

1 Which of the following places does Ahab NOT say he'll go to find Moby Dick?

- a Good Hope
- b the Horn
- c perdition
- d Nantucket

2 Who does not give Ahab total support?

- a Stubb
- b the harpooneers
- c the narrator
- d Starbuck

3 Why does Ahab want to kill Moby Dick?

- a because the whale is worth a lot of money
- b because he lost his leg to the whale
- c because the whale is very rare
- d because there is a prize for catching the whale

4 What does Ahab ask the steward to bring the men?

- a a large meal
- b a golden coin
- c a round of drinks
- d new, sharp weapons

Figurative Language

5 Work with a partner. Find one example of a simile, one example of a pun, and one example of personification in the passage.

Summarize

6 **First, fill in the graphic organizer based on the passage you read.**

Character(s)	Setting

Main Event(s)	Conflict

7 **Now, use your graphic organizer to summarize the passage with a partner.**

Listen

8 **Listen to a lecture about *Moby Dick*. Then, answer the questions.**

1 What is the speaker mostly talking about?

- **a** why Ishmael is a biased narrator
- **b** why Melville shouldn't have picked the narrator he did
- **c** why it's important to discuss narrators
- **d** why Ishmael was a good choice for narrator

2 How does the speaker organize her lecture?

- **a** by presenting two opposing opinions
- **b** by making a claim and supporting it
- **c** by refuting a common misconception
- **d** by explaining an author's reasoning

Analyze the Title

9 Find It.

Moby Dick is obviously important to the novel. In the passage, the reader learns a little bit about the whale. Go through the passage and underline every time one of the characters mentions the whale.

10 Think About It.

Using the underlined parts of the passage, write a paragraph explaining what you know about Moby Dick. Include as many details as possible.

11 Talk It Over.

Share your paragraph with a partner. Then, read your partner's paragraph. Compare and contrast your two descriptions. Add additional information to your description as needed. Then, as a class, discuss why you think Melville decided to name the book after the whale.

Analyze the Characters

12 Fill It In.

a. Listen to the first half of the lecture and use the words from the phrase bank to fill in the graphic organizer.

Phrase Bank

• natural goodness • religious
• inexperienced • introduce Ahab
• bloodthirsty • ship's owners
• harpooner • everyman • chief mate
• no fear of death • second mate • hates whales

Character	Role	Quality 1	Quality 2
Ishmael	narrator		
Peleg & Bildad		comic relief	
Queequeg		the "other"	
Starbuck		practical	
Stubb		joker	
Flask	third mate		

b. Listen to the second half of the lecture and use words from the phrase bank to fill in the Venn diagram.

Phrase Bank

• man • antagonist • invader • animal
• vengeful • wounded • in his element
• powerful • protagonist

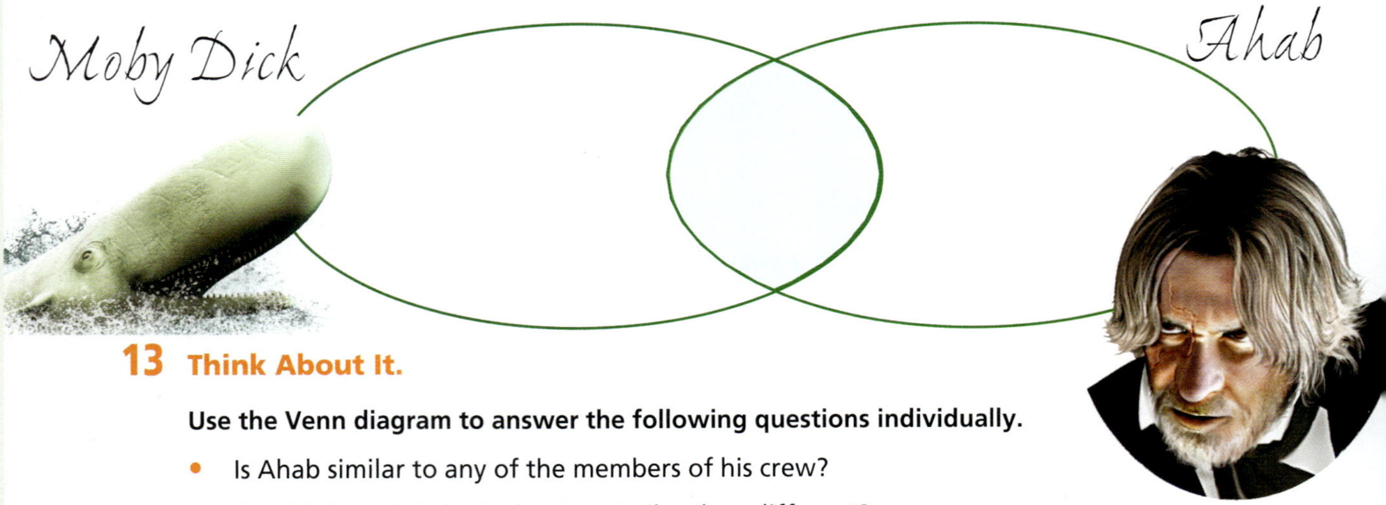

13 Think About It.

Use the Venn diagram to answer the following questions individually.

- Is Ahab similar to any of the members of his crew?
- Are Ahab and Moby Dick more similar than different?

14 Talk It Over.

Discuss the answers to the previous questions with a partner. Share your ideas with the class.

Analyze the Setting

15 Fill It In.

Listen to a lecture about the setting in *Moby Dick*. Then, use information from the lecture to fill in the graphic organizer.

Aspect of Setting	Importance in *Moby Dick*
time	
place	

16 Think About It.

With a partner answer the following questions.

Why do you think Melville chose to set his novel in this time and place? Could the story take place in a different setting?

17 Talk It Over.

As a class, discuss your answers to the previous questions.

Analyze the Symbols

18 Match It.

Moby Dick, the white whale, is the most important symbol in the novel. The whale means many different things to different people. Below are two columns. One column has some meanings of Moby Dick. The other column has lines from the book. Look at the two lists. Then, pick which lines you think go along with which ideas.

1 [ ] death
2 [ ] superstition
3 [ ] evil
4 [ ] revenge

A Ahab has "piled upon the whale's white hump the sum of all the general rage and hate felt by his whole race."

B Ahab says to Moby Dick, "To the last I grapple with thee; from hell's heart I stab at thee; for hate's sake I spit my last breath at thee."

C Ahab asks another sailor, "Hast seen the White Whale?" and the man responds, "No; only heard of him; but don't believe in him at all."

D The whale's whiteness reminds Ishmael of the "one visible aspect of the dead which most appals the gazer ... the marble pallor lingering there."

19 Think About It.

With a partner answer the following questions.

- Does Moby Dick mean the same thing to every person in the book?
- Do you think that Melville intended for Moby Dick to be an easy symbol to analyze? Why or why not?

20 Talk It Over.

As a class, discuss the following question.

Based on what you know about the book, which meaning do you think is most important? Why?

Analyze the Themes

21 Fill It In.

Use lines from the passage to fill in the graphic organizer.

Theme	Lines from Passage
revenge	
madness	

22 Think About It.

Which theme do you think is most important in this passage and why?

23 Talk It Over.

Discuss your answer to the previous question with a partner.

In-Depth Analysis: Foils

In literature, a foil is a character that is different than another in an important way. The author uses foils to illuminate certain character traits in both characters. In some cases, foils are very simple. For example, one character might be honorable and good and the other might be evil and cruel. Most of the time, however, foils are much more complex. Foils may share some similarities with one another. These similarities often serve to highlight characters' differences. In fact, a character might have more than one foil. Each foil can emphasize different aspects of a character's personality.

Starbuck serves as a foil to Ahab. In the passage, the two men act very differently. They have different objectives and goals. Starbuck's calm way of behaving and logical thought process makes Ahab look and sound all the more out of control and crazy. His insistence on whaling for profits shows how unreasonable Ahab's thirst for vengeance is.

This contrast is made all the stronger, however, by the similarities between the two men. This is a sign of a powerful foil character, since it is only really possible to contrast two things which are similar in some way.

24 **Read the In-Depth Analysis and reread the passage from *Moby Dick*. Then, use the words from the phrase bank to complete the Venn diagram.**

Phrase Bank

- angry
- wants money
- insane
- position of authority
- whaler
- calm
- wants revenge
- has experience
- in control

25 **Use your notes in Ex. 24 to compare and contrast the characters.**

26 **In groups of four, discuss your answers to Ex. 25. Then, as a group, talk about what Moby Dick represents to each man.**

Write

27 **Authors use foils to emphasize certain traits in a character. What trait or traits do you think Melville wanted to emphasize in Ahab through his foil, Starbuck, and what difference in attitude do they have towards Moby Dick? Using your answers from the sections above, write a 250- to 300-word essay about how Starbuck works as a foil to Ahab in the novel.**

VIDEO
See p. 216
for video activities & essay writing

7 Great Expectations

Objectives

By the end of this unit, you will:

• know about the author and the background information behind the novel • thoroughly understand the passage from the novel • be able to identify the point of view in the passage • be able to summarize the passage • be able to analyze the title, characters, setting, symbols, and themes of the novel • know about Victorian fiction in some depth • be able to use the passage to support your opinions and write a literature essay

VIDEO

Learn About ... Charles Dickens

Charles Dickens (1812-1870) was an English author. He wrote many famous books and created lots of memorable characters. His parents took him out of school at the age of eleven because they couldn't afford it, and shortly after his twelfth birthday, he started work in a factory. Shortly afterwards, his father was sent to debtors' prison. His terrible childhood did not discourage him, however. Instead, it made him determined to succeed. At the age of 24, his first book, *The Pickwick Papers*, was published, and his dream of success came true. He became a literary celebrity and enjoyed fame and financial security. He continued to write for the rest of his life. He also gave talks and readings to supplement his income. His work ethic was strong and he was often very busy. The most common themes in Dickens' work are those of social class, injustice, and the treatment of the poor. His novels told interesting stories, and at the same time they commented on the state of Victorian Britain.

Predict

Step 1

Discuss these questions with a partner.

1 Can two people from different social classes be friends? Why or why not?

2 What are some barriers that social class creates?

Step 2

Look at the key words from the *Great Expectations* **passage. With a partner, discuss the meaning of the words. Based on the words, predict the main ideas of the passage.**

Background Information

1 Read the text and answer the questions.

1. What happened to Pip's parents?
2. Why is Pip unsuitable for Estella?
3. Who does Pip think gave him the money to become a gentleman?
4. Who really gave Pip the money to become a gentleman?
5. In what way is *Great Expectations* like most of Dickens' other novels?

Great Expectations is one of Charles Dickens' most famous novels. It's set in early Victorian England (c. 1840-50) and tells the story of a young man named Pip. Pip is an orphan, and his older sister takes care of him. She is very mean to both him and her husband, Joe. One day, Pip meets a convict called Magwitch, who has escaped from prison. Pip helps the man and gives him some food and a file to remove the chains.

Some time later, Pip goes to play at Satis House, where the strange Miss Havisham lives. Miss Havisham is a old woman who always wears a wedding dress. She takes care of a beautiful little girl, Estella. Pip is soon in love with Estella, but he knows that he is not a gentleman, and will therefore never be with her. Furthermore, Estella is often mean to Pip.

Pip starts working as a blacksmith with Joe, but he dreams of being a rich gentleman. One day, his dreams come true. A lawyer tells him that some mysterious benefactor has given him a sum of money. Pip thinks that it must be Miss Havisham and is excited to become a gentleman for Estella. Pip moves to London, buys fancy clothes, and spends a lot of money on frivolous things. He forgets about his old friends, and when Joe comes to visit, Pip is embarrassed by his accent, manners, and appearance.

In the end, Pip finds out that it was Magwitch, and not Miss Havisham, who gave him the money. In addition, Miss Havisham does not want him to marry Estella. In fact, Miss Havisham hates men and only used Estella to make Pip feel bad. Eventually, Pip loses his fortune and leaves Britain. Before doing so, he makes up with Joe, who has married loving, kind Biddy, after Pip's cruel sister died. Pip works as a merchant in Egypt for eleven years to pay off his debts and, when he comes back, he runs into Estella. She is nice to him, for a change, and the book ends with them holding hands.

Like almost all of Dickens' works, *Great Expectations* is a story with a moral, warning of the dangers of easy money, a life of leisure and snobbishness. It promotes the simple values of friendship, honesty, and warmth, while hinting that social advancement is possible through hard work and education.

Listen & Read

2 **Listen to and read the passage from *Great Expectations*. First, read for general understanding. Then, reread the passage. As you read the second time, decide what emotions and conflicts Pip feels as he listens to Joe speak.**

In this passage, from Chapter 27, Joe has come to visit Pip in London. Joe wears his nicest clothes, which are still old-fashioned and shabby compared to everyone else Pip knows. Throughout the visit, Pip is embarrassed by Joe and his appearance. This is what Joe says when he leaves Pip.

"I have now concluded, sir," said Joe, rising from his chair, "and, Pip, I wish you ever well and ever prospering to a greater and a greater height."

"But you are not going now, Joe?"

"Yes I am," said Joe.

"But you are coming back to dinner, Joe?"

"No I am not," said Joe.

Our eyes met, and all the "Sir" melted out of that manly heart as he gave me his hand.

"Pip, dear old chap, life is made of ever so many partings welded together, as I may say, and one man's a blacksmith, and one's a whitesmith, and one's a goldsmith, and one's a coppersmith. Divisions among such must come, and must be met as they come. If there's been any fault at all to-day, it's mine. You and me is not two figures to be together in London; nor yet anywheres else but what is private, and beknown, and understood among friends. It ain't that I am proud, but that I want to be right, as you shall never see me no more in these clothes. I'm wrong in these clothes. I'm wrong out of the forge, the kitchen, or off th' meshes. You won't find half so much fault in me if you think of me in my forge dress, with my hammer in my hand, or even my pipe. You won't find half so much fault in me if, supposing as you should ever wish to see me, you come and put your head in at the forge window and see Joe the blacksmith, there, at the old anvil, in the old burnt apron, sticking to the old work. I'm awful dull, but I hope I've beat out something nigh the rights of this at last. And so GOD bless you, dear old Pip, old chap, GOD bless you!"

I had not been mistaken in my fancy that there was a simple dignity in him. The fashion of his dress could no more come in its way when he spoke these words than it could come in its way in Heaven. He touched me gently on the forehead, and went out. As soon as I could recover myself sufficiently, I hurried out after him and looked for him in the neighbouring streets; but he was gone.

Respond

3 Respond to the passage by answering these questions with a partner.

1 Was your prediction about the main ideas of the passage correct? Explain.

2 How did the author communicate the main ideas? Pick one (or more) and explain.

a with images b with dialogue c by explaining it directly

3 Who are the important people in this passage?

4 Which of the words in the phrase bank do you think best describe how Pip feels in the passage? Explain.

Phrase Bank

- embarrassed
- sad
- excited
- ashamed
- happy
- angry
- understanding

Understand

4 Read the questions and choose the correct answers.

1 What does Pip ask Joe?

a if he's ready to leave
b if he's coming to dinner
c if he'll buy new clothes
d if he'll leave Pip alone

2 Why does Joe use the comparison of metalworkers?

a to illustrate the kind of people he likes
b to show the divisions in his trade
c to explain the different classes of people
d to indicate how important blacksmiths are

3 Where does Joe say he and Pip should meet?

a in private
b in London
c in an area with lots of people
d in the marshes

4 Where does Joe feel most comfortable?

a in London
b with his wife
c in his forge
d with Pip

Point of View

5 Work with a partner. Does a first-person narrator or a third-person narrator tell the story? Is the narrator omniscient or limited? How do you know?

7

Summarize

6 **First, fill in the graphic organizer based on the passage you read.**

Character(s)	Setting

Main Event(s)	Conflict

7 **Now, use your graphic organizer to summarize the passage with a partner.**

Listen

8 **Listen to a lecture about *Great Expectations*. Then, answer the questions.**

1 What is the speaker mostly talking about?

- **a** a change that Dickens made to the novel
- **b** the life of Estella after the novel ends
- **c** reasons that Pip and Estella get married
- **d** the sad tone of the novel

2 Why did Dickens write a second ending?

- **a** because the first wasn't realistic
- **b** because he didn't like the first
- **c** because the first was too sad
- **d** because the publishers asked him to

Analyze the Title

9 Find It.

Look up the definitions of the words in the graphic organizer and fill in the empty column.

Word	Definition
great	
expectations	

10 Think About It.

For his title, Dickens chose two words that appear a number of times in the novel. This is a common novelistic device, and makes the words jump out at the reader when they come across them. Read this extract, in which the words first appear, and answer the questions.

"... the communication I have got to make is, that he has great expectations."

Joe and I gasped, and looked at one another.

"I am instructed to communicate to him," said Mr. Jaggers, throwing his finger at me sideways, "that he will come into a handsome property. Further, that it is the desire of the present possessor of that property, that he be immediately removed from his present sphere of life and from this place, and be brought up as a gentleman – in a word, as a young fellow of great expectations."

My dream was out; my wild fancy was surpassed by sober reality ...

- Who does the title clearly refer to?
- What are the "great expectations" referred to in this extract?
- Considering how the book turns out, how does the title sound?

11 Talk It Over.

As a class, discuss your answers to the previous questions. Then, talk about why you think Dickens chose to call the novel *Great Expectations*.

7

Analyze the Characters

12 Fill It In.

Listen to the lecture. Use the words above each graphic organizer to fill it in.

• grows and changes • feels compassion • unchanging • hardworking
• kind • learns from his mistakes

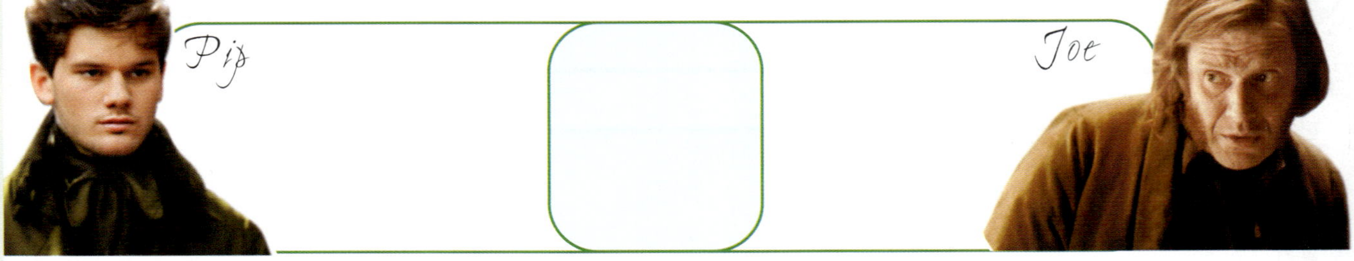

• wants revenge • ends up sorry • beautiful • rich • unkind • eccentric

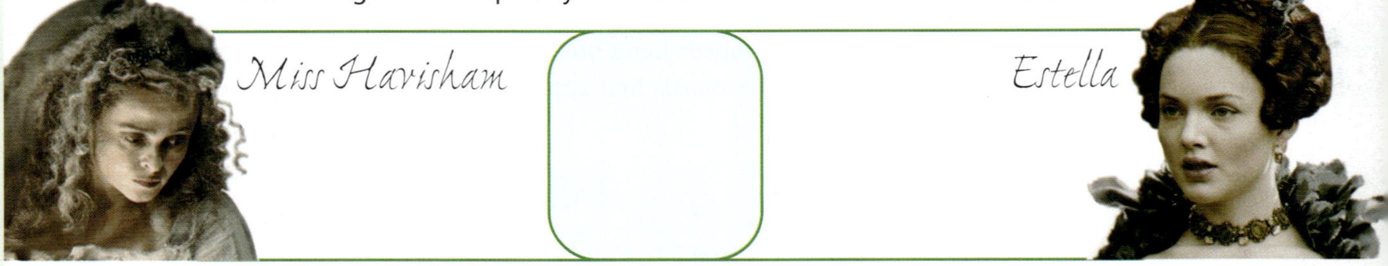

• went to jail • good at heart • bad to the core • Miss Havisham's former fiancé
• Estella's real father • forged signatures

13 Think About It.

Use the Venn diagram to answer the following questions individually.

- Which two characters are most similar, and which are most different?
- As the story progresses, does Pip become *more* like Joe, or less like Joe?

14 Talk It Over.

Discuss the answers to the previous questions with a partner. As a class, discuss the following question.

- Besides his part in the plot, what is Joe's importance in the story?

Analyze the Setting

15 Fill It In.

Listen to the following lecture about the setting in *Great Expectations*. Then, use information from the lecture to fill in the graphic organizer.

Aspect of Setting		Importance in *Great Expectations*
time		
place	Satis House	
	Joe's house	

16 Think About It.

With a partner, answer the following question.

- Could *Great Expectations* be set in the modern era?
- How do the two settings add to the main ideas of the novel?

17 Talk It Over.

As a class, discuss your answers to the previous question.

Analyze the Symbols

18 Match It.

Listen to the lecture and match the symbols to their meanings.

Symbol	Meaning
1 ☐ stopped clocks	A living in the past, refusing to move forward
2 ☐ the wedding cake	B decay
3 ☐ the wedding dress	C death

19 Talk It Over.

As a class, discuss the following questions.

- Which symbol do you think is the most important? Why?

Analyze the Themes

20 Fill It In.

Three important themes from *Great Expectations* are listed below. Fill in the graphic organizer with words or lines from the passage that relate to these themes.

Theme	Lines from Passage
appearance	
social class	
success	

21 Think About It.

Which theme do you think is most important in the passage and why?

22 Talk It Over.

Discuss your answer to the previous question with a partner.

In-Depth Analysis: Victorian Literature

The Victorian era in England lasted from 1837 to 1901. During this time, the most popular literary form was the novel. Indeed, the novel changed drastically during these times. Victorian novels are usually quite dense, with complicated plots, lots of characters, and realistic (and sometimes tediously detailed) physical descriptions. Charles Dickens' novels reflect these changes quite well. He writes stories with many different characters, twisting and turning plots that keep readers guessing, and very descriptive language that paints a picture of scenes of life in London.

All of these stylistic features are important, but there were thematic changes in novels as well. One of the most important themes in Victorian literature is the drive for social advancement. People in all groups and in all social classes wanted to move up. Things were changing in Victorian Britain. People were beginning to feel like they had more social mobility. It was becoming easier to make money, at least. Novels reflected this preoccupation with moving up. They told stories of people who fought and worked to achieve a better position. Again, Dickens' novels are great examples. Pip, from *Great Expectations*, wants to become a real gentleman. Although he does not succeed in this aim, he does move up into a new class – the middle class.

The emerging middle class is another important theme in Victorian literature. With the Industrial Revolution in full swing, a new group began to emerge in English society. These people were not poor or members of the working class. Nor were they nobility or members of the upper class. Instead, they were merchants, doctors, lawyers – in short, working professionals. Above the working poor, but below the aristocracy, this new group had to find a place for itself. Dickens captures this idea, as well. In *Great Expectations*, for example, Pip wants to be a member of the upper class – a gentleman. This doesn't work out, however. Instead, through his own hard work and perseverance, Pip is able to become part of the middle class, working as a merchant. This illustrates one of the most important values in the middle class: hard work. It also highlights a final feature of Victorian novels – they often contain a strong moral message.

Victorian novels reflect the times in which they were written. They're often long, complex, and deal with the social changes of the time and place in which they were written.

23 **Read the In-Depth Analysis. What are the characteristics of Victorian novels? Does** *Great Expectations* **have these characteristics?**

24 **In groups of four, discuss your answers to the previous questions. Then, as a group, write a short paragraph answering the following question. Use evidence from the In-Depth Analysis and the passage from** *Great Expectations* **to back up your answer.**

- *Great Expectations* was written in the Victorian Era. Is it a good example of a Victorian novel? Why or why not?

Write

25 **Joe's house and Miss Havisham's Satis House are very important settings in** *Great Expectations*. **Write a 250- to 300-word essay about their significance to the novel, and the role each plays in the moral lesson Pip has to learn.**

VIDEO See p. 217 for video activities & essay writing

8 Strange Case of Dr. Jekyll and Mr. Hyde

Objectives

By the end of this unit, you will:

• know about the author and the background information behind the novel • thoroughly understand the passage from the novel • be able to identify figurative language in the passage • be able to summarize the passage • be able to analyze the title, characters, setting, symbols, and themes of the novel • know about doppelgangers in some depth • be able to use the passage to support your opinions and write a literature essay

VIDEO

Learn About ... Robert Louis Stevenson

Robert Louis Stevenson (1850-1894) was a very important Scottish writer. Though his family expected him to go into the family business of lighthouse design, he knew he wanted to become a writer from an early age. Although his father was disappointed, he supported his son's decision.

Stevenson spent much of his life suffering from poor health. He moved from place to place in Europe, later to the USA, and finally to Samoa, to find a climate that would be good for his health condition. Samoa ended up being just the place for him, and he moved there with his wife and her children in 1890. He became a respected and loved member of the community and when he died in 1894, the local population grieved their loss. He was buried there on a hill overlooking the sea.

Stevenson is best known for his adventure and travel books as well as for the psychological thriller, *Strange Case of Dr. Jekyll and Mr. Hyde.*

Predict

Step 1

Discuss these questions with a partner.

1 Can someone be all good or all bad? Explain.

2 What are some ways that people deal with their "bad" or "evil" impulses?

Step 2

Look at the key words from the passage from *Strange Case of Dr. Jekyll and Mr. Hyde*. **With a partner, discuss the meaning of the words. Based on the words, predict the main ideas of the passage.**

Background Information

1 Read the text and answer the questions.

1. Why does Dr. Jekyll create the potion?
2. How does Dr. Jekyll feel about his transformation at the beginning?
3. What was the apparent cause of Dr. Jekyll/Mr. Hyde's death?
4. Who narrates the final chapter of the novel?
5. Who did not particularly care for *Strange Case of Dr. Jekyll and Mr. Hyde* at first?

Strange Case of Dr. Jekyll and Mr. Hyde takes place in London in the late 19th century. It tells the story of a scientist, Dr. Jekyll, who is a respectable, upstanding citizen. But he's bothered by the dark impulses that he feels, the urges he has to commit acts that he considers evil. Instead of acknowledging and dealing with these impulses, Jekyll invents a potion that he hopes will separate his good side from his bad side. By separating himself into two individual personalities, he feels he can indulge his dark side without his good side suffering terrible pangs of conscience.

When Jekyll first drinks the potion he has created, he realizes that he has transformed into a different person. He calls this other man Hyde. Hyde is completely evil; he's Jekyll's completely bad side. To turn back into Jekyll, Hyde must drink another potion. At first, Jekyll enjoys his new-found freedom. He transforms into Hyde and does all of the terrible things that he isn't allowed to do normally, and then he turns back into Jekyll and enjoys his respectable life. Over time, however, it takes more and more of the potion to turn Hyde back into Jekyll. Not only that: he begins to turn into Mr. Hyde without even taking it. The evil side of his personality has become more powerful than the good. The short novel ends with Jekyll's friends discovering Hyde's dead body in Jekyll's locked room. A letter from Jekyll explains it all and implies that Hyde will most likely kill himself rather than go on trial for the terrible things that he did; which is, it seems, what has happened.

Most of the novel is told by an omnipresent narrator from the perspective of Dr. Jekyll's lawyer, Utterson. He is trying to find out who the mysterious Mr. Hyde is, and what hold he has over Utterson's client. The last two chapters take the form of confessional letters, one from Dr. Jekyll's deceased friend Dr. Lanyon and the second Jekyll himself, which together provide the answer to the mystery.

Though it was not immediately embraced by literary critics, Stevenson's story was an instant popular success. Published in 1886, it was estimated to have sold 250,000 copies by 1901, which was a huge number at the time. It was soon adapted for the stage on both sides of the Atlantic, and versions have since been broadcast on the radio, on television, and in the cinema. In fact, there are over 123 film versions of the story alone.

Listen & Read

2 🎧 **Listen to and read the passage from** *Strange Case of Dr. Jekyll and Mr. Hyde*. **First, read for general understanding. Then, reread the passage. As you read the second time, underline the words Jekyll uses to describe Hyde.**

This passage comes from Chapter 10, where Dr. Jekyll confesses everything in a letter. His friend and lawyer Utterson finds this letter along with Hyde's dead body towards the end of the story. In this passage, Jekyll describes the first time that he transforms into the evil Mr. Hyde.

I must here speak by theory alone, saying not that which I know, but that which I suppose to be most probable. The evil side of my nature, to which I had now transferred the stamping efficacy, was less robust and less developed than the good which I had just deposed. Again, in the course of my life, which had been, after all, nine tenths a life of effort, virtue and control, it had been much less exercised and much less exhausted. And hence, as I think, it came about that Edward Hyde was so much smaller, slighter and younger than Henry Jekyll. Even as good shone upon the countenance of the one, evil was written broadly and plainly on the face of the other. Evil besides (which I must still believe to be the lethal side of man) had left on that body an imprint of deformity and decay. And yet when I looked upon that ugly idol in the glass, I was conscious of no repugnance, rather of a leap of welcome. This, too, was myself. It seemed natural and human. In my eyes it bore a livelier image of the spirit, it seemed more express and single, than the imperfect and divided countenance I had been hitherto accustomed to call mine. And in so far I was doubtless right. I have observed that when I wore the semblance of Edward Hyde, none could come near to me at first without a visible misgiving of the flesh. This, as I take it, was because all human beings, as we meet them, are commingled out of good and evil: and Edward Hyde, alone in the ranks of mankind, was pure evil.

I lingered but a moment at the mirror: the second and conclusive experiment had yet to be attempted; it yet remained to be seen if I had lost my identity beyond redemption and must flee before daylight from a house that was no longer mine; and hurrying back to my cabinet, I once more prepared and drank the cup, once more suffered the pangs of dissolution, and came to myself once more with the character, the stature and the face of Henry Jekyll.

Respond

3 Respond to the passage by answering these questions with a partner.

1. Was your prediction about the main ideas of the passage correct? Explain.
2. How did the author communicate the main ideas? Pick one (or more) and explain.
   - a with images
   - b with dialogue
   - c by explaining it directly
3. Who are the important people in this passage?
4. Which of the words from the phrase bank do you think best describe how Jekyll feels in the passage? Explain.

Phrase Bank

- happy
- scared
- excited
- confused
- horrified
- ashamed
- indifferent

5. Imagine you were Dr. Jekyll looking at yourself in a mirror as Mr. Hyde. Describe your feelings.

Understand

4 Read the questions and choose the correct answers.

1. What is true of Edward Hyde?
   - a He is taller than Jekyll.
   - b He is younger than Jekyll.
   - c He is more handsome than Jekyll.
   - d He is smarter than Jekyll.
2. How does Jekyll feel when he sees Hyde in the mirror?
   - a shocked
   - b disgusted
   - c afraid
   - d glad
3. Why is Hyde different than all other people?
   - a There is no good within him.
   - b His body is strangely deformed.
   - c His anger is overly powerful.
   - d There are two clear sides to his nature.
4. How do people react when they see Hyde?
   - a They are curious.
   - b They run away.
   - c They are uncomfortable.
   - d They don't talk to him.

Figurative Language

5 Work with a partner. Find two examples of organic imagery and two examples of kinesthetic imagery in the passage.

Summarize

6 **First, fill in the graphic organizer based on the passage you read.**

Character(s)

Setting

Main Event(s)

Conflict

7 **Now, use your graphic organizer to summarize the passage with a partner.**

Listen

8 **Listen to a lecture about** *Strange Case of Dr. Jekyll and Mr. Hyde*. **Then, answer the questions.**

1 What is the speaker mostly talking about?

- **a** important themes in *Jekyll and Hyde*
- **b** the historical context of *Jekyll and Hyde*
- **c** the setting of *Jekyll and Hyde*
- **d** the main conflict in *Jekyll and Hyde*

2 Why does the speaker mention Charles Darwin?

- **a** to explain how he influenced *Jekyll and Hyde*
- **b** to show the science behind *Jekyll and Hyde*
- **c** to tell where Stevenson got the idea for *Jekyll and Hyde*
- **d** to illustrate a common viewpoint from the time period of *Jekyll and Hyde*

Analyze the Title

9 Answer the Questions.

- Does the title resemble a newspaper headline, the title of a medical report, or the subject line of a police report?
- What impression do the different titles of the two men (**Dr.** Jekyll and **Mr.** Hyde) give you?
- Dr. Jekyll himself chooses the name "Hyde" for his alter ego. Why do you think he chooses this name?

10 Think About It.

What cover would you design for the book? Write a short paragraph describing what an appropriate cover for the book would look like. Then, compare your paragraph with your partner's.

....

....

....

....

....

....

....

11 Talk It Over.

As a class, discuss whether *Strange Case of Dr. Jekyll and Mr. Hyde* **is a good title for the book. What other titles might be suitable?**

Analyze the Characters

12 Fill It In.

Listen to the lecture. Then, use words from the bank to fill in the Venn diagram.

Phrase Bank

• tall • conflicted • pure evil • respectable
• free • small • ugly • deformed
• normal-looking • tormented by his desires
• does whatever he wants • has no regrets
• well-known • well-liked • respectable

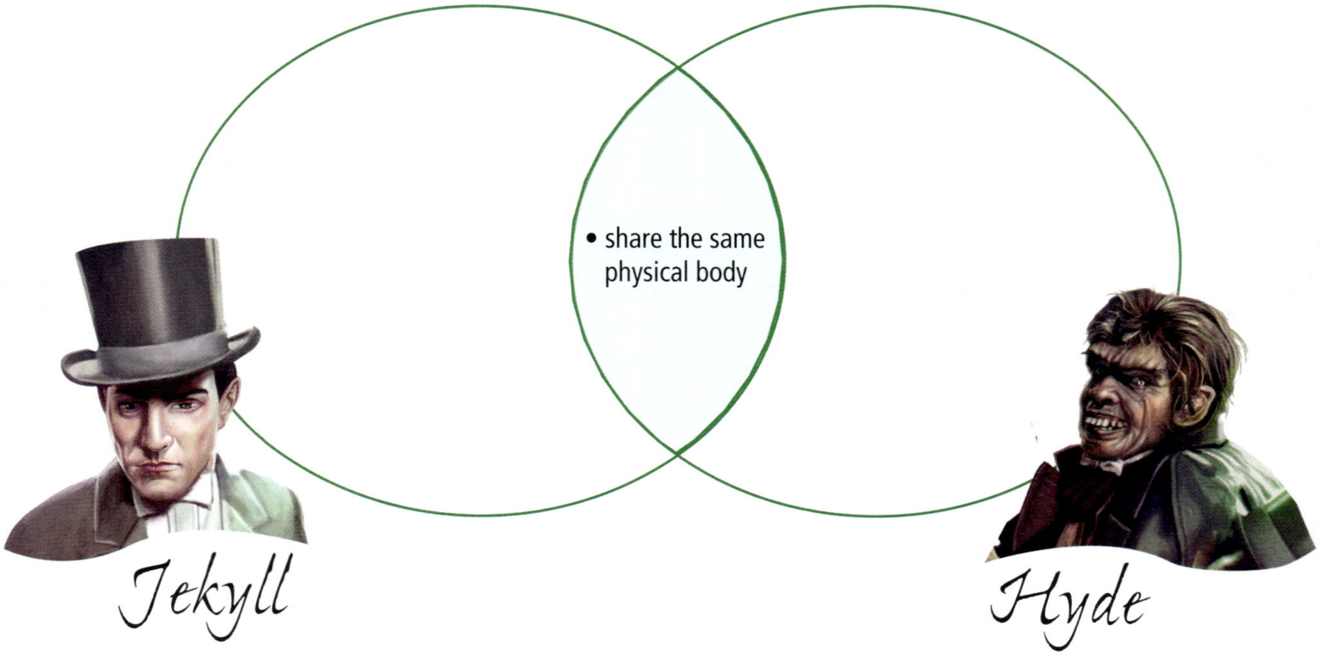

13 Think About It.

Use the Venn diagram to answer the following questions individually.

- How are the two characters the same?
- How are they different?

14 Talk It Over.

Discuss the answers to the previous questions with a partner. Share your ideas with the class. Then, as a class, discuss the following question.

What do you think the two characters represent?

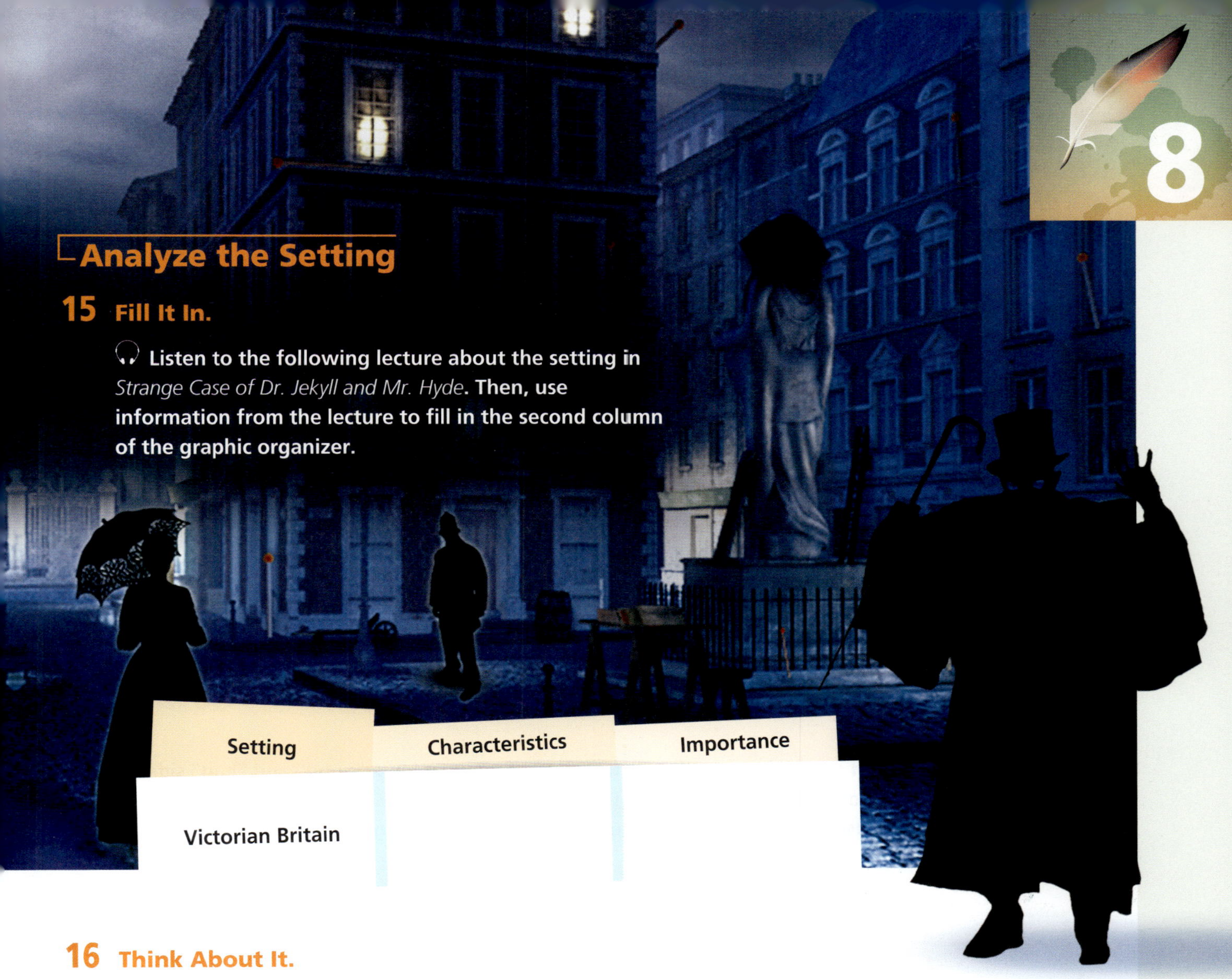

Analyze the Setting

15 Fill It In.

Listen to the following lecture about the setting in *Strange Case of Dr. Jekyll and Mr. Hyde*. Then, use information from the lecture to fill in the second column of the graphic organizer.

Setting	Characteristics	Importance
Victorian Britain		

16 Think About It.

With a partner, discuss the importance of the setting in *Strange Case of Dr. Jekyll and Mr. Hyde*. Then, fill in the last column of the graphic organizer.

17 Talk It Over.

As a class, discuss the graphic organizer. Then, answer the following question.

Could the story of Jekyll and Hyde take place in a different setting? Explain.

Analyze the Symbols

18 Match It.

The two most important symbols in the novel are Dr. Jekyll and Mr. Hyde themselves. Use what you know about the novel, its setting, and the passage to fill in the graphic organizer.

Character	Meaning
	the mind, civilization, bottled-up feelings, the oppressive nature of Victorian Britain
	the body, instinct, the animal side, freedom from the confines of societal pressures, the destructive nature of passion

19 Think About It.

With a partner, answer the following questions.

- What is the relationship between Dr. Jekyll and Mr. Hyde?
- What does this relationship suggest about the concepts the men represent?

20 Talk It Over.

As a class, discuss the following question.

How does Stevenson use the men as symbols to communicate the main ideas of the novel?

Analyze the Themes

21 Fill It In.

The duality of human nature (that is, the idea that people have "good" and "bad" sides) is one of the most important themes in the passage and *Strange Case of Dr. Jekyll and Mr. Hyde* **as a whole. Use lines from the passage to fill in the graphic organizer.**

Theme	Lines from Passage
the duality of human nature	

22 Think About It.

Which line from the passage is most important to the theme and why?

23 Talk It Over.

Discuss your answer to the previous question with a partner.

In-Depth Analysis: Doppelgangers

Doppelganger is a German word that literally means "double-goer." In other words, a doppelganger is a look-alike of a person. There's more to being a doppelganger than simply looking like another person, however. Doppelgangers often have a mysterious, supernatural component to them. In addition, they are also usually a bad sign or omen.

The idea of a doppelganger has been around for a long time. Although not called doppelgangers, obviously, similar ideas exist in Egyptian, Norse, and Finnish mythology. In the past, these doppelgangers were bad signs for people who saw them or of whom they were doubles. This idea hasn't really changed over the years. It's just become a little more complex.

In modern literature, doppelgangers often represent a part of a person that is being repressed or ignored. The doppelganger arises as a result of a character not addressing an important part of him or herself. In reaction to this perceived problem, the doppelganger creates lots of problems for the person. Sometimes, doppelgangers even try to kill their look-alikes.

Strange Case of Dr. Jekyll and Mr. Hyde is a part of this long tradition. In this novel, Hyde is Jekyll's doppelganger. Though the men don't look alike, they are still the same person. And Hyde represents a part of Jekyll's spirit that has been repressed. Because Hyde is evil, violent, and does what he wants, we can imagine that Jekyll has been reserved, calm, and concerned with propriety for a long time. He has neglected his more "wild" side.

Most doppelganger situations do not end well. The person usually must confront the doppelganger and kill it. In this case, since Jekyll and Hyde share the same body, both men die at the end, a somewhat unconventional way to end a doppelganger tale.

24 **Read the In-Depth Analysis and, with your answers to the Analyze the Characters section, answer the following questions.**

- What is a doppelganger?
- What are doppelganger stories normally about?
- What is the function of a doppelganger in modern literature?
- How is Hyde a doppelganger for Dr. Jekyll?

25 **Now, with a partner, discuss the following statement.**

Strange Case of Dr. Jekyll and Mr. Hyde is not a good example of a doppelganger story because the two characters don't actually look alike and they are the same person, not two separate people.

Take turns agreeing and disagreeing with the statement. Use points from the passage, the lesson, and the lectures to formulate your responses.

Write

26 **The duality of human nature is one of the most important themes in** *Strange Case of Dr. Jekyll and Mr. Hyde*. **The characters of Jekyll and Hyde give a physical representation of this idea. Write a 250- to 300-word essay about the duality of human nature in** *Strange Case of Dr. Jekyll and Mr. Hyde*. **Include what message the author communicates about this idea.**

VIDEO See p. 218 for video activities & essay writing

9

The Picture of Dorian Gray

Objectives

By the end of this unit, you will:

• know about the author and the background information behind the novel • thoroughly understand the passage from the novel • be able to identify figurative language in the passage • be able to summarize the passage • be able to analyze the characters, setting, symbols, and themes of the novel • know about Faustian themes in some depth • be able to use the passage to support your opinions and write a literature essay

VIDEO

Learn About ... Oscar Wilde

Oscar Wilde (1854-1900) was a famous Irish writer and celebrity. Today, he is best-known for his plays, poems, children's stories, and his one full-length novel, *The Picture of Dorian Gray*. In his time, however, he was very famous not only for his writing, but for his lectures and for his sometimes scandalous personal life. In addition, his plays were some of the most popular plays of his time.

When he was forty-one, he became involved in a scandal regarding his relationship with a young man. He ended up in prison because of it. Though he continued to write while imprisoned, the hard labor, poor food, and wretched conditions destroyed his health. After his release, he moved to the Continent, and never returned to Britain. He died in Paris a little over three years later, with no money and few remaining friends. He was buried in Paris, and his grave is visited by hundreds of admirers every year. He is still an intriguing character to many people in modern times.

Predict

Step 1

Discuss these questions with a partner.

1 Would you like to live forever? Why or why not?

2 Is it more important to be beautiful or to be good? Explain.

Step 2

Look at the key words from the passage from *The Picture of Dorian Gray*. **With a partner, discuss the meaning of the words. Based on the words, predict the main ideas of the passage.**

Background Information

1 Read the text and answer the questions.

1 What first sparks Lord Henry Wotton's interest in Dorian?

2 Why doesn't Dorian get older?

3 Why does Dorian kill Basil?

4 Why does the painting look worse after Dorian does good things?

5 What happens after Dorian stabs the portrait?

Oscar Wilde's only novel, *The Picture of Dorian Gray*, tells the story of a young man's descent into immorality. Dorian Gray is a sweet and innocent young man at the beginning of the novel. His friend, Basil Hallward, who is painting his picture, describes him as being beautiful and good. Basil's friend, Lord Henry Wotton, sees the unfinished picture and expresses interest in meeting Dorian.

Later, Dorian comes to Basil's house to sit for the painting. Lord Henry is still there, so the two men talk for some time. In the course of a few hours, Dorian starts to adopt Lord Henry's view of life – that people can and should do whatever they want regardless of the consequences as long as it brings them pleasure. Basil finishes the painting and gives it to Dorian, who expresses the wish that the painting would age instead of him.

Dorian begins to live a life of pleasure, and one which values beauty above all else. He recklessly pursues pleasure without any thought of the consequences of his deeds, leaving his home for days and weeks. Strangely, he notices that he is not getting any older. Instead, the painting is taking on all the signs of aging and moral corruption.

Over time, Dorian's behavior gets worse and worse. His old friend, Basil, comes to visit him one night. Basil asks Dorian if the terrible rumors about him are true. Dorian admits to it and shows Basil the portrait, which looks awful. Suddenly, he becomes furious with Basil for making the painting, and stabs him to death.

Eventually, Dorian decides he wants to be good, not because he has a genuine change of heart, but because he is obsessed with the beauty of the portrait. He wonders if it will look nice again once he starts to do good things. But after doing some good deeds, the portrait looks worse than ever. In a fit of rage, Dorian stabs the portrait with a knife. The servants hear a noise coming from upstairs and race to see what happened. They see the portrait of Dorian Gray, as beautiful as when it was first painted, and a strange, old, evil-looking man dead on the floor, with a knife through his heart. It is the body of Dorian Gray.

The novel caused quite a scandal at the time, due to the lightness with which Wilde dealt with what the Victorians considered extremely serious subject matter, and for containing too strong an argument in favor of an immoral lifestyle. Wilde even had to make some major changes before his publishers would agree to bring it out.

Listen & Read

2 **Listen to and read the passage from *The Picture of Dorian Gray*. First, read for general understanding. Then, reread the passage, noting down what Dorian thinks about the portrait.**

In this passage, from Chapter 11, Dorian compares his outwardly flawless appearance with the increasingly ugly and old appearance of his portrait. He has been living a life of pleasure-seeking for years at this point, and he still looks as young and beautiful as he did at the beginning of the novel.

Often, on returning home from one of those mysterious and prolonged absences that gave rise to such strange conjecture among those who were his friends, or thought that they were so, he [Dorian Gray] himself would creep upstairs to the locked room, open the door with the key that never left him now, and stand, with a mirror, in front of the portrait that Basil Hallward had painted of him, looking now at the evil and aging face on the canvas, and now at the fair young face that laughed back at him from the polished glass. The very sharpness of the contrast used to quicken his sense of pleasure. He grew more and more enamoured of his own beauty, more and more interested in the corruption of his own soul. He would examine with minute care, and sometimes with a monstrous and terrible delight, the hideous lines that seared the wrinkling forehead or crawled around the heavy sensual mouth, wondering sometimes which were the more horrible, the signs of sin or the signs of age. He would place his white hands beside the coarse bloated hands of the picture, and smile. He mocked the misshapen body and the failing limbs.

There were moments, indeed, at night, when, lying sleepless in his own delicately scented chamber, or in the sordid room of the little ill-famed tavern near the docks which, under an assumed name and in disguise, it was his habit to frequent, he would think of the ruin he had brought upon his soul with a pity that was all the more poignant because it was purely selfish. But moments such as these were rare. That curiosity about life which Lord Henry had first stirred in him, as they sat together in the garden of their friend, seemed to increase with gratification. The more he knew, the more he desired to know. He had mad hungers that grew more ravenous as he fed them.

Respond

3 Respond to the passage by answering these questions with a partner.

1 Was your prediction about the main ideas of the passage correct? Explain.

2 How did the author communicate the main ideas? Pick one (or more) and explain.

a with images b with dialogue c by explaining it directly

3 Who are the important people in this passage?

4 Which of the words from the phrase bank do you think best describe how Dorian feels in the passage? Explain.

Phrase Bank

- excited
- scared
- ashamed
- upset
- sad
- interested
- indifferent

Understand

4 Read the questions and choose the correct answers.

1 How does Dorian feel about the portrait?

a It scares him.

b It repulses him.

c It fascinates him.

d It embarrasses him.

2 What brings Dorian particular pleasure?

a the contrast between himself and the portrait

b his unchanging and timeless beauty

c the skill with which the painting was made

d the beauty that is revealed in the painting

3 What does Dorian NOT note in the painting?

a lines on the forehead

b bloated hands

c misshapen body

d dirty appearance

4 What does Dorian desire more of?

a life

b youth

c knowledge

d sleep

Figurative Language

5 Work with a partner. Find one example of olfactory imagery and one example of oxymoron in the passage.

9

Summarize

6 **First, fill in the graphic organizer based on the passage you read.**

Character(s)

Setting

Main Idea(s)

Conflict

7 **Now, use your graphic organizer to summarize the passage with a partner.**

Listen

8 **Listen to a lecture about** *The Picture of Dorian Gray*. **Then, answer the questions.**

1 What is the speaker mostly talking about?

- **a** beauty and goodness in the novel
- **b** how the transformation of Dorian takes place
- **c** the sources of the story of Dorian Gray
- **d** why Dorian Gray never aged or looked bad

2 How does Wilde symbolize Dorian's soul?

- **a** with his outward looks
- **b** with the changes in the painting
- **c** with the words of his friends
- **d** with his inner thoughts

About the Title

The Picture of Dorian Gray is a fairly straightforward title, although it has two possible interpretations. For one thing, the title refers to the actual portrait of Dorian that Basil painted. The title can also refer to the novel itself. That is, the novel is actually a "picture" of Dorian Gray. Many titles play with words like this, and have a double meaning. Both pictures (the actual portrait and the novel) reveal things about Dorian that the rest of the world cannot see. The readers are the only people who know how degraded Dorian truly is – with the exception of Dorian himself. So the picture in the title refers to the true picture of Dorian's inner self.

Another interesting observation about the title is that it emphasizes the "picture," not a "tale" or a "story." The image takes center stage in the title. This reflects Dorian's obsession with the portrait and its beauty (or lack thereof). It also brings to mind the central theme of the novel: the difference between appearance and truth.

9 **Do you think Wilde chose a good title for his novel? Would you choose a different one?**

Analyze the Characters

10 Fill It In.

Listen to the lecture. Then, use words from the phrase bank to fill in the graphic organizer. You may use words more than once.

Phrase Bank

- beautiful • a tempter
- obsessed with beauty • has no regrets
- immoral • pleasure-seeking
- does not care about right and wrong
- innocent • young

Character	Description
Dorian	
Lord Henry	
Basil	

11 Think About It.

Use the graphic organizer to answer the following questions individually.

- What do the characters have in common?
- How are the men different?

12 Talk It Over.

Discuss the answers to the previous questions with a partner. Share your ideas with the class. Then, as a class, discuss the following question.

Why do you think that Dorian gave in to Lord Henry and didn't listen to his friend Basil?

Analyze the Setting

13 Fill It In.

Listen to the following lecture about the setting in *The Picture of Dorian Gray*. Then, use information from the lecture to fill in the second column of the graphic organizer.

Aspect of setting	Importance
Time	
Place	

14 Think About It.

With a partner, discuss the importance of the setting in *The Picture of Dorian Gray*.

15 Talk It Over.

As a class, discuss the graphic organizer. Then, answer the following question.

- Could the story of Dorian Gray take place in a different setting? Explain.

Analyze the Symbols

16 Fill It In.

The most important symbol in the novel is the portrait of Dorian Gray. Use lines from the passage that describe the painting and fill in the middle column of the graphic organizer.

Symbol	Definition	How it makes you feel ...
the portrait		

17 Think About It.

Share your answers to the previous activity with a partner. Then, discuss what you think the meaning of the painting is. Fill in the last column of the graphic organizer with your own ideas.

18 Talk It Over.

As a class, discuss the following question.

- How does the author use the painting in the novel?

Analyze the Themes

19 Fill It In.

Find lines in the passage that relate to each of the three themes from *The Picture of Dorian Gray* and fill in the graphic organizer.

Theme	Lines from Passage
good and evil	
beauty/appearance	
mortality and aging	

20 Think About It.

Which theme do you think is most important to the novel and why?

21 Talk It Over.

Discuss your answer to the previous question with a partner.

9

In-Depth Analysis: Faustian Themes

There is an old German tale about a man named Faust. He is very smart and a serious student. But he's not satisfied. He wants to know more. So he makes a deal with an evil spirit. Faust gets unlimited knowledge. In exchange, after an agreed number of years, the Devil takes Faust's soul.

For years, Faust enjoys his limitless knowledge in self-serving ways. He doesn't use his powers for good. He doesn't even use them to do great things. Instead, he plays silly pranks on people. Faust enjoys his pranks, but his happiness does not last forever. Eventually, the evil spirit comes to claim Faust's soul. Though he begs for mercy, the spirit does not give in. Faust dies and spends eternity in Hell.

This legend is incredibly popular, both inside and outside Germany. It has inspired countless retellings and adaptations. People have written books, plays, movies, and even music based on the story of Faust. It is an important and recognizable theme in the literary world.

The Faustian theme shows people that they should not overstep their natural boundaries. That is, people should not try to achieve more than they can naturally achieve. People should be satisfied with what they do have and accept their limitations. This is Faust's fatal flaw: being dissatisfied with his own knowledge. Certainly, the pursuit of knowledge is not bad in and of itself. But this desire superseded everything else in Faust's life – even his own sense of morals. When a character acts in such a way, people should immediately think of Faust.

The Picture of Dorian Gray is a kind of Faustian story. Dorian Gray gives up his soul in order to have eternal youth and beauty. It's never said who or what the agent of this exchange is. But the reader does know that Dorian has unnaturally extended his life and his good looks. Nothing good can come of this.

Dorian's crime is different than Faust's in that he does not immediately seek knowledge. His main motivation is retaining his beauty and his youth. Still, the main idea is the same. Dorian, like Faust, is dissatisfied with a natural limitation of being a human. He leaves behind what is normal and right to pursue something abnormal. And in the end, he pays for it.

Why are Faustian tales so popular? The answer is likely to be that they resonate with a lot of people. The desire for more knowledge, eternal life, and eternal beauty are things that many people have experienced. In a Faustian story, people go after these things and are always punished. It shows people that although these are things that people would like to have, pursuing them is unnatural and will lead to problems. In this way, Faustian tales are cautionary stories that warn people against going too far to get what they want.

22 **Read the In-Depth Analysis and, with your answers to the Analyze the Characters section, answer the following questions.**

- What is the story of Faust?
- How is *The Picture of Dorian Gray* related to the story of Faust?
- In what way is Dorian similar to Faust?
- How is Dorian different from Faust?

23 **Now, with a partner, discuss the following statement.**

The Picture of Dorian Gray is a modern example of a Faustian tale. Although the main character does not enter into an agreement with any spirit, the message and the consequences of his actions are still the same as in the original tale.

Take turns agreeing and disagreeing with the statement. Use points from the passage, the unit, and the lectures to formulate your responses.

24 **As a class, discuss the statement from the previous exercise.**

Write

25 **The ideas of good and evil, and beauty and ugliness are very important in** *The Picture of Dorian Gray*. **In addition, good and evil are connected to the ideas of beauty and ugliness. In a 250- to 300-word essay, discuss the relationship between these two sets of opposites in the novel.**

VIDEO See p. 219 for video activities & essay writing

10 The Time Machine

Objectives

By the end of this unit, you will:

• know about the author and the background information behind the novel • thoroughly understand the passage from the novel • be able to identify figurative language in the passage • be able to summarize the passage • be able to analyze the characters, setting, symbols, and themes of the novel • know about genre in some depth • be able to use the passage to support your opinions and write a literature essay

VIDEO

Learn About ... H.G. Wells

Herbert George Wells (1866-1946) was an English writer. He wrote many different things during his lifetime, including novels, textbooks, and social commentaries. Today, however, he is best-known for his science fiction stories and novels. In fact, he is often referred to as "the Father of Science Fiction." Though this title is shared with other writers of the time, it is undeniable that Wells helped create the science fiction genre.

Wells worked as a teacher for much of his early life. This allowed him to support himself and still have time to write. He had several best-sellers, both fiction and non-fiction, during his life. His works deal with a wide variety of different and recognizable themes, such as alien invasions, future dystopias, and time travel. After achieving fame, he left teaching to write and lecture full time.

Wells' impact on modern science fiction cannot be overstated. Even today, his writings continue to inspire and fascinate readers worldwide.

Predict

Step 1

Discuss these questions with a partner.

1 Do you think that the world will be better or worse in the future? Explain.

2 Why do people enjoy thinking about and imagining the future of the world?

Step 2

Look at the key words from the passage from *The Time Machine*. **With a partner, discuss the meaning of the words. Based on the words, predict the main ideas of the passage.**

Background Information

1 **Read the text and answer the questions.**

1. What are the Eloi like?
2. Where does the time traveler believe the Eloi came from at first?
3. What is the time traveler's second theory, after he discovers the existence of the Morlocks?
4. What is the true relationship between the Eloi and the Morlocks?
5. What life does the time traveler see in the time of the dying sun?

The Time Machine is about a man who travels into the future. He builds a time machine (Wells was the first author to use the term "time machine") and goes to the year 802,701 AD. When he arrives, he sees futuristic, though run-down buildings. There is also a race of people there called the Eloi. They're small, childlike, and don't appear to work or do much of anything. The time traveler tries to talk to them, but they're not really interested.

He does, however, make friends with one, a woman named Weena. Weena follows the time traveler around and the two spend a lot of time together as the time traveler studies the land and people around him. He concludes that the Eloi are a peaceful, communist race who evolved to not need intellect or strength to survive. He takes this as an indication of their superior state.

Later, the time traveler realizes that his time machine is missing. As he looks for it, he discovers that there are creatures living under the ground. They're ape-like and primitive, and called Morlocks. Underground, where the Morlocks live, is all the machinery that keeps the surface world functioning. The time traveler thinks that humanity must have split into two different species: the idle Eloi and the hard-working Morlocks.

Soon, the time traveler changes his hypothesis again. He sees the Morlocks attack, kill, and eat one of the Eloi. He realizes that the Eloi are nothing but a food source for the Morlocks, and leaves, horrified. Next he goes forward millions of years, to a time when the sun is dying. There is no sign of civilization, and the only animals he sees are giant white butterflies and huge red crabs. He returns home and tells his friends, but no one believes him. He disappears in the time machine again to bring back proof, and never returns.

The Time Machine was hailed as a masterpiece from its first release. Written 36 years after Charles Darwin published *On the Origin of Species*, it takes as law his theory of the evolution of the human race. Like many of Wells' other works, it contains both bold predictions about the future and critical commentary on the social and political structures that existed in Wells' own time.

Listen & Read

2 **Listen to and read the passage from *The Time Machine*. First, read for general understanding. Then, reread the passage. As you read the second time, ask yourself: how did the time traveler feel about the place on his first arrival, and to what extent was he right?**

In this passage, from Chapter 10, the time traveler has come to understand what is really happening on the Earth of 802,701 AD, and the true relationship between the Eloi and the Morlocks. He gives his theory as to what has happened and why.

'About eight or nine in the morning I came to the same seat of yellow metal from which I had viewed the world upon the evening of my arrival. I thought of my hasty conclusions upon that evening and could not refrain from laughing bitterly at my confidence. Here was the same beautiful scene, the same abundant foliage, the same splendid palaces and magnificent ruins, the same silver river running between its fertile banks. The gay robes of the beautiful people moved hither and thither among the trees. Some were bathing in exactly the place where I had saved Weena, and that suddenly gave me a keen stab of pain. And like blots upon the landscape rose the cupolas above the ways to the Under-world. I understood now what all the beauty of the Over-world people covered. Very pleasant was their day, as pleasant as the day of the cattle in the field. Like the cattle, they knew of no enemies and provided against no needs. And their end was the same.

'I grieved to think how brief the dream of the human intellect had been. It had committed suicide. It had set itself steadfastly towards comfort and ease, a balanced society with security and permanency as its watchword, it had attained its hopes – to come to this at last. Once, life and property must have reached almost absolute safety. The rich had been assured of his wealth and comfort, the toiler assured of his life and work. No doubt in that perfect world there had been no unemployed problem, no social question left unsolved. And a great quiet had followed.

'It is a law of nature we overlook, that intellectual versatility is the compensation for change, danger, and trouble. An animal perfectly in harmony with its environment is a perfect mechanism. Nature never appeals to intelligence until habit and instinct are useless. There is no intelligence where there is no change and no need of change. Only those animals partake of intelligence that have to meet a huge variety of needs and dangers.

'So, as I see it, the Upper-world man had drifted towards his feeble prettiness, and the Under-world to mere mechanical industry. But that perfect state had lacked one thing even for mechanical perfection – absolute permanency. Apparently as time went on, the feeding of the Under-world, however it was effected, had become disjointed. Mother Necessity, who had been staved off for a few thousand years, came back again, and she began below. The Under-world being in contact with machinery, which, however perfect, still needs some little thought outside habit, had probably retained perforce rather more initiative, if less of every other human character, than the Upper. And when other meat failed them, they turned to what old habit had hitherto forbidden. So I say I saw it in my last view of the world of Eight Hundred and Two Thousand Seven Hundred and One. It may be as wrong an explanation as mortal wit could invent. It is how the thing shaped itself to me, and as that I give it to you.'

Respond

3 Respond to the passage by answering these questions with a partner.

1 Was your prediction about the main idea of the passage correct? Explain.

2 How did the author communicate the main ideas? Pick one (or more) and explain.

a with images   b with dialogue   c by explaining them directly

3 Who are the important people in this passage?

4 Which of the words from the phrase bank do you think best describe how the time traveler feels in the passage? Explain.

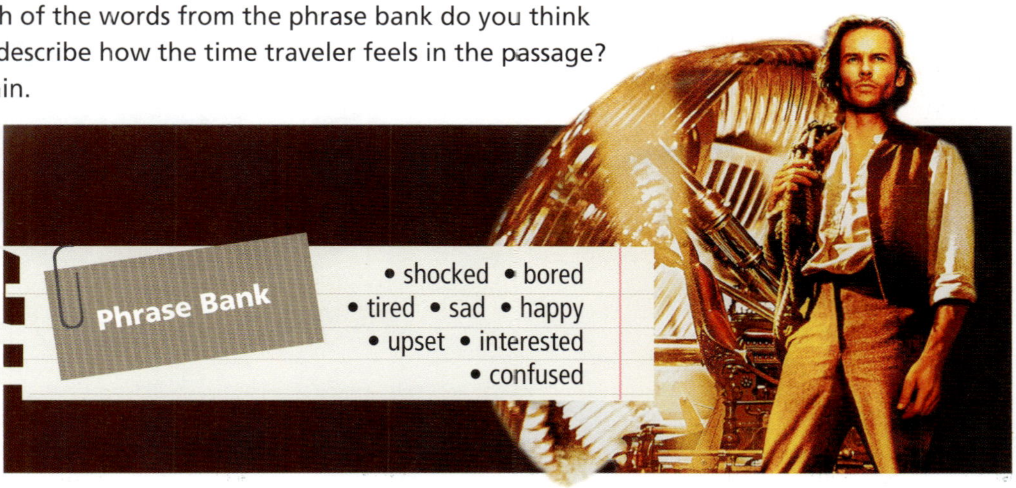

Understand

4 Read the questions and choose the correct answers.

1 To what does the time traveler compare the Over-world people?

a people from his time

b ruins

c cattle

d the Under-world people

2 Why does the time traveler think that people lost their intellectual abilities?

a People didn't have to work anymore.

b There was no unemployment.

c People became richer.

d Life became too easy.

3 What does the time traveler conclude about the "perfect state" that existed before?

a People were unhappy then.

b It couldn't last forever.

c No one knew what would happen.

d It was a very happy time.

4 What is NOT true of the Under-world people?

a They learned to grow food.

b They are more intelligent than the Over-world people.

c They operate the machinery underground.

d They use the Over-world people for food.

Figurative Language

5 Work with a partner. Find one example of simile and two examples of personification in the passage.

10

Summarize

6 **First, fill in the graphic organizer based on the passage you read.**

Character(s)

Main Idea(s)

Main Event(s)

7 **Now, use your graphic organizer to summarize the passage with a partner.**

Listen

8 **Listen to a lecture about** *The Time Machine*. **Then, answer the questions.**

1 What is the speaker mostly talking about?

a the historical and social setting of *The Time Machine*

b the differences between the two human species in *The Time Machine*

c the way that *The Time Machine* represents human evolution

d the reasons that people became less intelligent in *The Time Machine*

2 How does Wells relate to Darwin's ideas?

a He misunderstands them.

b He contradicts them.

c He interprets them in a new way.

d He sets out to prove that they are wrong.

About the Title

H.G. Wells was not the first person to imagine time travel. He was, however, the first person to use the term "time machine" and the first to think of such a device. The time machine is some kind of mountable machine that allows the traveler to travel rapidly forwards through time. In addition, the traveler can also come back to his own time. This idea, which is commonplace today, was completely new in Wells' time. Perhaps this is why Wells decided to name the book after the time machine rather than the time traveler.

9 **What title would you give the novel? Explain.**

Analyze the Characters

10 Fill It In.

Listen to the lecture. Then, use words from the phrase bank to fill in the text in the box and the Venn diagram.

Phrase Bank

• beautiful • ape-like
• childlike • inventor
• main character
• unintelligent • intelligent
• eat meat • eat fruit • wear clothes
• go naked • name • used to be humans

The Time Traveler

Although the time traveler is the 1) .... in the novel, we don't even find out his 2) .... All we do discover is that he is a(n) 3) .... and a scientist.

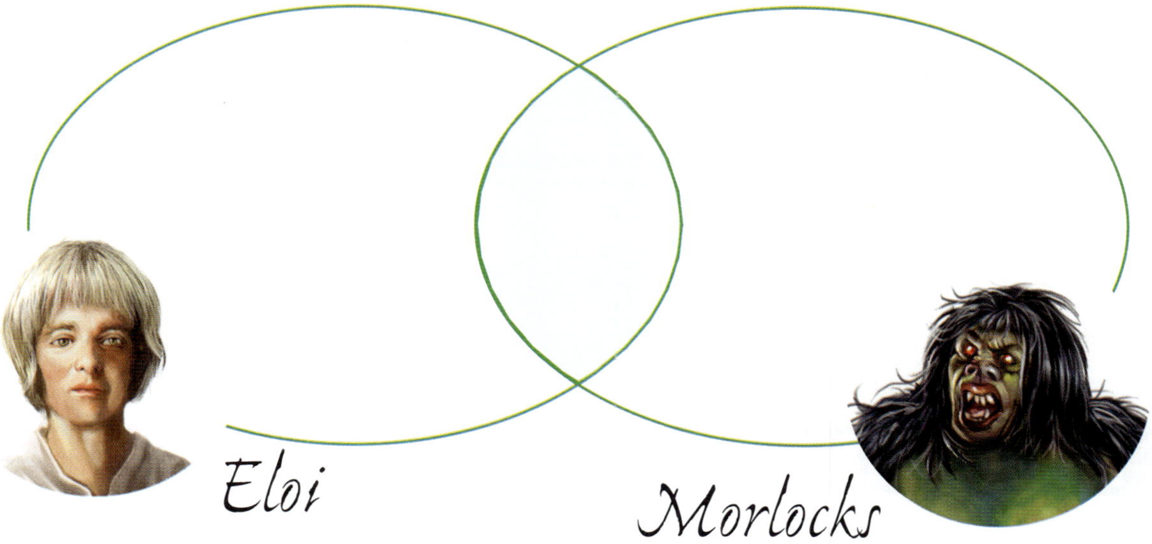

11 Think About It.

Use the Venn diagram to answer the following questions individually.

- How are the Eloi like the Morlocks? How are they different?
- What do the differences imply about the lives of people in the future?

12 Talk It Over.

Discuss the answers to the previous questions with a partner. Share your ideas with the class.

Analyze the Setting

13 Fill It In.

Listen to the following lecture about the setting in *The Time Machine*. Then, use information from the lecture to fill in the graphic organizer.

Setting	Time	Place	Importance
First setting			
Second setting			

14 Think About It.

Answer the following questions with a partner.

- How are the time periods in which the story takes place important to the ideas in the novel?
- How is the place in which the story takes place important to the ideas in the novel?
- How would the story be different if the time or place changed?

15 Talk It Over.

As a class, discuss your answers to the previous questions.

Analyze the Symbols

16 Fill It In.

First, listen to the lecture, and then complete the graphic organizer.

Symbol	Meaning
fire	
flowers	

17 Think About It.

What do the two symbols say about humanity in the novel?

18 Talk It Over.

Discuss your answer to the previous question with a partner.

Analyze the Themes

19 Fill It In.

Three important themes in *The Time Machine* are social class, technology, and passivity – that is, the state of being inactive. Use lines from the passage to complete the graphic organizer.

Theme	Lines from Passage
social class	
technology	
passivity	

20 Think About It.

Which theme do you think is most important in this section and why?

21 Talk It Over.

Discuss your answer to the previous question with a partner.

10

In-Depth Analysis: Genre

A genre is a kind or style of literature. The most basic genres are prose, poetry, and drama. Within these broad categories, there are additional ways to classify a work of literature. For example, a play can be a comedy or a tragedy. And, of course, these genres have more specialized sub-genres. A comedy, for instance, can be a comedy of manners or a satire.

Learning to identify the genre of a literary work can help people to understand that work better. It puts the work in a larger context. Authors who write in the same genre often use similar techniques and conventions. In addition, they also may have similar ideas about what they want to say. For this reason, paying attention to genre is an important step for a reader.

The Time Machine is very clearly a part of the science fiction genre. Indeed, H.G. Wells is one of the founders of science fiction. There are several defining characteristics of this genre. For one thing, science fiction usually deals with situations that are in the realm of possibility given our current knowledge of the world. For instance, a science fiction novel might describe space travel to distant galaxies, because, someday, this may be possible. A science fiction novel would not, however, focus on wizards and magic spells, as these things are not possible according to human knowledge. Clearly *The Time Machine* is a possibility. Someday people might learn to travel through time. And the Eloi and Morlocks could evolve from humans. It's possible, so it's science fiction.

Science fiction also allows authors to introduce important issues from a more removed point of view. That is, some issues and topics are very sensitive. For this reason, people might feel uncomfortable talking about them. But in many science fiction novels, writers distance the issues from their source. For example, in *The Time Machine*, Wells talks about issues of social class and idleness. But instead of addressing the issues directly, he allows the reader to make a comparison between societal organization in the future and in the present.

Finally, science fiction often addresses the question of our planet's future. People are always very concerned about what will happen to Earth and how people and animal life will fare. Different books have different ideas. In the case of *The Time Machine*, Earth slowly fades away as the sun burns out and leaves the surface of the Earth empty and cold. This is actually a common convention in a sub-genre of science fiction called the "Dying Earth" genre. Unlike in some sub-genres of science fiction, in the Dying Earth genre, people don't cause the destruction of the planet. Instead, natural processes eventually lead to its decline. This deemphasizes the human component and highlights the insignificance of human life to the Earth.

22 **Read the In-Depth Analysis and answer the following questions individually.**

- What is a genre?
- What is science fiction?
- What is the "Dying Earth" genre?
- Why is it important to think about genre when studying a literary work?

23 **List three characteristics of the science fiction genre.**

- ....
- ....
- ....

24 **For each of the characteristics listed above, write how** *The Time Machine* **fulfills it.**

- ....
- ....
- ....

Write

25 **In the passage from** *The Time Machine*, **the time traveler explains how the world of the Eloi and the Morlocks works. Write a 250- to 300-word essay comparing and contrasting the Eloi and the Morlocks. Be sure to include the significance of their similarities and differences.**

VIDEO See p. 220 for video activities & essay writing

11 The Hound of the Baskervilles

Objectives

By the end of this unit, you will:

• know about the author and the background information behind the novel • thoroughly understand the passage from the novel • be able to identify figurative language in the passage • be able to summarize the passage • be able to analyze the title, characters, setting, symbols, and themes of the novel • know about tension in some depth • be able to use the passage to support your opinions and write a literature essay

VIDEO

Learn About ... Sir Arthur Conan Doyle

Sir Arthur Conan Doyle (1859-1930) was a Scottish writer. He is famous for creating one of the best-known detectives of all time, Sherlock Holmes. In addition, he was a writer of other short stories, historical novels, plays, poetry, and fantasies.

When he was a child, Conan Doyle's Irish mother told him vivid stories. These stories helped distract the young man from what was very often a stressful home life. He noted that they were very important to him and had a tremendous influence on him as a writer and as a person.

At the age of nine, his wealthy relatives paid for Conan Doyle to go to boarding school, which he very much disliked. Again, however, storytelling became a means of escape as the boy shared stories with his classmates.

Conan Doyle went on to medical school and became a practicing physician. But he was never a very successful one, and while he waited for patients, he wrote short stories and other pieces for magazines. In time, he became one of the most well-known writers in Britain.

Predict

Step 1

Discuss these questions with a partner.

1 Do you believe in the supernatural? Do you feel that everything has a logical explanation? Explain.

2 What things make you nervous or afraid? Explain.

Step 2

Look at the key words from the passage from *The Hound of the Baskervilles*. With a partner, discuss the meaning of the words. Based on the words, predict the mood of the passage.

Background Information

1 **Read the text and answer the questions.**

1. Who tells the story?
2. What do people think was the cause of Sir Charles Baskervilles' death?
3. Who is Sir Henry?
4. Who was really responsible for Sir Charles' death?
5. Why was it hard to perform the story in the theater?

The Hound of the Baskervilles is the third of the four novel-length stories Conan Doyle wrote about Sherlock Holmes, and it is one of the most famous Sherlock Holmes mysteries. As with most of the stories, it is narrated by Holmes' right-hand man and friend, Dr. Watson. In it, Sherlock Holmes is asked to help solve a strange murder. A man, Sir Charles Baskerville, has been found dead. People believe that the Baskerville family has a curse on it and that Sir Charles' death is related to an evil supernatural dog. The dog is thought to be part of the curse.

Holmes and Watson go to the Baskervilles' home. The last known surviving Baskerville, Sir Henry, has also come to the house. Since he is the last Baskerville known to be alive, he will inherit the large house. But because of the curse he is in danger.

By finding a series of important clues and using his brilliant mind, Sherlock Holmes unravels the mystery. There is no curse, nor is there a ghost dog. Holmes determines that the culprit is a previously unknown relative of Sir Henry's (his cousin, in fact – the son of Sir Charles Baskerville's long-lost brother), who has been living under a false name nearby. He had trained a huge dog to chase down Sir Charles Baskerville, using a special chemical to make it look like flames were coming from it, adding to its hellish appearance. Once Sir Charles was out of the way, he needed Sir Henry to die too so that he could inherit the family house. He used the hound so that superstitious locals will blame the deaths on the curse of the Baskervilles.

Huge ghostly dogs are common in folk tales from all over Britain and Ireland, and the inclusion of one in the book adds another layer of mystery and suspense to this murder story (even if the dog turns out not to be of supernatural origin). With the addition of the moors and the ancient family of the Baskervilles, this made *The Hound of the Baskervilles* Conan Doyle's most Gothic detective story. Though the fact that the story centered around a dog made it difficult to stage, the book has been adapted for radio, film, and television many times.

11

Listen & Read

2 **Listen to and read the passage from** *The Hound of the Baskervilles*. **First, read for general understanding. Then, reread the passage. As you read the second time, note down how the author creates a sense of suspense in the passage.**

In this passage, from Chapter 14, Holmes, Watson, and Lestrade, a police officer, wait outside for Sir Henry to walk by, hoping he will tempt the "ghost dog" to attack. Holmes thinks he knows what's going on, but he needs proof.

There was a thin, crisp, continuous patter from somewhere in the heart of that crawling bank. The cloud was within fifty yards of where we lay, and we glared at it, all three, uncertain what horror was about to break from the heart of it. I was at Holmes's elbow, and I glanced for an instant at his face. It was pale and exultant, his eyes shining brightly in the moonlight. But suddenly they started forward in a rigid, fixed stare, and his lips parted in amazement. At the same instant Lestrade gave a yell of terror and threw himself face downward upon the ground. I sprang to my feet, my inert hand grasping my pistol, my mind paralyzed by the dreadful shape which had sprung out upon us from the shadows of the fog.

A hound it was, an enormous coal-black hound, but not such a hound as mortal eyes have ever seen. Fire burst from its open mouth, its eyes glowed with a smouldering glare, its muzzle and hackles and dewlap were outlined in flickering flame. Never in the delirious dream of a disordered brain could anything more savage, more appalling, more hellish be conceived than that dark form and savage face which broke upon us out of the wall of fog.

With long bounds the huge black creature was leaping down the track, following hard upon the footsteps of our friend. So paralyzed were we by the apparition that we allowed him to pass before we had recovered our nerve. Then Holmes and I both fired together, and the creature gave a hideous howl, which showed that one at least had hit him. He did not pause, however, but bounded onward. Far away on the path we saw Sir Henry looking back, his face white in the moonlight, his hands raised in horror, glaring helplessly at the frightful thing which was hunting him down.

But that cry of pain from the hound had blown all our fears to the winds. If he was vulnerable he was mortal, and if we could wound him we could kill him. Never have I seen a man run as Holmes ran that night. I am reckoned fleet of foot, but he outpaced me as much as I outpaced the little professional. In front of us as we flew up the track we heard scream after scream from Sir Henry and the deep roar of the hound. I was in time to see the beast spring upon its victim, hurl him to the ground, and worry at his throat. But the next instant Holmes had emptied five barrels of his revolver into the creature's flank. With a last howl of agony and a vicious snap in the air, it rolled upon its back, four feet pawing furiously, and then fell limp upon its side. I stooped, panting, and pressed my pistol to the dreadful, shimmering head, but it was useless to press the trigger. The giant hound was dead.

Sir Henry lay insensible where he had fallen. We tore away his collar, and Holmes breathed a prayer of gratitude when we saw that there was no sign of a wound and that the rescue had been in time. Already our friend's eyelids shivered and he made a feeble effort to move. Lestrade thrust his brandy flask between the baronet's teeth, and two frightened eyes were looking up at us.

"My God!" he whispered. "What was it? What, in heaven's name, was it?"

"It's dead, whatever it is," said Holmes. "We've laid the family ghost once and forever."

Respond

3 Respond to the passage by answering these questions with a partner.

1. Was your prediction about the main idea of the passage correct? Explain.
2. How did the author create the mood? Pick one (or more) and explain.
   a with images b with dialogue c by explaining it directly
3. Who are the important people in this passage?
4. Which of the words from the phrase bank do you think best describe how Watson feels in the passage? Explain.

Phrase Bank

- happy
- nervous
- excited
- afraid
- sad
- relieved
- indifferent

Understand

4 Read the questions and choose the correct answers.

1. Who is NOT in the group of three lying in wait?
   a Watson
   b Holmes
   c Lestrade
   d Sir Henry
2. Which is NOT true of the hound?
   a It was black.
   b It seemed to glow.
   c It was a spirit.
   d It was very large.
3. Who kills the hound?
   a Holmes
   b It's impossible to tell.
   c Watson
   d No one; it escapes.
4. What is true of Sir Henry after the hound's attack?
   a He's badly injured.
   b He's temporarily unconscious.
   c He cannot wake up.
   d He's been accidentally shot.

Figurative Language

5 Work with a partner. Find two examples of onomatopoeia and two examples of alliteration in the passage.

Summarize

6 **First, fill in the graphic organizer based on the passage you read.**

Character(s)

Main Event(s)	Setting

7 **Now, use your graphic organizer to summarize the passage with a partner.**

Listen

8 **Listen to a lecture about** *The Hound of the Baskervilles*. **Then, answer the questions.**

1 What is the speaker mostly talking about?
- a the symbolism of dogs in world folklore
- b legends of the British Isles
- c a story that Conan Doyle retold
- d the inspiration for the character of Holmes

2 What makes the Scottish dog stand out?
- a its color
- b its temperament
- c its size
- d its call

Analyze the Title

9 **The hound is obviously important to the story, and in the passage, the reader meets him face to face for the first time. Go through the passage, underlining each time the animal is mentioned, and then answer the questions.**

- How many times does Conan Doyle use the word ' hound"?
- What other words does he use to refer to the animal?
- Look up the word "hound" in a dictionary. Why did Conan Doyle use this word in the title and passage, and never simply "dog"?

10 Think About It.

With a partner, discuss the following questions.

- Baskerville is a real surname in Britain. It is a very old aristocratic name of French origin, and came across the channel with the Norman invasion of England in 1066. Why did Conan Doyle chose this name and not a more common name like Smith or Williams for the cursed family in *The Hound of the Baskervilles*?
- Conan Doyle could have called the book *The Baskervilles' Hound* rather than *The Hound of the Baskervilles* with no change in meaning. Why do you think Conan Doyle chose the form he did?
- Look at the following possible titles for Conan Doyle's novel. Are any of them suitable alternatives for *The Hound of the Baskervilles*? Why/Why not?

Sherlock Holmes Solves Another Mystery

The Curse of the Baskervilles

The Fake Ghost Dog

The Mystery of the Strange and Tragic Death of Sir Charles Baskerville

Dr. Watson and the Hound of the Moors

11 Talk It Over.

As a class, discuss the following question.

Is *The Hound of the Baskervilles* the best title the novel could have, or could it be improved upon?

Analyze the Characters

12 Fill It In.

a. Listen to the first part of the lecture. Use words from the phrase bank to fill in the first Venn diagram.

Phrase Bank

• intelligent • observant • single-minded • kind • sympathetic • brilliant • has normal relationships • not interested in relationships • rude • selfish • cold • interested in puzzles • admires his friend

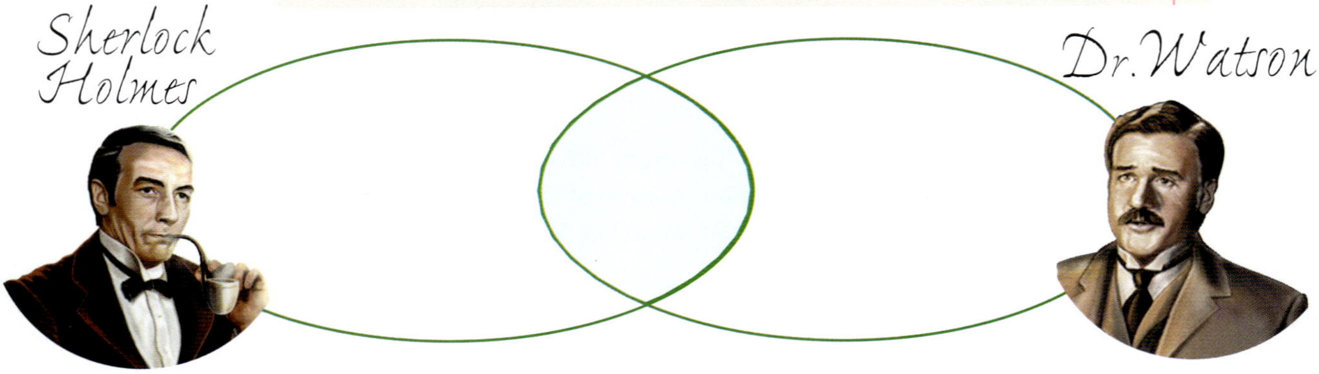

b. Listen to the second part of the lecture and use words from the phrase bank to fill in the second Venn diagram.

Phrase Bank

• around thirty years old • strong • cruel • the killer • thin • fair complexion • member of Baskerville family • dark features • brave • appears ordinary • gentleman • violent • kind-hearted • careful planner

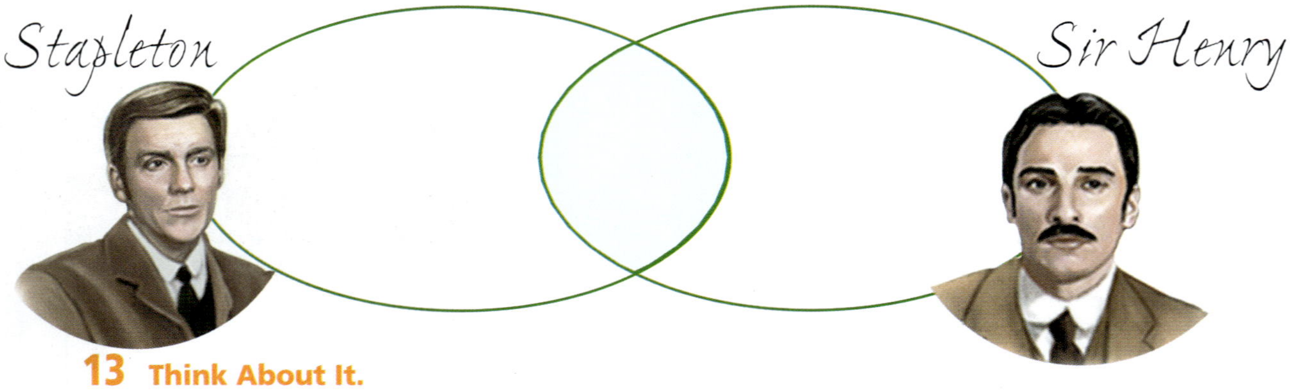

13 Think About It.

Use the Venn diagram to answer the following questions individually.

- How are Holmes and Watson alike? How are they different? What about Sir Henry and Stapleton?
- Do the two men seem to make a good team? Why or why not?

14 Talk it Over.

Discuss the answers to the previous questions with a partner. Share your ideas with the class.

Analyze the Setting

15 Fill It In.

Listen to the following lecture about the setting in *The Hound of the Baskervilles*. Then, use information from the lecture to fill in the graphic organizer.

Aspect of setting	Importance
time	
place	

16 Think About It.

Answer the following questions with a partner.

- How is the time period in which the story takes place important to the ideas in the novel?
- How is the place in which the story takes place important to the ideas in the novel?
- How would the story be different if the time or place changed?

17 Talk It Over.

As a class, discuss your answers to the previous questions.

11

Analyze the Symbols

18 Match it.

Some of the important symbols in the story are the hound, the moors, and light. Match the symbols to their meanings.

Symbol	Meaning
1 ☐ the hound	A mystery, the unknown, the natural world
2 ☐ the moors	B superstition, the supernatural
3 ☐ light	C illumination, knowledge, truth

19 Think About It.

With a partner, discuss your answers to the previous section. Explain why you chose the answers that you did.

20 Talk It Over.

As a class, discuss the following question.

- Based on what you know about the novel, which symbol do you think is most important? Why?

Analyze the Themes

21 Fill It In.

Two important themes in *The Hound of the Baskervilles* are fear and rational thought versus superstition. Use lines from the passage to complete the graphic organizer.

Theme	Lines from Passage
fear	
rational thought versus superstition	

22 Think About It.

Which theme do you think is most important in this section and why?

23 Talk It Over.

Discuss your answer to the previous question with a partner.

In-Depth Analysis: Tension

When authors sit down to write a story, one of their main concerns is how to keep the reader engaged. No one wants to read a book that is boring! The trick is to create a story that compels people to keep reading. In order to do this, authors build a sense of tension, or suspense, in their work. This is a feeling on the reader's part of anticipation and wanting to know the outcome. Authors do this in many different ways.

Sometimes, authors create tension by placing their characters in danger. These dangerous situations – often with horrible potential outcomes – can keep a reader on the edge of their seat while waiting to see what happens. If characters are at risk of being harmed or even killed, a reader will be very likely to keep reading.

To go along with the point above, authors also create tension by creating characters that the reader will care about. If the characters are in danger but are not sympathetic, readers will not care what happens to them. On the other hand, if the reader has bonded with the characters, he or she will be a lot more emotionally invested in their stories. Of course, this doesn't only apply when a character is in danger. Readers who care about the characters in a story will want to know what happens to them in any situation or circumstance.

Another method of creating tension is to withhold information from the reader. This is very common in mystery and detective stories. For example, if there is some crime or some problem with no obvious solution, a reader will be motivated to continue reading simply to discover the answer.

24 **Read the In-Depth Analysis and answer the following questions with a partner.**

- What is tension?
- What is the goal of tension in literature?

25 **List three ways in which authors create tension in a work of literature.**

- ....
- ....
- ....

26 **For each of the methods listed above, give an example from** *The Hound of the Baskervilles*.

- ....
- ....
- ....

Write

27 **Detective stories and mysteries need a lot of tension to keep readers in suspense about what will happen next.** *The Hound of the Baskervilles* **is no exception. Write a 250- to 300-word essay about how Sir Arthur Conan Doyle creates tension in** *The Hound of the Baskervilles*. **Where possible, include quotations from the passage to support your points.**

VIDEO
See p. 221
for video activities & essay writing

Words of Wisdom

A wise man should have money in his head, but not in his heart.
Jonathan Swift

Blessed is he who expects nothing, for he shall never be disappointed. **Jonathan Swift**

Every man desires to live long, but no man wishes to be old. **Jonathan Swift**

There is nothing like staying at home for real comfort. **Jane Austen**

There is no charm equal to tenderness of heart.
Jane Austen

What is right to be done cannot be done too soon.
Jane Austen

There are people, who the more you do for them, the less they will do for themselves. **Jane Austen**

Honest people don't hide their deeds. **Emily Brontë**

If I could I would always work in silence and obscurity, and let my efforts be known by their results.
Emily Brontë

It is better to fail in originality than to succeed in imitation. **Herman Melville**

He who has never failed somewhere, that man can not be great. **Herman Melville**

Truth is in things, and not in words. **Herman Melville**

Have a heart that never hardens, and a temper that never tires, and a touch that never hurts.
Charles Dickens

We forge the chains we wear in life.
Charles Dickens

'Tis love that makes the world go round.
Charles Dickens

It opens the lungs, washes the countenance, exercises the eyes and softens the temper; so cry away.
Charles Dickens

We are all travelers in the wilderness of this world, and the best we can find in our travels is an honest friend. **Robert Louis Stevenson**

You can give without loving, but you can never love without giving. **Robert Louis Stevenson**

No man is rich enough to buy back his past.
Oscar Wilde

What really matters is what you do with what you have. **H.G. Wells**

Our true nationality is mankind. **H.G. Wells**

History is a race between education and catastrophe.
H.G. Wells

If you fell down yesterday, stand up today.
H.G. Wells

Any truth is better than indefinite doubt.
Arthur Conan Doyle

Drama

(1597-1895)

1

Romeo and Juliet

Objectives

By the end of this unit, you will:

• know about the author and the background information behind the play • thoroughly understand the passage from the play • be able to identify figurative language in the passage • be able to summarize the passage • be able to put the passage into modern English • be able to analyze the characters, meter, setting, and themes of the play • know about similes and metaphors in some depth • be able to use the passage to support your opinions and write a literature essay

VIDEO

Learn About ... William Shakespeare

William Shakespeare (1564-1616) was a famous English playwright. Not much is known about Shakespeare's early life. We do know, however, that he was born in Stratford-upon-Avon, a small town about 160 kilometers north-west of London. Shakespeare clearly attended school, most likely in Stratford, but probably did not attend university. When he was eighteen, he married a woman named Anne Hathaway, who had a daughter soon after, then twins two years later. Following the baptism of the twins in Stratford, there are no records for Shakespeare for about seven years. The next time he shows up in historical documents is in the context of the London theatrical scene. There is no indication of when or why he started writing plays, or of why he moved to London. He had great success in London, working as a playwright and even owning his playing company, a group of actors that performed plays, as well as building and running the Globe Theatre. In his later years, Shakespeare enjoyed a high level of financial security, buying the second-largest house in Stratford in 1597. He died when he was only 52.

Despite this lack of solid facts about Shakespeare's life, he's probably the most important author in the history of the English language. His plays are familiar to most people in some form or another.

Predict

Step 1

Discuss these questions with a partner.

1 Why are people willing to do so much for love?

2 When you hear the word "tragedy," what do you think of?

Step 2

Look at the key words from the passage from *Romeo and Juliet*. **With a partner, discuss the meaning of the words. Based on these words, predict the main ideas of the passage.**

Background information

1 Read the text and answer the questions.

1. What stands in the way of Romeo and Juliet getting married?
2. Why don't the Capulets recognize Romeo at their party?
3. Why does Romeo have to leave Verona?
4. Who dies first, Romeo or Juliet?
5. What was innovative about *Romeo and Juliet*?

R*omeo and Juliet* tells the story of two young people who fall in love. There's a problem, however. They come from two different families of Verona, Italy – the Montagues (Romeo) and the Capulets (Juliet) – and these two families are feuding. This means that the members of each family hate and want to kill the members of the other, and that neither Romeo's nor Juliet's parents would agree to their marrying.

Romeo and his friends hear about a party at the Capulets' house. They decide to go, their faces disguised with masks. At the party, Romeo meets Juliet and falls in love. The two talk, and Juliet feels the same way. When they realize that they're from enemy families, they're devastated.

That same night, Romeo sneaks into Juliet's garden and sees her on her balcony. There follows "the balcony scene," perhaps the most famous love scene in literature. By the end of it, they have agreed to get married in secret, which they do the next day. But then, Romeo kills Juliet's violent cousin Tybalt, in revenge for his killing Romeo's close friend Mercutio, and Verona's ruler exiles him from the city. At the same time, Juliet learns that her parents have arranged for her to marry someone else, a man named Paris.

Romeo is in Mantua, a nearby city, but is trying to return to Verona. In the meantime, Juliet decides to drink a potion to make her look like she's dead, so that she will not be forced to marry Paris. The potion will last for forty-two hours, after which time she will wake up. Romeo doesn't know about the plan, but hears of Juliet's "death." He rushes back to Verona, kills Paris, and then kills himself in Juliet's tomb. When Juliet wakes up, she finds Romeo's dead body and decides to kill herself, too, using Romeo's dagger.

Romeo and Juliet was a huge hit in its day, and today it's still one of Shakespeare's most famous and frequently performed plays, while also being the Shakespeare play adapted for the screen the most often. The story comes from Italy, but Shakespeare added his own touch and style. Indeed, until the play became popular, people did not really consider romance a serious enough topic for tragedy. Today, of course, this attitude has changed – and it's mostly due to this play.

Listen & Read

2 **Listen to and read the passage from *Romeo and Juliet*. First, read for general understanding. Then, reread the passage. As you read the second time, underline the different terms Romeo uses to refer to Juliet.**

In this passage, from Act 2, Scene 2, Romeo has climbed into Juliet's garden after meeting her at the party. He sees her come out onto her balcony.

ROMEO
But, soft ! what light through yonder window breaks?
It is the east, and Juliet is the sun.
...
It is my lady, O, it is my love!
O, that she knew she were!
She speaks yet she says nothing: what of that?
Her eye discourses; I will answer it.
I am too bold, 'tis not to me she speaks:
Two of the fairest stars in all the heaven,
Having some business, do entreat her eyes
To twinkle in their spheres till they return.
What if her eyes were there, they in her head?
The brightness of her cheek would shame those stars,
As daylight doth a lamp; her eyes in heaven
Would through the airy region stream so bright
That birds would sing and think it were not night.
See, how she leans her cheek upon her hand!
O, that I were a glove upon that hand,
That I might touch that cheek!

JULIET
Ay me!

ROMEO
She speaks:
O, speak again, bright angel! for thou art
As glorious to this night, being o'er my head
As is a winged messenger of heaven
Unto the white-upturned wondering eyes
Of mortals that fall back to gaze on him
When he bestrides the lazy-pacing clouds
And sails upon the bosom of the air.

JULIET
O Romeo, Romeo! wherefore art thou Romeo?
Deny thy father and refuse thy name;
Or, if thou wilt not, be but sworn my love,
And I'll no longer be a Capulet.

ROMEO
[Aside] Shall I hear more, or shall I speak at this?

JULIET
'Tis but thy name that is my enemy;
Thou art thyself, though not a Montague.
What's Montague? it is nor hand, nor foot,
Nor arm, nor face, nor any other part
Belonging to a man. O, be some other name!
What's in a name? that which we call a rose
By any other name would smell as sweet;
So Romeo would, were he not Romeo call'd,
Retain that dear perfection which he owes
Without that title. Romeo, doff thy name,
And for that name which is no part of thee
Take all myself.

ROMEO
I take thee at thy word:
Call me but love, and I'll be new baptized;
Henceforth I never will be Romeo.

JULIET
What man art thou that thus bescreen'd in night
So stumblest on my counsel?

ROMEO
By a name
I know not how to tell thee who I am:
My name, dear saint, is hateful to myself,
Because it is like an enemy to thee;
Had I it written, I would tear the word.

JULIET
My ears have not yet drunk a hundred words
Of that tongue's utterance, yet I know the sound:
Art thou not Romeo and a Montague?

ROMEO
Neither, fair saint, if either thee dislike.

JULIET
How camest thou hither, tell me, and wherefore?
The orchard walls are high and hard to climb,
And the place death, considering who thou art,
If any of my kinsmen find thee here.

ROMEO
With love's light wings did I o'er-perch these walls;
For stony limits cannot hold love out,
And what love can do that dares love attempt;
Therefore thy kinsmen are no stop to me.

JULIET
If they do see thee, they will murder thee.

ROMEO
Alack, there lies more peril in thine eye
Than twenty of their swords: look thou but sweet,
And I am proof against their enmity.

Respond

3 **Respond to the selection by answering these questions with a partner.**

1. Was your prediction about the main ideas of the passage correct? Explain.
2. How did the author communicate the main ideas? Pick one (or more) and explain.

   a with images **b** with dialogue **c** by explaining them directly
3. Who are the important people in the passage?
4. Which adjectives from the phrase bank best descr be how Romeo might feel in this part of the play? What about Juliet? Explain.

Phrase Bank

- nervous • excited
- angry • sad
- happy • scared
- indifferent

Understand

4 **Read the questions and choose the correct answers.**

1. Which of the following is a comparison that Romeo does NOT make?

   a Juliet to the sun

   b Juliet's eyes to lamps

   c the brightness of Juliet's cheek to daylight

   d Juliet to an angel
2. What does Romeo wish that he was?

   a a glove

   b a bird

   c a cloud

   d an angel
3. What does Juliet wish that Romeo would do?

   a propose to her

   b kiss her

   c give up his name

   d change his attitude
4. How does Juliet recognize Romeo?

   a by his face

   b by his clothes

   c by his hair

   d by his voice

Figurative Language

5 **Work with a partner. Find one example of an oxymoron and one example of olfactory imagery in the passage.**

1

Summarize

6 **First, fill in the graphic organizer based on the passage you read.**

Character(s)

Setting

Main Event(s)

Conflict

7 **Now, use your graphic organizer to summarize the passage with a partner.**

Listen

8 **Listen to a lecture about *Romeo and Juliet*. Then, answer the questions.**

1 What aspect of *Romeo and Juliet* is the speaker discussing?

- **a** its themes
- **b** its characters
- **c** its structure
- **d** its genre

2 What happens in Act 3?

- **a** Romeo and Juliet get married.
- **b** The play turns much more serious.
- **c** There are many jokes and puns.
- **d** The play becomes overly depressing.

Translate

9 **Shakespeare wrote *Romeo and Juliet* sometime before 1600. The language he used is very different from the English that people use today. Look at the example below. Use it as a guide to translate the rest of the speech into modern English on a separate piece of paper with a partner.**

Original	Modern
But soft, what light through yonder window breaks?	But, wait. What's that light coming through the window over there?
It is the east, and Juliet is the sun.	It's the east, and Juliet is the sun.
…	…
It is my lady, oh it is my love.	It is my lady, oh, it is my love!
Oh, that she knew she were.	Oh, if she only knew that she was my love.

About the Title

10 ***Romeo and Juliet* is based on older stories. The earliest-known version comes from Italy and is a story entitled** *Mariotto and Gianozza*, **from a larger volume written in 1496. It tells the story of two young people in love who get married in secret and later meet tragic ends. In 1530, another man rewrote the story and called it** *Giulietta e Romeo*. **In this version, the poison is first introduced, as are many of the other supporting characters. Another Italian wrote a third version in 1554, which was translated into French. From French, a man translated it into English in the form of a poem. It was called** *The Tragicall Historye of Romeus and Juliet*. **This is most likely the source that Shakespeare used to write his play, as it is unlikely that he could read Italian, though he was probably familiar with the Italian stories.**

- Why do you think that Shakespeare chose to name the play *Romeo and Juliet*, not *Juliet and Romeo* as the Italians did?
- The poem that Shakespeare consulted had a longer title than Shakespeare's play. Why do you think Shakespeare shortened it?
- What name would you give the play? Explain.

Analyze the Characters

11 Fill It In.

a. Listen to the first part of the lecture. Then, use words from the phrase bank to fill in the first Venn diagram.

Phrase Bank

- intense • emotional • young
- level-headed • logical • rash • impulsive
- intelligent • not controlled by feelings
- in love • reacts without thinking
- brave • thinks before acting

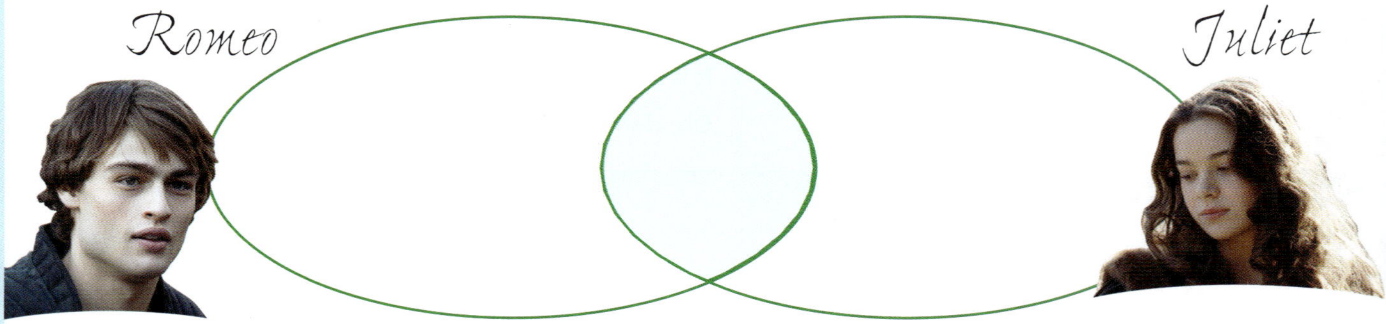

b. Listen to the second part of the lecture and use words from the phrase bank to fill in the second Venn diagram.

Phrase Bank

- quick-tempered • loyal • dies
- Romeo's friend • loses their sword fight
- Juliet's cousin • likes to fight • arrogant
- wants to prove himself

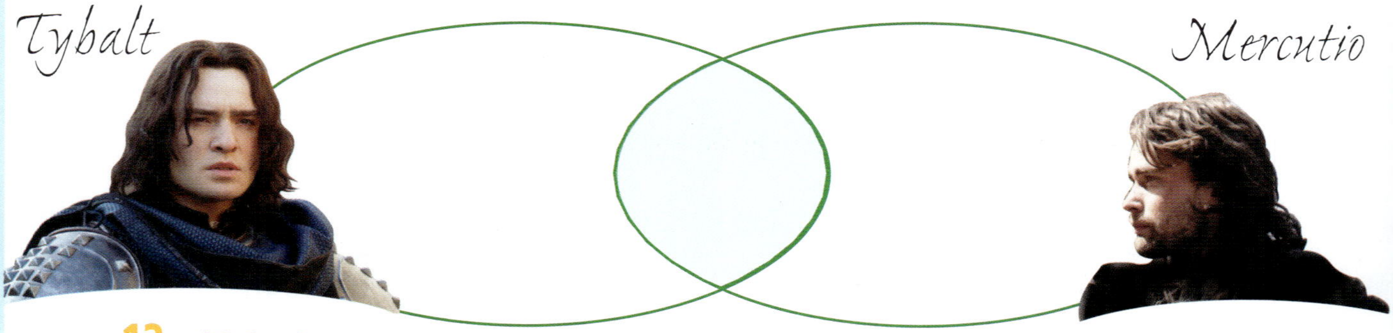

12 Think About It.

Use the Venn diagram to answer the following questions individually.

- How are Romeo and Juliet similar? How are they different? What about Tybalt and Mercutio?
- How do you think that the characters of Romeo and Juliet influenced the outcome of the play? What about the characters of Tybalt and Mercutio?

13 Talk It Over.

Discuss the answers to the previous questions with a partner. Share your ideas with the class.

Analyze the Meter

14 Mark It Up.

Look at the following lines from the passage from *Romeo and Juliet*. Circle the syllables that are emphasized. Listen to a recording of the lines and check your work.

- But soft, what light through yonder window breaks?
- It is my lady, O, it is my love!
- I am too bold, 'tis not to me she speaks.

Shakespeare's characters often talked in verse during serious speeches. Verse means that the lines had a particular rhythmic pattern. The most popular pattern that Shakespeare used was iambic pentameter. Each line of iambic pentameter has ten syllables. The pattern of iambic pentameter is an unstressed syllable followed by a stressed syllable.
Though this is the most common meter in Shakespeare's plays, he doesn't always stick to it perfectly.

15 Think About It.

Answer the following questions with a partner.

- In these lines, what is the pattern of stressed and unstressed syllables?
- Does the rest of the passage follow this pattern?
- Do all of the lines in the passage have the same number of syllables?

16 Talk It Over.

As a class, discuss the following questions.

- Why do you think Shakespeare uses iambic pentameter in this passage?
- Does Shakespeare use perfect iambic pentameter throughout the passage? Why do you think this is?
- Does the rhythm of the passage change the way in which you read it?

Analyze the Setting

17 Match It.

Listen to the lecture. Then, answer the following questions with a partner.

- Why is the setting less important in *Romeo and Juliet* than in other works?
- Can the story make sense in any time or place?
- What do *indoors* and *outdoors* represent within the play?

Analyze the Themes

18 Fill It In.

Love is the most important theme in the passage. Romeo and Juliet both talk about love and why they love one another. Reread the passage and fill in the graphic organizer with lines from the passage for each character.

Theme	Romeo	Juliet
love		

19 Think About It.

Do Romeo and Juliet seem to have the same views about love? Explain.

20 Talk It Over.

Discuss your answer to the previous question with the rest of the class.

In-Depth Analysis: Similes and Metaphors

Figures of speech are important in literature. They help the author communicate ideas in unique and interesting ways. In particular, similes and metaphors allow the author to compare two things that might otherwise seem dissimilar.

Similes and metaphors are very similar, but there is one major difference. Similes compare two things using the words "like" or "as." Metaphors, on the other hand, do not use these words. For example, the phrase, "She is like an angel" is a simile, while the corresponding metaphor would be: "She is an angel."

Shakespeare used both similes and metaphors to great effect in the famous balcony scene. In this passage, Romeo reveals his true feelings about Juliet and uses very beautiful language to do so. This adds to the emotional quality of the scene.

21 **Read the In-Depth Analysis and reread the passage from *Romeo and Juliet*. Identify three similes and three metaphors. Keep in mind that sometimes they are not stated outright. That is, some inference is necessary.**

Simile	Metaphor

22 **For each simile and metaphor listed above, explain which two things are being compared.**

Simile comparisons	Metaphor comparisons

23 **Pick one simile and explain what you think it means. Do the same for one metaphor. Share your answers with the class.**

Write

24 **In the balcony scene from *Romeo and Juliet*, we learn a lot about the two characters' love for each other. In a 250- to 300-word essay, discuss the different ways that Romeo and Juliet view love. Where possible, include direct quotations from the passage.**

VIDEO See p. 222 for video activities & essay writing

2 *Hamlet*

VIDEO

Objectives

By the end of this unit, you will:

• know about the author and the background information behind the play • thoroughly understand the speech from the play • be able to identify figurative language in the speech • be able to summarize the speech • be able to put the speech into modern English • be able to analyze the title, characters, setting, metaphors, meter, and themes of the play • know about Man versus Self conflict in some depth • be able to use the speech to support your opinions and write a literature essay

Learn About ... William Shakespeare

William Shakespeare (1564-1616) was one of the most important English writers of all time. His most famous works are his plays and his sonnets. Today, people continue to perform, study, and enjoy his writings, and his place in English literature is widely recognized and admired. Shakespeare gave people such memorable characters as Romeo and Juliet, Macbeth, and, of course, Hamlet. Not only that, but he also helped shape modern drama by refining ideas of plot and character development in his plays. For example, Shakespeare was one of the first playwrights to allow the audience to see the inner workings of the characters' minds by making them speak their thoughts out loud. Finally, Shakespeare's language shaped the way that people talk today. Hundreds of figures of speech can be traced back to his plays. Perhaps no other writer before or since has had such an overreaching or long-lasting influence on English literature as Shakespeare has.

Predict

Step 1

Discuss these questions with a partner.

1 What are some things that can make a person give up hope?

2 When you are discouraged, what keeps you going?

Step 2

Look at the key words from the speech from *Hamlet*. With a partner, discuss the meaning of the words. Based on these words, predict the mood of the speech.

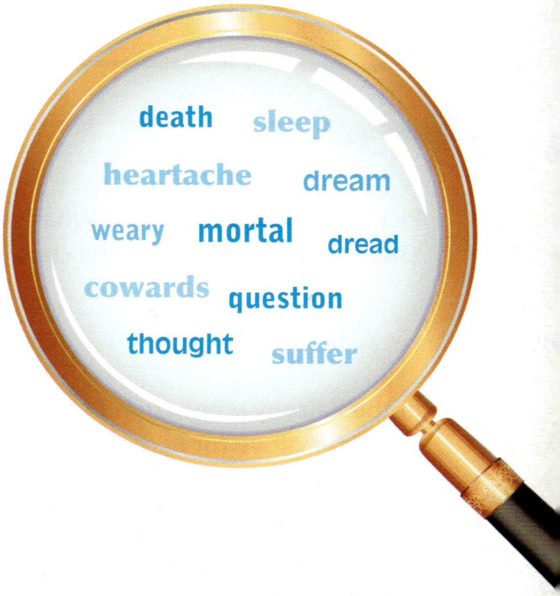

Hamlet, which Shakespeare wrote between the years of 1599 and 1602, is one of his tragedies and probably his most famous play. It tells the story of a royal family in Denmark, and seems to take place during the same time period in which it was written, though this is never explicitly stated. Shortly before the play begins, Hamlet's father, the King of Denmark, dies. Claudius, Hamlet's uncle, marries Gertrude, Hamlet's mother, after the death. Already saddened by his father's death and upset by his mother's hasty wedding, Hamlet becomes even more distraught when he speaks with his dead father's ghost. The ghost tells him that Claudius poisoned him in order to gain the throne and the Queen. Once Hamlet hears this terrible accusation, the rest of the play is largely devoted to his difficulty in trying to decide what he should do next.

Uncertain of his uncle's guilt, Hamlet hires some actors to put on a play in front of the court, a play which re-enacts the murder scene the ghost described to Hamlet – where Claudius poured poison into Hamlet's father's ear to kill him while he slept. When Claudius rushes out of the room in shock, Hamlet is convinced he is truly guilty, and finally decides to act. However, he first accidentally kills the wrong man, Polonius, thinking him to be his uncle, which triggers the madness and suicide of the man's daughter, Ophelia – the woman Hamlet has been courting. Hamlet is banished for the crime, but returns after surviving an assassination attempt upon him directed by Claudius. Ophelia's brother Laertes, who wants revenge for his father's and sister's deaths, fences with Hamlet with a poisoned blade, and fatally wounds him. Before he dies, however, he manages to kill Claudius and explain his actions to Fortinbras, the Norwegian prince whom Hamlet has named as his heir.

Despite being his longest play, *Hamlet* was still one of Shakespeare's most popular in his day, and remains among his most performed today. The title role of Hamlet is considered the pinnacle of a male actor's career, and has been played on screen by the biggest actors of stage or screen, including Laurence Olivier, Mel Gibson, and Kenneth Branagh. It contains the "To be or not to be" speech, probably the most famous soliloquy in English literature, as well as hundreds of lines that have become part of the English language.

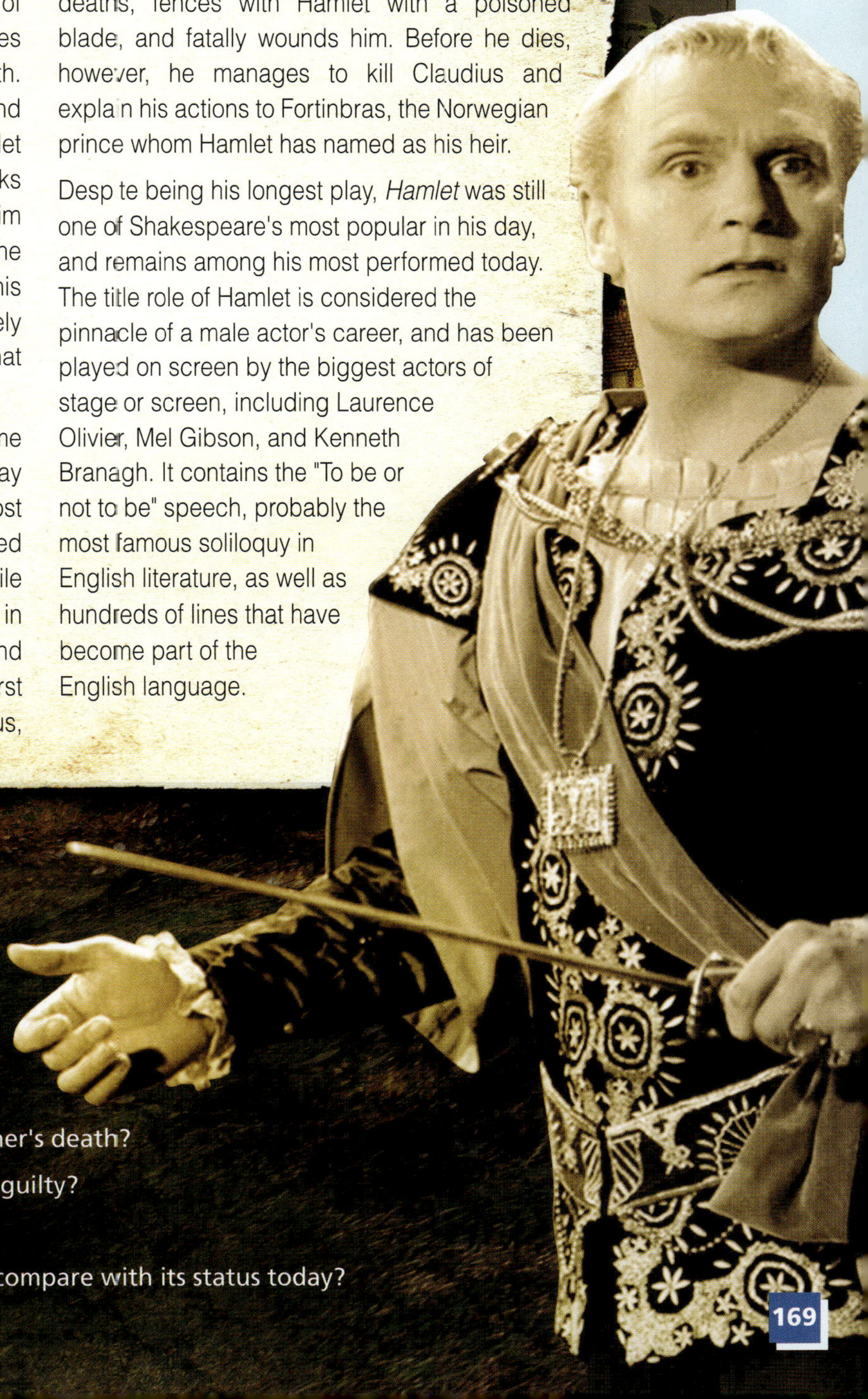

Background information

1 Read the text and answer the questions.

1. Why is Hamlet sad as the play begins?
2. Who is responsible for Hamlet's father's death?
3. How does Hamlet prove his uncle is guilty?
4. Who kills Hamlet, and why?
5. How does Hamlet's early reception compare with its status today?

Listen & Read

2 🎧 **Listen to and read the speech from *Hamlet*. First, read for general understanding. Then, reread the speech. As you read the second time, decide which kind of conflict Hamlet is experiencing.**

In this speech, from Act 3, Scene 1, Hamlet is talking to himself about death and suicide.

Hamlet

To be, or not to be, that is the question:
Whether 'tis nobler in the mind to suffer
The slings and arrows of outrageous fortune,
Or to take arms against a sea of troubles,
And by opposing end them? To die: to sleep;
No more; and by a sleep to say we end
The heart-ache and the thousand natural shocks
That flesh is heir to, 'tis a consummation
Devoutly to be wish'd. To die, to sleep;
To sleep: perchance to dream: ay, there's the rub;
For in that sleep of death what dreams may come
When we have shuffled off this mortal coil,
Must give us pause: there's the respect
That makes calamity of so long life;
For who would bear the whips and scorns of time,
The oppressor's wrong, the proud man's contumely,
The pangs of despised love, the law's delay,
The insolence of office and the spurns
That patient merit of the unworthy takes,
When he himself might his quietus make
With a bare bodkin? who would fardels bear,
To grunt and sweat under a weary life,
But that the dread of something after death,
The undiscover'd country from whose bourn
No traveller returns, puzzles the will
And makes us rather bear those ills we have
Than fly to others that we know not of?
Thus conscience does make cowards of us all;
And thus the native hue of resolution
Is sicklied o'er with the pale cast of thought,
And enterprises of great pith and moment
With this regard their currents turn awry,
And lose the name of action.

Respond

3 Respond to the speech by answering these questions with a partner.

1 Was your prediction about the main ideas of the speech correct? Explain.

2 How did the author communicate the main ideas? Pick one (or more) and explain.

a with images b with dialogue c by explaining them directly

3 Which adjectives from the phrase bank best describe how Hamlet feels in this part of the play? Explain.

Phrase Bank

- nervous
- hopeless
- angry
- sad
- scared
- conflicted
- indifferent

Understand

4 Read the questions and choose the correct answers.

1 To what does Hamlet compare death?

a sleeping
b dreaming
c suffering
d fighting

2 What does Hamlet say makes people cowardly?

a enterprises
b resolution
c conscience
d thought

3 Why does Hamlet decide not to take his life?

a He doesn't want to leave his family.
b He's afraid of what happens after death.
c He thinks that it is a cowardly thing to do.
d He doesn't think it will end his suffering.

4 What does Hamlet NOT say is a problem with life?

a unreturned love
b rudeness of others
c insults of proud men
d work with no reward

Figurative Language

5 Work with a partner. Find one example of auditory imagery and two examples of alliteration in the speech.

2

Summarize

6 **First, fill in the graphic organizer based on the speech you read.**

Character(s)	Setting

Main Event(s)	Conflict

7 **Now, use your graphic organizer to summarize the speech with a partner.**

Listen

8 **Listen to a lecture about *Hamlet*. Then, answer the questions.**

1 What is the speaker mainly talking about?

a who Shakespeare based Hamlet's character on

b how *Hamlet* is different from other plays

c Shakespeare's sources for *Hamlet*

d who wrote the original version of *Hamlet*

2 Why does the speaker mention the ghost?

a to prove the originality of Shakespeare's *Hamlet*

b to point out what the stories have in common

c to explain where Shakespeare got an idea

d to show how the legend changed over time

Translate

9 **Shakespeare wrote *Hamlet* sometime around 1600. The language he used is very different from the English that people use today. Look at the example below. Use it as a guide to translate the rest of the speech into modern English on a separate piece of paper with a partner.**

Original	Modern
To be, or not to be, that is the question: Whether 'tis nobler in the mind to suffer The slings and arrows of outrageous fortune, Or to take arms against a sea of troubles, And by opposing end them?	To live, or not to live? That's the question: Do we find it nobler to suffer through the attacks that fate throws at us, or do we fight back against the sea of troubles and, in doing so, end it once and for all?

Analyze the Title

Shakespeare named this play after the most important character: Hamlet. This was not unusual for Shakespeare. Many of his other tragedies were also named in this way, including *Romeo and Juliet*, *Macbeth*, and *King Lear*. The comedies, like *Measure for Measure*, were often named after lines in the plays and not after individual characters. This is because the comedies are generally about more than one protagonist. That is, there is no identifiable main character. The tragedies, on the other hand, are much more tightly focused on one person (or two people, as in the case of *Romeo and Juliet*). The tragedies are given the name of the protagonist to emphasize that person's importance to the play.

10 Fill It In.

Look at the list of Hamlet's character traits. Review the speech to find lines that support each of the character traits. Use the lines to fill in the second column of the graphic organizer.

Character trait	Evidence from the play	What kind of person is Hamlet?
depression		
indecision		
low self-esteem		

11 Think About It.

Now, think about what kind of person Hamlet is. Fill in the third column of the table with your own ideas.

12 Talk It Over.

With a partner, answer the following questions.

- Does Hamlet seem like a typical protagonist or main character? Why or why not?

Analyze the Characters

13 Fill It In.

First, listen to the lecture. Then, use phrases from the phrase bank to complete the Venn diagrams.

Phrase Bank

- acts • reacts • thinks • depressed
- submissive • looks after status
- goes mad • power-hungry
- loves Hamlet • relies on others • moral
- self-destructive • no conscience
- sensitive • confused • upset

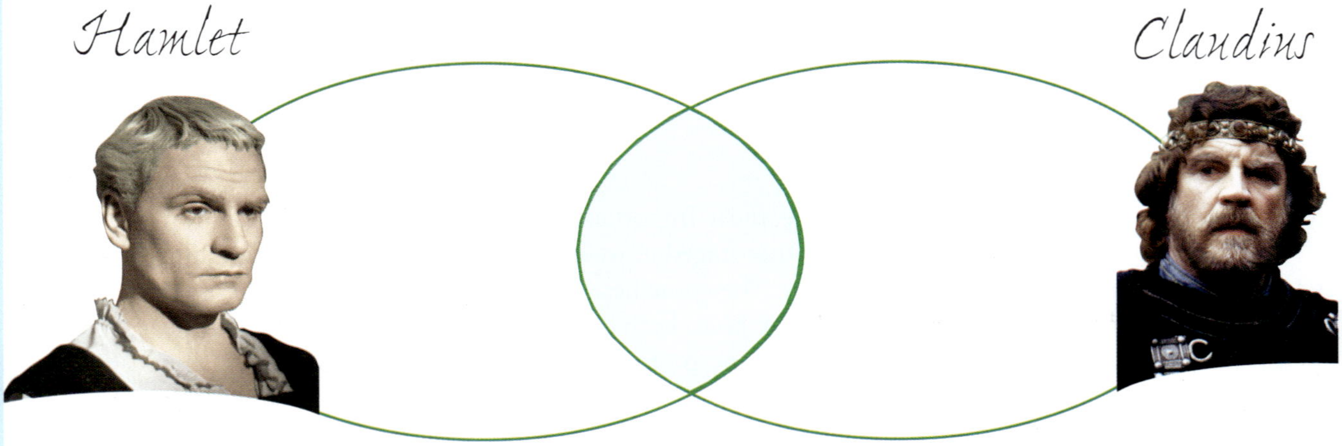

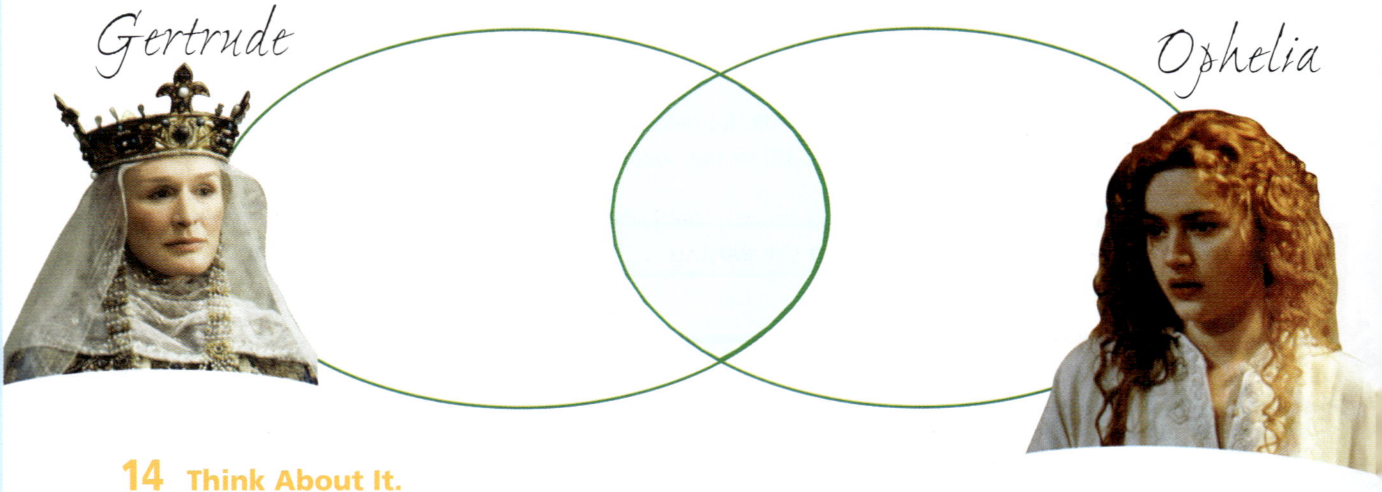

14 Think About It.

Use the Venn diagrams to answer the following questions individually.

- What do the characters have in common?
- How are the characters different?

15 Talk It Over.

Discuss the answers to the previous questions with a partner. Share your ideas with the class.

Analyze the Setting

16 Fill It In.

First, listen to the lecture. Then, read the following lines from different scenes in Hamlet. Write what the lines reveal about the setting.

Lines	Setting
Enter Bernardo and Francisco, two sentinels, [meeting]. *BERNARDO* Who's there? *FRANCISCO* Nay, answer me. Stand and unfold yourself.	
HAMLET The air bites shrewdly; it is very cold. *HORATIO* It is a nipping and an eager air.	
Enter two Clowns [with spades and mattocks]. *HAMLET* Has this fellow no feeling of his business, 'a sings in grave-making?	

17 Think About It.

With a partner, discuss the answers to the following question.

- What can you tell about the setting in each of the previous lines?

18 Talk It Over.

Discuss the following question as a class.

- Why do you think that the scenery was not that important in Shakespeare's time?

Analyze the Metaphors

19 Fill It In.

The table lists several important metaphors from Hamlet's speech. For each line from the speech, write what you think Hamlet is referring to.

Hamlet says ...	Hamlet means ...
"the slings and arrows of outrageous fortune"	
"For in that sleep of death what dreams may come"	
"The undiscover'd country from whose bourn/ No traveller returns"	

20 Think About It.

Answer the following questions individually.

- Why do you think Shakespeare chose these metaphors? Which is most effective? Why?

21 Talk It Over.

In groups of four, discuss your answers to the previous questions. Choose one group member to report the group's ideas to the rest of the class.

2

Analyze the Meter

Iambic pentameter is a special kind of rhythm, or meter. An iamb is a pattern of an unstressed syllable followed by a stressed syllable. The prefix penta- means five. So lines of iambic pentameter have five iambs – five groups made of an unstressed and a stressed syllable.

Shakespeare often uses iambic pentameter. It is also the most common kind of meter in English poetry. This is because is a very natural-sounding rhythm. Shakespeare does not always stick strictly to iambic pentameter. It varies throughout speeches, but the iamb (the pattern of an unstressed and a stressed syllable) is the most common pattern in the lines of verse.

Generally, Shakespeare uses iambic pentameter when his characters are discussing something important or profound. Other times, the characters may speak with no real recognizable rhythm – in prose.

22 Mark It Up.

Look at the following lines from Hamlet's speech. Circle the syllables that are emphasized. Listen to a recording of the lines and check your work.

For in that sleep of death what dreams may come
When we have shuffled off this mortal coil,
Must give us pause; there's the respect
That makes calamity of so long life

23 Think About It.

Answer the following questions individually.

- In these lines, what is the pattern of stressed and unstressed syllables?
- Does the rest of the speech follow this pattern?
- Do all of the lines in the speech have the same number of syllables?

24 Talk It Over.

As a class, discuss the following questions.

- Why do you think Shakespeare uses iambic pentameter in this speech?
- Does Shakespeare use perfect iambic pentameter throughout the speech? Why do you think this is?
- Does the rhythm of the speech change the way in which you read it?

Analyze the Themes

25 Fill It In.

There are many different themes in Hamlet's speech. The graphic organizer lists some of the most important. Find lines from the speech that are related to each of the themes.

Theme	Lines from Speech
death	
indecision	
fear	

26 Think About It.

Which theme do you think is most important to this speech and why?

27 Talk It Over.

Discuss your answer to the previous question with the rest of the class.

In-Depth Analysis: Man versus Self conflict

Conflict is an important part of most literary works. If there were no conflicts in a story, people would become bored very quickly. Authors include many different kinds of conflicts in their works. For example, a character can have a conflict with another character, with the natural world, with society, and even with himself. It is this final kind of conflict that we see in Hamlet's famous speech, and it is known as Man versus Self conflict.

In the "To be or not to be" speech, Hamlet argues with himself about what to do. The speech sets up the conflict very early on when he asks, "To be or not to be?" Hamlet's conflict is deciding whether or not he should commit suicide.

28 Read the In-Depth Analysis and fill in the graphic organizer. Use lines from the speech to list Hamlet's arguments for and against suicide.

Argument for Life	Argument for Suicide

29 With a partner, evaluate Hamlet's arguments by answering the following questions.

- Does Hamlet present a better case for life or for death?
- Which option does Hamlet choose? Why does he choose this?

Write

30 In the "To be or not to be" speech, Hamlet has a conflict with himself. He tries to decide if he should kill himself or not. He presents arguments for both sides. Write a 250- to 300-word essay explaining which argument you think is stronger. Use quotations from the speech to support your opinion.

VIDEO See p. 223 for video activities & essay writing

3 As You Like It

Objectives

By the end of this unit, you will:

• know about the author and the background information behind the play • thoroughly understand the speech from the play • be able to identify figurative language in the speech • be able to summarize the speech • be able to put the speech into modern English • be able to analyze the characters, meter, setting, and themes of the play • know about extended metaphors in some depth • be able to use the speech to support your opinions and write a literature essay

VIDEO

Learn About ... William Shakespeare

William Shakespeare (1564-1616) was a famous English playwright. His tragedies, such as *Hamlet* and *King Lear*, are among his most famous plays. His comedies are equally as important, however. In these plays, romance always plays a big role. There are also other playful elements, like disguises and cases of mistaken identity. Shakespeare's tragedies often focus on one or two main characters. The comedies, on the other hand, have large casts with many different characters of equal importance. The comedies combine fun and festive settings with sharp social commentary. Even though they are lighthearted, Shakespeare's comedies still give the audience or reader something to think about when the play is over.

Predict

Step 1

Discuss these questions with a partner.

1 Do you act the same way all of the time, or do you act differently in different situations? Explain.

2 How do people's lives change as they age?

Step 2

Look at the key words from the speech from *As You Like It*. **With a partner, discuss the meaning of the words. Based on these words, predict the main ideas of the speech.**

Background information

1 **Read the text and answer the questions.**

1. What connection does *As You Like It* have to ancient Greek literature?
2. Why have most protagonists gone to the Forest of Arden?
3. Why do Rosalind and Celia disguise themselves?
4. How have critics reacted to *As You Like It*?
5. What criticism does Shakespeare have of civilized life in *As You Like It*?

As You Like It is one of Shakespeare's most well-known comedies and, with a number of songs included, it is actually a musical comedy. He most likely wrote it between 1598 and 1600, the last years of Queen Elizabeth's reign. In spite of when it was written, the play is actually part of a much older tradition. It is written in the pastoral tradition, a form of literature that emphasizes how simple and peaceful life is in a natural setting, and how those who live the country life are truly free. This form has its roots in the literature of ancient Greece.

As You Like It tells the story of a group of people who flee Duke Frederick's court (his place of residence, probably a castle, and the town surrounding it) to go live in the Forest of Arden, for a variety of reasons. Orlando goes to the forest because his older brother wants to kill him. Duke Senior also lives in the forest to escape his evil brother, with an informal "court" of lords, including musician Amiens and the philosophical Jacques. Rosalind, whose story the play follows, is Duke Senior's daughter, and she moves to the forest when her uncle becomes angry with her. Celia is Rosalind's cousin, and goes with Rosalind because they are best friends. Since it would be dangerous to stay in the forest as young noblewomen, they both disguise themselves, Rosalind as a man called Ganymede, Celia as a poor woman called Aliena. Eventually, all of these characters meet one another, and great complications ensue. For example, Rosalind loves Orlando, but she can't tell him because he thinks she's a boy. A shepherdess named Phebe loves Ganymede (though Ganymede is in reality Rosalind in disguise). Silvius, a shepherd, loves Phebe. Finally, at the end of the play, Orlando's brother has a change of heart. So does Duke Senior's brother, restoring the throne to Duke Senior. Rosalind reveals herself, and she and Orlando get married. Celia falls in love with Orlando's brother. Silvius and Phebe also get married. Everyone moves back to the court.

As You Like It has divided critics through the ages, with some speculating that it was written as a crowd-pleaser rather than a serious piece of work. It certainly proved popular, and has continued to be so, but Shakespeare does use the lightness of comedy to make some serious points about society. In the forest, the breakdown of barriers of class and gender allow the characters to speak and love far more freely than they could in the stiff and formalized atmosphere of "civilized life" in the court.

3

Listen & Read

2 🎧 **Listen to and read the speech from** *As You Like It*. **First, read for general understanding. Then, reread the passage. As you read the second time, underline each word that refers to the theater.**

In this passage, from Act 2, Scene 7, Jacques is speaking. He is a member of Duke Senior's court, and he's generally in a bad mood.

JACQUES
All the world's a stage,
And all the men and women merely players;
They have their exits and their entrances,
And one man in his time plays many parts,
His acts being seven ages. At first, the infant,
Mewling and puking in the nurse's arms.
And then the whining school-boy, with his satchel
And shining morning face, creeping like snail
Unwillingly to school. And then the lover,
Sighing like furnace, with a woeful ballad
Made to his mistress' eyebrow. Then a soldier,
Full of strange oaths and bearded like the pard,
Jealous in honour, sudden and quick in quarrel,
Seeking the bubble reputation
Even in the cannon's mouth. And then the justice,
In fair round belly with good capon lined,
With eyes severe and beard of formal cut,
Full of wise saws and modern instances;
And so he plays his part. The sixth age shifts
Into the lean and slipper'd pantaloon,
With spectacles on nose and pouch on side,
His youthful hose, well saved, a world too wide
For his shrunk shank; and his big manly voice,
Turning again toward childish treble, pipes
And whistles in his sound. Last scene of all,
That ends this strange eventful history,
Is second childishness and mere oblivion,
Sans teeth, sans eyes, sans taste, sans everything.

Respond

3 Respond to the passage by answering these questions with a partner.

1. Was your prediction about the main ideas of the speech correct? Explain.
2. How did the author communicate the main ideas? Pick one (or more) and explain.
   a with images   b with dialogue   c by explaining them directly
3. Which adjectives from the phrase bank do you think best describe how Jacques feels in this part of the play? Explain.

Phrase Bank

- sad
- happy
- thoughtful
- angry
- hopeful
- tired
- bored

Understand

4 Read the questions and choose the correct answers.

1. To what does Jacques compare the world?
   a a stage
   b a story
   c a cycle
   d a fight
2. How many parts do people play?
   a three
   b five
   c seven
   d nine
3. Which is a characteristic of soldiers?
   a They are often sad.
   b They give good advice.
   c They care about reputation.
   d They have full stomachs.
4. What is the last age of people?
   a extreme old age
   b childhood
   c respectability
   d death

Figurative Language

5 Work with a partner. Find one example of hyperbole and one example of gustatory imagery in the speech.

Summarize

6 First, fill in the graphic organizer based on the speech you just read.

Character(s)

Setting

Main Event(s)

7 Now, use your graphic organizer to summarize the speech with a partner.

Listen

8 **Listen to a lecture about *As You Like It*. Then, answer the questions.**

1 What aspect of *As You Like It* is the speaker discussing?

a an important theme

b the characters

c the setting

d its history

2 Why does the speaker mention Celia?

a to explain how the play ends

b to contrast her with Rosalind

c to give an example of friendship

d to show the climax of the play

Translate

9 **Shakespeare wrote *As You Like It* sometime around 1600. The language he used is very different from the English that people use today. Look at the example below. Use it as a guide to translate the rest of the speech into modern English on a separate piece of paper with a partner.**

Original	Modern
All the world's a stage, And all the men and women merely players: They have their exits and their entrances; And one man in his time plays many parts, His acts being seven ages.	The whole world is a stage, And men and women are nothing but actors. They come on stage, and then they leave, And a person plays many different roles in life. He has seven main periods of life altogether.

About the Title

10 **Sometimes, it's hard to understand what Shakespeare meant by his titles. In the case of *As You Like It*, he gives us a hint at the end of the play. Rosalind comes back on stage, alone. She says, "I charge you/…to like as much/ of this play as please you." To "charge" means to ask someone to do something. So Rosalind asks the audience to like as much of the play as they want. Shakespeare seems to tell the audience that they can take his play or leave it. They should only like the parts of the play that were entertaining to them.**

Answer the following questions with a partner.

- What does the title of *As You Like It* mean?
- Why do you think Shakespeare chose to give the play this name?
- What name would you have given the play?

Analyze the Characters

11 Fill It In.

First, listen to the lecture. Then, complete the character map.

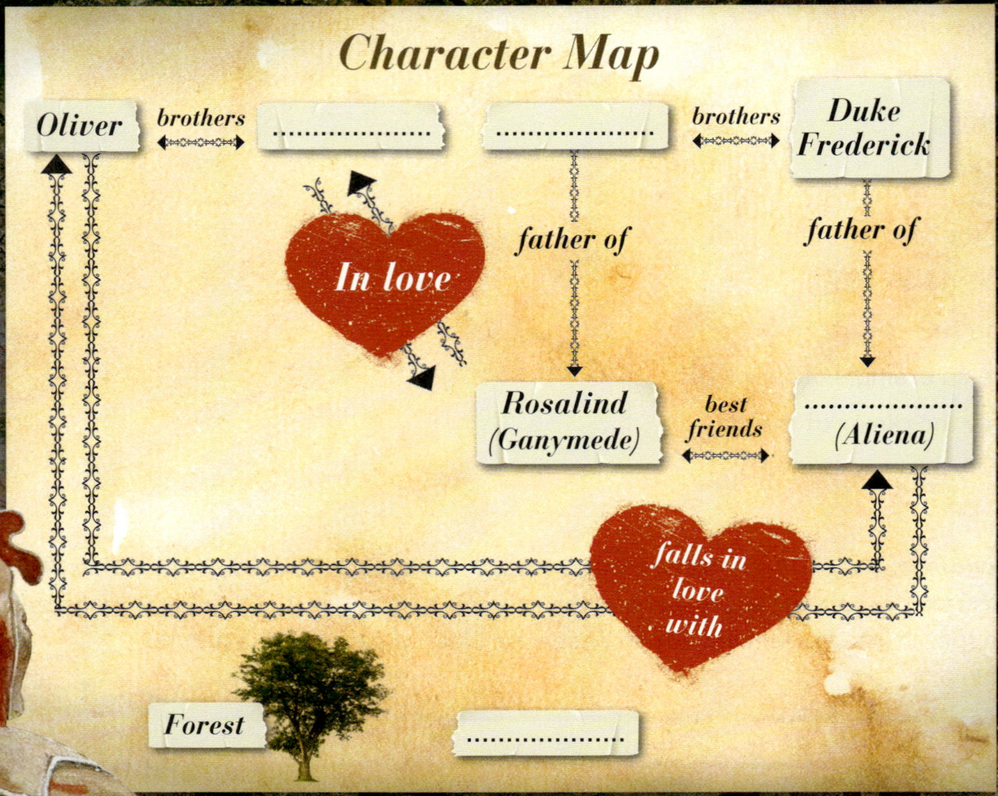

12 Think About It.

Use the character map to answer the following questions individually.

- What are the relationships that you see in the map?
- Based on the number of connections to others, which character seems to be at the center of the action?

13 Talk It Over.

Discuss the answers to the previous questions with a partner. Share your ideas with the class.

Analyze the Meter

Shakespeare's plays sometimes use prose – without any special rhythm or form – and sometimes use verse – with a special rhythm or form. When Shakespeare uses verse, he most commonly uses iambic pentameter. Iambic pentameter is a very popular rhythm in English poetry because it closely mimics the natural rhythm of human speech. A line of iambic pentameter consists of five groups of two syllables. These groups are made up of an unstressed syllable followed by a stressed syllable. Since there are five groups of two syllables, each line has ten syllables.

Even when writing in verse, Shakespeare doesn't always stick to iambic pentameter. Sometimes, he adds an extra syllable, or leaves one out. This is intentional, and adds to the realism of the play, since normal people do not speak in perfect iambic pentameter all of the time.

14 Mark It Up

Look at the following lines from Jacques' speech. Circle the syllables that are emphasized. Listen to a recording of the lines and check your work.

And all the men and women merely players

They have their exits and their entrances

And one man in his time plays many parts

15 Think About It.

Answer the following questions individually.

- In these lines, what is the pattern of stressed and unstressed syllables?
- Does the rest of the speech follow this pattern?
- Do all of the lines in the speech have the same number of syllables?

16 Talk It Over.

As a class, discuss the following questions.

- Why do you think Shakespeare uses iambic pentameter in this speech?
- Does Shakespeare use perfect iambic pentameter throughout the speech? Why do you think this is?
- Does the rhythm of the speech change the way in which you read it?

3

Analyze the Setting

17 Fill It In.

First, listen to the lecture. Then fill in the graphic organizer.

Setting	Meaning
the forest	
the court	

18 Think About It.

With a partner, discuss the following questions.

- What does the forest represent?
- What does the court represent?

19 Talk It Over.

Discuss the following question as a class.

- What does Shakespeare suggest about the court and the forest in *As You Like It*?

Analyze the Themes

20 Fill It In.

There are many different themes in Jacques' speech. The graphic organizer lists some of the most important. Find lines from the speech that are related to each of the themes.

Theme	Lines from Speech
life as a play	
the inevitability of death/old age	
the universality of the human experience	

21 Think About It.

Which theme do you think is most important to this speech and why?

22 Talk It Over.

Discuss your answer to the previous question with the rest of the class.

In-Depth Analysis

Extended Metaphors

A metaphor is a comparison between two things. The two things usually don't seem to have much in common. By comparing them, the author forces the reader to think about them in a different way. Unlike a simile, a metaphor does not use the words "like" or "as." For example, a simile is "Love is like a rose." The same idea expressed through a metaphor is: "Love is a rose." Obviously, love is not literally a rose. And love is an abstract idea, not a physical object like a rose. So when a reader encounters a metaphor, they must think and analyze it to understand what point the author is trying to make.

Jacques' speech is one of the most famous examples of metaphor in the English language. In this speech, Jacques uses a technique called an extended metaphor. Instead of simply making one comparison and moving on, Jacques spends a lot of time developing his metaphor and adding more details to it. This makes for a very interesting commentary on life. Of course, for an extended metaphor to work, it has to be convincing each and every step of the way, which is why most writers do not attempt them, and many who do end up creating metaphors which sound forced. In his "All the world's a stage" speech, Shakespeare controls and completes the extended metaphor beautifully.

23 **Read the In-Depth Analysis and reread the speech. Underline any portions that you think are metaphors.**

24 **Share your answers with a partner. Then, answer the following questions.**

- What do you think is the central metaphor of Jacques' speech?
- What are some secondary metaphors in the speech?

25 **Discuss the following question as a class.**

- What does the metaphor in Jacques' speech mean? That is, what is Jacques attempting to say about human life by using this metaphor?
- Is Jacques' metaphor effective?

Write

26 **In Jacques' speech, he compares the world to a stage. This extended metaphor continues throughout the rest of his speech. In a 250- to 300-word essay, discuss the use of this metaphor and to what extent it fits with the message of the play.**

VIDEO See p. 224 for video activities & essay writing

4 Doctor Faustus

Objectives

By the end of this unit, you will:

• know about the author and the background information behind the play • thoroughly understand the speech from the play • be able to identify figurative language in the speech • be able to summarize the speech • be able to put the speech into modern English • be able to analyze the characters, setting, symbols, and themes of the play • know about tragic heroes in some depth • be able to use the speech to support your opinions and write a literature essay

VIDEO

Learn About ... Christopher Marlowe

Christopher Marlowe (1564-1593) was an English playwright, poet, and translator, but much of his life is a mystery. He was born in the same year as William Shakespeare, and his writing influenced Shakespeare a great deal. Marlowe was a poet, a playwright, and a translator. He attended college and received a Master of Arts degree in 1587. In the following years, he wrote several successful plays that were widely performed in England. He also wrote poetry and translated Roman poetry.

For some reason, in May 1593, the courts issued a warrant for Marlowe's arrest. The charge was most likely blasphemy – or the writing of things that went against official church teachings – but no one knows for sure. Ten days after the warrant was issued, a man named Ingram Frizer stabbed Marlowe to death. Some people think that this was related to his arrest. Others say it was a simple fight over money they owed at an inn or tavern. Despite his early death, the influence of Marlowe on English literature is immense.

Predict

Step 1

Discuss these questions with a partner.

1 What motivates people to learn new things?

2 Do you think that one kind of knowledge can be better than another? Explain.

Step 2

Look at the key words from the speech from *Doctor Faustus*. **With a partner, discuss the meaning of the words. Based on these words, predict the main ideas of the speech.**

Background information

1 Read the text and answer the questions.

1. How did people react to *Doctor Faustus* originally?
2. What deal does Faustus strike with Mephastophilis?
3. What makes Mephastophilis sympathetic to the audience?
4. How much does Faustus worry about what will happen to him after twenty-four years?
5. How is Faustus flawed as a character?

Doctor Faustus is the most famous of Christopher Marlowe's plays, and caused enormous controversy and even scandal when it was first performed because of its content. It tells the story of Doctor Faustus' tragic downfall. Faustus is very smart. He is already an expert in philosophy, medicine, law, and religion, but he wants more. He decides to turn to black magic in order to gain more power. This, he thinks, will give him the ability to do and learn nearly anything.

Faustus summons an evil spirit, Mephastophilis. This spirit is a servant to Lucifer, the Devil. Faustus tells Mephastophilis what he wants: unlimited knowledge and power. Mephastophilis tells Faustus that he can have it. For twenty-four years, Faustus will be able to do and have whatever he wants. After the time is up, however, Mephastophilis will take Faustus to Lucifer. Faustus will have to live forever in Lucifer's terrible kingdom.

Mephastophilis urges Faustus not to go forward with this plan. He talks about his lifetime of servitude to Lucifer and says that if he had known how awful it would be, he never would have agreed to it. In this way, Mephastophilis is a tragic character as well. He made a bad decision and regrets it. His thirst for power led to his eternal suffering. Mephastophilis' fate foreshadows what will eventually happen to Faustus, but Faustus dismisses Mephastophilis' warnings without much thought. Faustus signs a contract with Lucifer (using his own blood as ink), and Mephastophilis becomes Faustus' personal servant.

At first, Faustus tries to learn everything that he can. After all, his first motivation was to gain knowledge. Over time, however, Faustus stops trying. He spends his time doing meaningless things, like summoning Helen of Troy to his side so that he can kiss her. During this whole period, Faustus does not think much about his eventual fate. Even when he receives warnings from his friends, he continues down his path of destruction. Although a good and a bad angel appear time and again to advise Faustus (indicating that he could still take the path of good) he ignores the sign. Throughout the entire play, Faustus is blind to the fact that he could be saved from his terrible punishment. He simply doesn't seem to think about it.

At the end, Mephastophilis comes to take Faustus away. He spends his last minutes worrying and hoping that he will not have to die. But he never regrets his decision or asks for forgiveness. It is implied that all Faustus would have to do is ask and he would be saved. He never does this, and his blindness to the possibility of his own salvation is one of Faustus' tragic flaws. Mephastophilis drags Faustus off the stage, and takes him to his master, Lucifer.

The play had a profound effect on the audiences of the time, with some even reporting the appearance of evil spirits in the theater. It was the first time such a controversial subject had been addressed in English drama, and it has helped make the story of Faust one of the most commonly told in English literature.

Listen & Read

2 **Listen to and read the speech from** *Doctor Faustus*. **First, read for general understanding. Then, reread the speech. As you read the second time, ask yourself: what kind of a person is Faustus?**

This speech comes from Act 1, Scene 1, at the very beginning of the play. It takes place in Faustus' home (in Wittenberg, Germany) in the late 16th century. Here, Faustus talks about all of the things that he has learned and studied. One by one, he dismisses them for different reasons. In the end, he realizes that only one subject interests him: black magic.

FAUSTUS

Settle thy studies, Faustus, and begin
To sound the depth of that thou wilt profess:
Having commenced, be a divine in show,
Yet level at the end of every art,
And live and die in Aristotle's works.
Sweet *Analytics*, 'tis thou hast ravished me:
Bene disserere est finis logices.
Is to dispute well logic's chiefest end?
Affords this art no greater miracle?
Then read no more, thou hast attained the end;
A greater subject fitteth Faustus' wit.
Bid on kai me on farewell; Galen come:
Seeing, *ubi desinit philosophus, ibi incipit medicus.*
Be a physician, Faustus, heap up gold,
And be eternized for some wondrous cure.
Summum bonum medicinae sanitas.
The end of physic is our body's health.
Why Faustus, hast thou not attained that end?
Is not thy common talk found aphorisms?
Are not thy bills hung up as monuments,
Whereby whole cities have escaped the plague,
And thousand desperate maladies been eased?
Yet art thou still but Faustus, and a man.
Couldst thou make men to live eternally,
Or, being dead, raise them to life again,
Then this profession were to be esteemed.
Physic farewell! Where is Justinian?
Si unaeademque res legatur duobus
Alter rem, alter valorem rei, etc.
A petty case of paltry legacies:
Exhereditare filium non potest pater nisi…
Such is the subject of the Institute,
And universal body of the law:
This study fits a mercenary drudge
Who aims at nothing but external trash!
Too servile and illiberal for me.
When all is done, divinity is best:
Jerome's Bible, Faustus, view it well:
Stipendium peccati mors est: ha! Stipendium, etc.
The reward of sin is death? That's hard.
Si pacasse negamus, fallimur, et nulla est in nobis veritas. If we say that we have no sin,
We deceive ourselves, and there's no truth in us.
Why then belike we must sin,
And so consequently die.
Ay, we must die an everlasting death.
What doctrine call you this? *Che serà, serà*
What will be, shall be! Divinity, adieu!
These metaphysics of magicians,
And necromantic books are heavenly!
Lines, circles, schemes, letters, and characters!
Ay, these are those that Faustus most desires.
O what a world of profit and delight,
Of power, of honor, or omnipotence
Is promised to the studious artisan!
All things that move between the quiet poles
Shall be at my command: emperors and kings
Are but obeyed in their several provinces,
Nor can they raise the wind, or rend the clouds;
But his dominion that exceeds in this
Stretcheth as far as doth the mighty mind of man:
A sound magician is a mighty god.
Here Faustus, try thy brains to gain a deity.

Respond

3 Respond to the speech by answering these questions with a partner.

1. Was your prediction about the main ideas of the speech correct? Explain.
2. How did the author communicate the main ideas? Pick one (or more) and explain.
   a with images b with dialogue c by explaining them directly
3. Which of the words from the phrase bank do you think best describe how Faustus feels in the speech? Explain.

Phrase Bank

- excited
- scared
- ashamed
- upset
- sad
- interested
- worried

Understand

4 Read the questions and choose the correct answers.

1. What does Faustus say is the goal of logic?
   a to perform miracles
   b to argue well
   c to help people
   d to get rich
2. What can you deduce about Faustus?
   a He is a well-known doctor.
   b He has no children of his own.
   c He enjoys his job.
   d He does not have many friends.
3. What does Faustus dislike about the subject of law?
   a It inspires greed in people.
   b It cannot make a person famous.
   c It is unimportant and tedious.
   d It takes too much time to learn.
4. What does Faustus NOT hope to get from black magic?
   a riches
   b fame
   c political position
   d god-like power

Figurative Language

5 Work with a partner. Find one example of personification and one example of a metaphor in the speech.

Summarize

6 First, fill in the graphic organizer based on the speech you read.

Character(s)

Setting

Main Idea(s)

7 Now, use your graphic organizer to summarize the speech with a partner.

Listen

8 Listen to a lecture about *Doctor Faustus*. Then, answer the questions.

1 What aspect of *Doctor Faustus* is the speaker discussing?
   - a its symbols
   - b its themes
   - c its characters
   - d its background

2 Why does the speaker mention Germany?
   - a to show where the play takes place
   - b to explain where the idea for the play came from
   - c to point out an important detail in the play
   - d to illustrate the global influence of the play

Translate

9 **Marlowe wrote** *Doctor Faustus* **sometime shortly before his death in 1593. The language he used is very different from the English that people use today. Look at the example below. Use it as a guide to translate the rest of the speech into modern English on a separate piece of paper with a partner. Leave the ancient Greek and Latin as they are.**

Original	Modern
Settle thy studies, Faustus, and begin To sound the depth of that thou wilt profess; Having commenced, be a divine in show, Yet level at the end of every art, And live and die in Aristotle's works. Sweet *Analytics*, 'tis thou hast ravished me: Bene disserere est finis logices. Is to dispute well logic's chiefest end? Affords this art no greater miracle? Then read no more, thou hast attained the end; A greater subject fitteth Faustus' wit. Bid on kai me on farewell; Galen come:	Decide on your studies, Faustus, and start To measure the extent of what you will declare; Having begun, be a theologian in appearance, But aim at the goal of every art, And live and die in Aristotle's works. Sweet *Analytics*, you have swept me off my feet: Bene disserere est finis logices. Is arguing well the main goal of logic? Does this subject hold no greater miracle? Then read no more, you have reached the goal; Faustus' intellect is worthy of a greater subject. Say goodbye to on kai me on; come here, Galen:

About the Title

The story of Faust, the man who sold his soul for knowledge, power and wealth, has been told and retold in book, poem, and on film. It comes from a German legend that had been translated into English in 1592, so the story would have been very familiar to audiences in Marlowe's time. The Faustian theme tells people that they should not overstep their natural boundaries. That is, people should not try to achieve more than they can naturally achieve. People should be satisfied with what they do have and accept their limitations. This is Faust's fatal flaw: being dissatisfied with the limits of his own knowledge. Certainly, the pursuit of knowledge is not bad in and of itself. But when Faustus comes up to the edge of knowledge, he wants to go beyond, and this desire supersedes everything else in his life – even his own sense of morals. When a character acts in such a way, people immediately think of Faust, and understand the consequences.

10 *Doctor Faustus* **is the shortened name of the play. The real name is** *The Tragicall History of the Life and Death of Doctor Faustus*. **Over time, the name of the play was shortened. Answer the following questions with a partner.**

- Why do you think that the name of the play was shortened?
- Why do you think Marlowe chose the name *Doctor Faustus*, rather than just calling the play (and character) *Faust*?
- If you could choose a new name for the play, what would it be?

4

Analyze the Characters

11 Fill It In.

First, listen to the lecture. Then, complete the graphic organizer.

Character	Attributes	Conflict
Faustus		
Mephastophilis		

12 Think About It.

Use the graphic organizer to write a short descriptive paragraph about Faustus. Write another about Mephastophilis.

13 Talk It Over.

Share your paragraph with a partner. As a class, discuss the paragraphs.

Analyze the Setting

14 Fill It In.

First, listen to the lecture. Then, fill in the graphic organizer.

Aspect of Setting	Importance
time	
place	

15 Think About It.

With a partner, discuss the importance of the setting in *Doctor Faustus*.

16 Talk It Over.

As a class, discuss the graphic organizer. Then, answer the following question.

- Could the play take place in a different setting?

Analyze the Symbols

17 Match It.

Some of the important symbols in the play are blood, the good and bad angels, and Faustus' contract. Match the symbols with their meanings.

Symbols

1 ☐ Faustus' blood
2 ☐ good and bad angels
3 ☐ Faustus' contract

Meanings

A the duality of human nature, Faustus' conscience
B Faustus' descent into black magic, the permanency of his decision
C Faustus' soul, his inner spirit

18 Think About It.

Share your answers to the previous activity with a partner. Then, discuss why you chose the answers that you did.

19 Talk It Over.

As a class, discuss the following question.

- Which symbol is most important to the play and why?

About the Meter

20 **Answer the following question with a partner.**

Though *Doctor Faustus* was published later than many of Shakespeare's plays, it was performed before them all. Marlowe was, in fact, the first playwright to use blank verse in the English language, and it is virtually certain that he inspired the other Elizabethan playwrights to do so too. Like Shakespeare, Marlowe uses unrhymed iambic pentameter. Interestingly, his characters only use it in the serious scenes. In the comic scene that follows every serious scene, prose is used.

- Why do you think Marlowe chose to use verse and prose in the way he did?

Analyze the Themes

21 Fill It In.

There are many different themes in Faustus' speech. The graphic organizer lists some of the most important. Find lines from the speech that are related to each of the themes.

Theme	Lines from Speech
knowledge	
rejection of the past	
magic and the supernatural	

22 Think About It.

Which theme do you think is most important to this speech and why?

23 Talk It Over.

Discuss your answer to the previous question with the rest of the class.

In-Depth Analysis: Tragic Hero

Doctor Faustus is a tragedy. The main character in a tragedy is a "tragic hero." Thus, Faustus, who is the main character in the play, is a tragic hero. These characters follow a specific pattern – one that was laid out many years ago by the ancient Greeks.

There are three important characteristics of tragic heroes. First of all, they must have something wrong with them. That is, they must have a tragic flaw. Usually, the tragic hero is not completely immoral or bad. Instead, they have this one little problem that they need to work on. Inevitably, it is this problem that causes their downfall. In Faustus' case, it is his unceasing and overreaching quest for knowledge. It's important to remember that Faustus is not the villain in the play. That is, he is not, in himself, an evil person. He just wants to push the limits of human understanding a little too far. He is still the protagonist, or main character, of the play, and as such the audience are on his side despite his shortcomings.

Secondly, the hero's tragic flaw must result in ruin for the tragic hero. A tragedy is not a simple and easily fixable mistake. Instead, it is a total transformation of the tragic hero's life. He loses everything, for example, or he even dies. In Faustus' case, he ends up selling his soul and gaining very little. Understanding Faustus' character arc – or the changes that his character goes through in the story – reveals a lot about his ruin. At the beginning of the play, Faustus is a very smart man who wants to learn everything that he can. He's well-respected and important. Over the course of the play, however, he becomes nothing more than a prankster. He loses the respect of his colleagues. In addition, he loses his own soul. Obviously, Faustus' tragic flaw is directly related to his eventual ruin.

Finally, the audience must feel a mixture of fear and pity for the tragic hero. Audience members should be afraid because they can see some of themselves in the tragic hero. They should feel sorry for the hero for the same reason. Tragedies should remind people that no one is perfect. Everyone has flaws, and sometimes those flaws lead to serious consequences. Doctor Faustus is a sympathetic character in many ways. The audience can certainly relate to his attempt to improve his place in the world and his desire for fame and knowledge.

24 **Read the In-Depth Analysis. What are three characteristics of a tragic hero?**

- ....
- ....
- ....

25 **Explain how each of the characteristics listed above relates to Faustus.**

- ....
- ....
- ....

26 **With a partner, write a paragraph explaining why Faustus is or isn't a tragic hero.**

VIDEO See p. 225 for video activities & essay writing

Write

27 **The passage from *Doctor Faustus* is the first speech the audience hear from the main character. Write a 250- to 300-word essay explaining how the speech shows Faustus to be a tragic hero, using direct quotations where possible.**

5 The Importance of Being Earnest

Objectives

By the end of this unit, you will:

- know about the author and the background information behind the play
- thoroughly understand the passage from the play
- be able to identify figurative language in the passage
- be able to summarize the passage
- be able to analyze the title, characters, setting, symbols, and themes of the play
- know about social class in some depth
- be able to use the passage to support your opinions and write a literature essay

VIDEO

Learn About ... Oscar Wilde

Oscar Wilde (1854-1900) was a famous Irish playwright, poet, and novelist, whose plays began to gain recognition in the early 1890s. The plays generally dealt with life in Victorian society and were mostly comedies. In these plays, Wilde gently poked fun at Victorian social mores, but in such a way as not to be offensive. In fact, his plays were very successful commercially. At the height of his success, Wilde wrote *The Importance of Being Earnest*. Audiences loved it and it became very popular. Unfortunately, Wilde was involved in a scandal which led to his imprisonment, and despite its immense popularity, the play was cancelled after only eighty-six performances. Today, *The Importance of Being Earnest* is probably Wilde's most enduringly popular work. It is still performed, and remains a very amusing and enjoyable play.

Predict

Step 1

Discuss these questions with a partner.

1 When choosing a marriage partner, does it matter if the two people have different backgrounds? Why or why not?

2 Who should decide who a person marries: that person, or his or her parents? Explain.

Step 2

Look at the key words from the passage from *The Importance of Being Earnest*. With a partner, discuss the meanings of the words. Then, predict the main ideas of the passage.

Background information

1 Read the text and answer the questions.

1. Why does Jack sometimes use a different name?
2. What makes Lady Bracknell unwilling to allow Jack to marry Gwendolen?
3. Where does Algernon first meet Cecily?
4. How does Lady Bracknell realize that Jack is her nephew?
5. When did Wilde's works begin to gain popularity again?

The Importance of Being Earnest is Oscar Wilde's most famous play. It takes place in the 1890s in Britain and tells the story of two young men: Jack and Algernon. Jack is in love with Algernon's cousin, Gwendolen. He asks Algernon if he can pursue Gwendolen romantically. Algernon says yes, so Jack spends some time alone with Gwendolen. He tells her that his name is Ernest. This is the name that he has always used in London, so that he can act as he wishes without damaging his reputation. At home in the countryside, when he's caring for his ward, Cecily (a ward is a person that someone else is obligated to care for), he goes by the name of Jack and says that the wild Ernest is his brother.

Gwendolen agrees to marry Jack. However, she thinks his name is Ernest and is so impressed by and obsessed with the name that Jack decides to change his name legally to Ernest. Next, he talks to Gwendolen's mother, Lady Bracknell, about marrying Gwendolen. At first, she seems agreeable, but then she realizes that Jack was found abandoned at a train station as a baby and she withdraws her consent.

In the meantime, Algernon has met Jack's ward, Cecily. In order to see her, he has visited Jack's home in the countryside, claiming to be Ernest, Jack's brother. Cecily is very interested in meeting Ernest, about whom she has heard so many stories. The two talk, fall in love, and agree to marry. Algernon decides to change his name to Ernest as well. Later, both girls realize that the men have lied about their names.

Algernon tells Lady Bracknell of his intention to marry Cecily. She agrees, because Cecily is rich. But Jack refuses to give his consent unless Lady Bracknell allows him to marry Gwendolen. This is unacceptable to Lady Bracknell – until she sees Cecily's governess and recognizes her. When Lady Bracknell's sister's baby was first born, the same woman – his nursemaid at the time – left him at a train station by accident. This means that Jack is actually Algernon's brother and Lady Bracknell's nephew. Because he is now known to be a legitimate person, and not a strange orphan, Lady Bracknell agrees for him to marry Gwendolen. It is also revealed that Jack's given name is actually Ernest.

The opening night was described by Allen Aynesworth, who played Algernon and had a fifty-three-year career in theatre, as the greatest triumph he had ever witnessed. Due to Wilde's imprisonment, however, the play was forced to close. After Wilde's death in 1900, his reputation as an author slowly began to be resurrected. His plays have regularly been performed ever since, with *The Importance of Being Earnest* always being the most popular. It has been performed on television and radio numerous times, and there are three film versions, the most recent being in 2002, with Colin Firth, Judy Dench, and Reese Witherspoon all appearing.

Listen & Read

2 🎧 **Listen to and read the passage from *The Importance of Being Earnest*. First, read for general understanding. Then, reread the passage. As you read the second time, decide what Lady Bracknell believes about social class.**

This passage comes from Act 1 of the play. In this extract, Lady Bracknell interviews Jack about his social standing. She is trying to determine if he will be a good match for Gwendolen.

Lady Bracknell: Are your parents living?
Jack: I have lost both my parents.
Lady Bracknell: To lose one parent, Mr. Worthing, may be regarded as a misfortune; to lose both looks like carelessness. Who was your father? He was evidently a man of some wealth. Was he born in what the Radical papers call the purple of commerce, or did he rise from the ranks of the aristocracy?
Jack: I am afraid I really don't know. The fact is, Lady Bracknell, I said I had lost my parents. It would be nearer the truth to say that my parents seem to have lost me ... I don't actually know who I am by birth. I was ... well, I was found.
Lady Bracknell: Found!
Jack: The late Mr. Thomas Cardew, an old gentleman of a very charitable and kindly disposition, found me, and gave me the name of Worthing, because he happened to have a first-class ticket for Worthing in his pocket at the time. Worthing is a place in Sussex. It is a seaside resort.
Lady Bracknell: Where did the charitable gentleman who had a first-class ticket for this seaside resort find you?
Jack: [Gravely.] In a hand-bag.
Lady Bracknell: A hand-bag?
Jack: [Very seriously.] Yes, Lady Bracknell. I was in a hand-bag—a somewhat large, black leather hand-bag, with handles to it—an ordinary hand-bag in fact.
Lady Bracknell: In what locality did this Mr. James, or Thomas, Cardew come across this ordinary hand-bag?
Jack: In the cloak-room at Victoria Station. It was given to him in mistake for his own.
Lady Bracknell: The cloak-room at Victoria Station?
Jack: Yes. The Brighton line.
Lady Bracknell: The line is immaterial. Mr. Worthing, I confess I feel somewhat bewildered by what you have just told me. To be born, or at any rate bred, in a hand-bag, whether it had handles or not, seems to me to display a contempt for the ordinary decencies of family life that reminds one of the worst excesses of the French Revolution. And I presume you know what that unfortunate movement led to? As for the particular locality in which the hand-bag was found, a cloak-room at a railway station might serve to conceal a social indiscretion —has probably, indeed, been used for that purpose before now—but it could hardly be regarded as an assured basis for a recognised position in good society.
Jack: May I ask you then what you would advise me to do? I need hardly say I would do anything in the world to ensure Gwendolen's happiness.
Lady Bracknell: I would strongly advise you, Mr. Worthing, to try and acquire some relations as soon as possible, and to make a definite effort to produce at any rate one parent, of either sex, before the season is quite over.
Jack: Well, I don't see how I could possibly manage to do that. I can produce the hand-bag at any moment. It is in my dressing-room at home. I really think that should satisfy you, Lady Bracknell.
Lady Bracknell: Me, sir! What has it to do with me? You can hardly imagine that I and Lord Bracknell would dream of allowing our only daughter—a girl brought up with the utmost care—to marry into a cloak-room, and form an alliance with a parcel? Good morning, Mr. Worthing!

Respond

3 Respond to the passage by answering these questions with a partner.

1. Was your prediction about the main ideas of the passage correct? Explain.
2. How did the author communicate the main idea?

   Pick one (or more) and explain.

   a with images b with dialogue c by explaining them directly
3. Who are the major characters in the passage?
4. Which of the words from the phrase bank do you think best describes how Jack feels in the passage? What about Lady Bracknell? Explain.

Phrase Bank

• happy • nervous
• excited • frustrated
• sad • relieved
• indifferent

Understand

4 Read the questions and choose the correct answers.

1. What is true of Jack's parents?
   - a They died.
   - b They don't like him.
   - c They lost him somehow.
   - d They gave him up for adoption.
2. Where was Jack found?
   - a on a train
   - b in a town by the sea
   - c in a piece of luggage
   - d on a doorstep
3. How did Jack get his last name?
   - a It was on the train ticket of the man who found him.
   - b It is the same last name as the man who found him.
   - c It's the name of the city in which he was found.
   - d It's the name of the train station in which he was found.
4. What is Lady Bracknell's advice to Jack?
   - a not to worry about his lack of relatives
   - b to ask Thomas Cardew to adopt him
   - c not to tell anyone about his past
   - d to find at least one parent

Figurative Language

5 Work with a partner. Find one example of an oxymoron and one example of hyperbole in the passage.

5

Summarize

6 **First, fill in the graphic organizer based on the passage you read.**

Character(s)	Setting

Main Idea(s)	Conflict

7 **Now, use your graphic organizer to summarize the passage with a partner.**

Listen

8 **Listen to a lecture about** ***The Importance of Being Earnest*****. Then, answer the questions.**

1 What is the speaker mostly talking about?
- a different dramatic genres
- b qualities present in a farce
- c Wilde's use of humor in his plays
- d comedy in Victorian England

2 What is true of Lady Bracknell?
- a She is to be taken seriously.
- b She is based on a real person.
- c She holds the same values as Wilde.
- d She represents a real attitude of the time.

Analyze the Title

Puns

A pun is a kind of wordplay, where a humorous or rhetorical effect is achieved because of the resemblance between two words. For example, the first line of William Shakespeare's *Richard III* contains a pun which plays on the resemblance between the words "son" and "sun":

Gloucester: Now is the winter of our discontent made glorious summer by this son of York ...

Oscar Wilde also liked to use puns in his plays, along with other rhetorical devices.

9 Look It Up.

Look at the three quotations from *The Importance of Being Earnest* below. Working with a partner, decide what the pun is in each one. Use a dictionary where necessary.

1 **Jack:** My dear Algy, you talk exactly as if you were a dentist. It is very vulgar to talk like a dentist when one isn't a dentist. It produces a false impression. *(Act I)*

2 **Gwendolen:** Personally I cannot understand how anybody manages to exist in the country, if anybody who is anybody does. The country always bores me to death.

Cecily: Ah! This is what the newspapers call agricultural depression, is it not? *(Act II)*

3 **Lady Bracknell:** Mr. Worthing, is Miss Cardew at all connected ... with any of the larger railway stations in London? I merely desire information. Until yesterday I had no idea that there were any families or persons whose origin was a Terminus. *(Act III)*

10 Think About It.

There are two different meanings to the play's title and they depend on a pun. Look at the definitions.

DEFINITIONS

earnest (adj): intensely serious and sincere

Ernest (proper noun): a man's name

- What are the two different meanings of the play's title? Explain why it's important to be both "earnest" and "Ernest" in the play.

11 Talk It Over.

Discuss your answers to the previous question as a class.

Analyze the Characters

12 Fill It In.

Look at the character map as you listen to the lecture. Then, fill in the missing names in the character map.

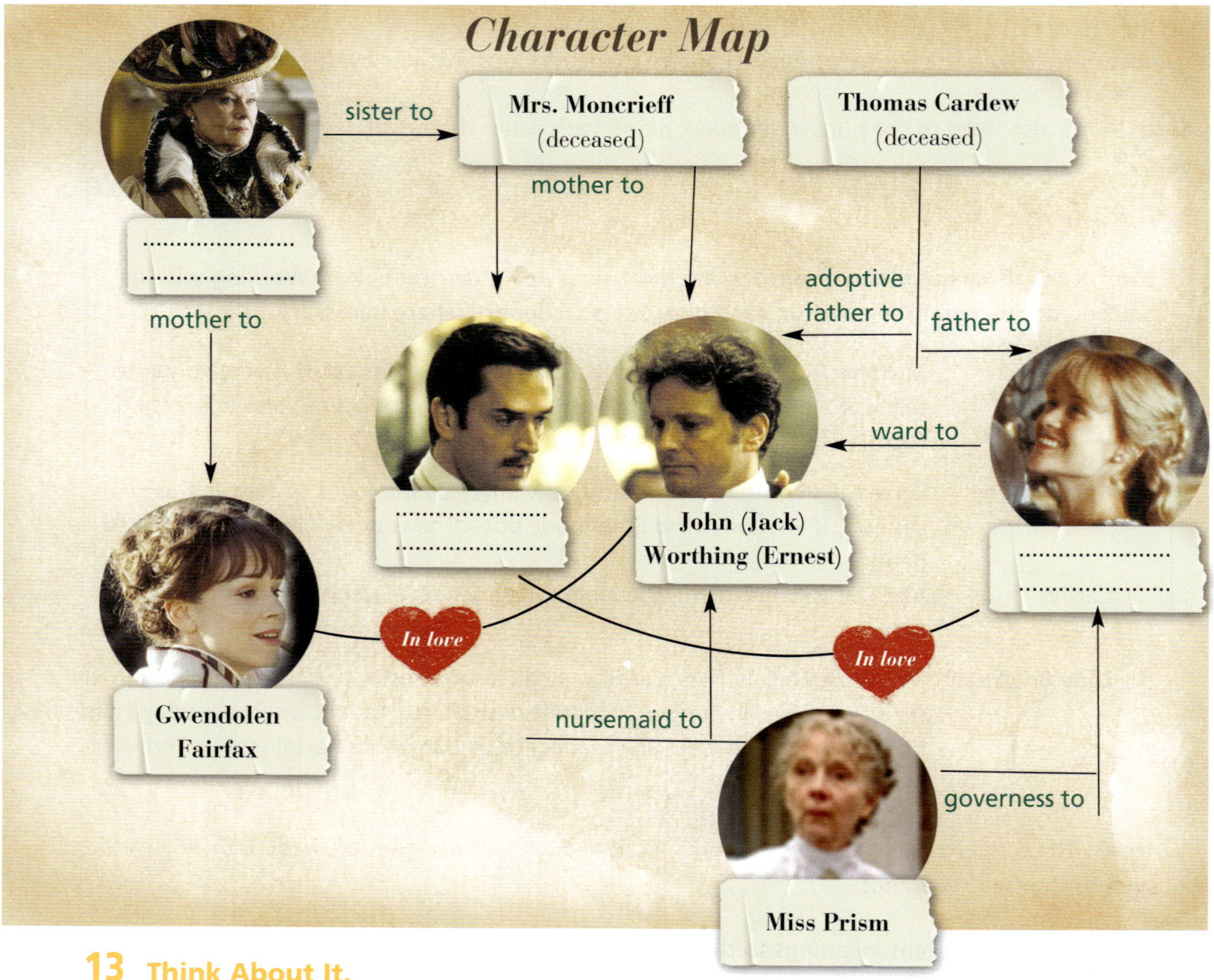

13 Think About It.

Use the character map to answer the following questions individually.

- What kinds of relationships do you see on the map?
- Around the time of the play, London's population was close to 6.7 million people. How likely do you think it would have been for these people to meet in real life?
- Based on the number of connections to other people, which character seems to be at the center of the action? Explain.

14 Talk It Over.

Discuss the answers to the previous questions with a partner. Share your ideas with the class.

Analyze the Setting

15 Fill It In.

Listen to the following lecture about the setting in *The Importance of Being Earnest*. Then, use information from the lecture to fill in the graphic organizer.

Aspect of Setting	Importance
time	
place	

16 Think About It.

Answer the following questions with a partner.

- How are the time and place in which the play occurs important to the story?
- How would the play be different if the time or place changed?

17 Talk It Over.

As a class, discuss your answers to the previous questions.

Analyze the Symbols

18 Match It.

Some of the important symbols in the play are the name "Ernest" and the hand-bag. Match the symbols to their meanings.

Symbols

1 ☐ Ernest
2 ☐ the hand-bag

Meanings

A deception, a double life
B class and status, social mobility

19 Think About It.

With a partner, discuss your answers to the previous question. Explain why you chose the answers that you did.

20 Talk It Over.

As a class, discuss the following question.

- Based on what you know about the play, which symbol do you think is most important? Why?

Analyze the Themes

21 Fill It In.

Two important themes in *The Importance of Being Earnest* are social status and marriage. Use lines from the passage to complete the graphic organizer.

Theme	Lines from passage
social status	
marriage	

22 Think About It.

Which theme do you think is most important in this passage and why?

23 Talk It Over.

Discuss your answer to the previous question with a partner.

In-Depth Analysis: Social Class

Most large societies have some concept of social class. People are placed in different groups according to their education, wealth, occupation, and ancestry, among other things. These divisions have been around as long as people have organized themselves into communities. In many places, these groups have become more sharply separated as time goes on. In some cases, new class divisions arise. When this happens, there is often conflict and uncertainty while people rearrange themselves into the new groups.

In Victorian Britain, social class was very important. In the past, there were basically only two classes in Britain: the upper class, or aristocracy, and the lower class, or peasantry. Members of the upper class owned land. The members of the lower class worked the land. With the start of the Industrial Revolution, however, more options became available to people. A new class, the middle class, began to develop. Sometimes, members of the middle class were richer than their upper class counterparts. The upper class was nervous about these newcomers. They were afraid that their position at the top of society was being threatened.

At the same time, the middle class recognized this antagonism and reacted against it. Instead of lauding idleness and frivolity as virtues, the middle class extolled hard work, being a self-made person, and adhering to such values as frugality, perseverance, and respectability. They rebelled against the upper class by rejecting the things that the upper class held dear.

In *The Importance of Being Earnest*, social class is of the utmost importance. Jack's adoptive family is not part of the aristocracy. Therefore, Lady Bracknell objects to his marriage to Gwendolen. At the same time, Algernon wishes to marry Cecily, who is below his station. To this, Lady Bracknell does not object – because of Cecily's wealth. And she of course relents when it is revealed that Jack is her own nephew. Wilde uses this play to poke fun at the upper class and demonstrate how hypocritical some of its values were. A play that deals with society in this way is often called a "comedy of manners"; this type of play has a long tradition in English literature.

24 **Read the In-Depth Analysis and answer the following questions individually.**

- What is social class?
- How did social class change in Victorian England?
- What were the results of this change?

25 **With a partner, discuss the role of social class in** *The Importance of Being Earnest* **by answering the following questions.**

- Which characters in the play are members of the upper class? Which are members of the middle class?
- What conflicts arise in the play as a result of the changing social structure in Victorian Britain?

26 **As a class, discuss the following question.**

- Does Oscar Wilde portray the upper class in a flattering or an unflattering way? Explain.

Write

27 **Social class is one of the most important themes in Oscar Wilde's play,** *The Importance of Being Earnest*. **At the time the play was written, society was changing. This led to lots of new conflicts and opportunities for misunderstandings. In a 250- to 300-word essay, discuss the role of social class in** *The Importance of Being Earnest*.

VIDEO See p. 226 for video activities & essay writing

Video Activities & Essay Writing

Poetry

1 | Sonnet 18

Video Activities

1 Watch the video and answer the questions.

1. Where was Shakespeare born?
2. How many sonnets did he write?
3. What is the main theme of *Sonnet 18*?
4. In which ways are Ovid's works similar to *Sonnet 18* by Shakespeare?
5. How many lines does *Sonnet 18* contain?
6. What rhythm is *Sonnet 18* written in?
7. What does Shakespeare compare his beloved to?
8. In which film does *Sonnet 18* appear?

2 Watch again and choose the correct words to complete the summary.

Shakespeare is best known for his plays and **1) prose/poetry.** His sonnets talk about love, time, beauty, and **2) life/death.** The first seventeen procreation sonnets focus on marriage and **3) children/families.** *Sonnet 18* is the first of the **4) Fair/Four** Youth sequence and has romance as its main theme.

The sonnet's first **5) ten/twelve** lines are divided into **6) three/four** quatrains of four lines each. The last two lines are the rhymed **7) meter/couplet.** In this sonnet, Shakespeare attributes qualities of everlasting beauty and **8) life/love** to his beloved, whose immortality is thus ensured.

Writing

Who is the most important person in the poem *Shall I Compare Thee to a Summer's Day?*, **the poet or the beloved?**

2 | She Walks in Beauty

Video Activities

1 **Watch the video and mark the sentences *T* (true) or *F* (false).**

1. Lord Byron's real name was George Gordon Byron. ....
2. Lord Byron was born in York, England. ....
3. He only wrote narrative poems. ....
4. *She Walks in Beauty* was written in 1814. ....
5. The poem contains 20 lines. ....
6. Light and darkness are the themes of the poem. ....

2 **Watch again and complete the summary.**

Lord Byron was born in England in **1)** .... He started writing poetry as a young **2)** .... He was a member of the **3)** .... movement. Lord Byron was a prolific writer. His most famous poem, *She Walks in Beauty*, is thought to be about either his cousin or his half-sister Augusta, or a metaphor for art's **4)** .... The poem begins with the description of a woman walking. The poet uses enjambment for the first four lines. This means he presents a line without **5)** .... and explains that same line with the next one. Byron compares the woman with the starry **6)** .... , showing the contrast between light and **7)** .... , a theme prevalent throughout the poem. Byron shows that these two separate things can come together to create **8)** ....

Writing

What idea of female beauty does Byron present in his poem *She Walks in Beauty*?

3 | Ulysses

Video Activities

1 Watch the video and answer the questions.

1 When was Alfred, Lord Tennyson born?
2 When did he start writing poetry?
3 In which collection did *Ulysses* appear?
4 Who wrote the *Odyssey*?
5 What do Ulysses in the *Odyssey* and Ulysses in *Inferno* have in common?
6 How many lines does *Ulysses* consist of?
7 What is the type of long speech Tennyson uses called?
8 What are the poem's main themes?

2 Watch again and choose the correct words to complete the summary.

Lord Tennyson was born in **1) Somersby/Plymouth**, England. He won the Chancellor's **2) Gold/Silver** Medal while still at college. He became Poet Laureate and took a seat in the House of **3) Poets/ Lords.** *Ulysses* was written during the **4) 1840s/1850s.** It is based on Odysseus, an ancient **5) Greek/Roman** king of Ithaca. The poem is written in unrhymed **6) trochaic/iambic** pentameter. Ulysses is making a speech recounting his emotions about coming back to Ithaca and how he would like to continue **7) fighting/traveling** although he is old. Simple but strong language is used together with enjambment to show Ulysses' **8) strength/anxiety** and unhappiness. Ulysses is a hero. Tennyson presents him as **9) cunning/brave** and determined. He possesses all the qualities that Tennyson respects, qualities which reflect the **10) Victorian/Elizabethan** ideals of the time.

Writing

To what extent is the Ulysses in Tennyson's poem a typical hero, and to what extent is he an unusual one?

Prose

1 | Robinson Crusoe

Video Activities

VIDEO

1 Watch the video and mark the sentences *T* (true) or *F* (false).

1 Daniel Defoe was born in 1760. ....
2 He was a merchant before he began political and journalistic writing. ....
3 *Robinson Crusoe* was published in 1731. ....
4 "Robinsonade" is a genre that includes a desert island story. ....
5 Defoe's sequel to *Robinson Crusoe* was a huge success. ....
6 Films such as 2000's Oscar-nominated *Castaway* and the highly rated show *Lost* have been influenced by *Robinson Crusoe*. ....

2 Watch again and complete the summary.

Daniel Defoe was born in London, England. In the **1)** .... he started writing novels. *Robinson Crusoe,* a novel about a **2)** .... experiences on a distant island, is mostly associated with real-life Scottish sailor and castaway Alexander Selkirk. This book has been deemed to be the first **3)** .... in the English language. The novel is set during the **4)** .... and the main part of the story takes place on an island close to South America. After setting off to collect African slaves, Robinson Crusoe becomes **5)** .... on the isolated Caribbean island in 1659. There, he has to fend for himself. Twenty-four years later he discovers that he shares the island with native **6)** .... However, he becomes friends with an escaped native that he names **7)** .... , who represents all the native peoples that were oppressed by European **8)** .... The ideas of society, **9)** .... , and colonization, and the rules and order that go along with them, are demonstrated by Crusoe's **10)** .... , use of European tools and weapons, and his attempt to make his native friend more "civilized."

Writing

From your reading of *Robinson Crusoe*, do you feel that Defoe meant it to be a moral tale? Why/Why not?

2 | Gulliver's Travels

Video Activities

1 Watch the video and answer the questions.

1. Where was Jonathan Swift born?
2. Who was he mainly brought up by?
3. What was his first job after he graduated university?
4. When and why did he die?
5. What was *Gulliver's Travels* inspired by?
6. What is Gulliver like?
7. Which places does Gulliver visit?
8. Which terms used in the book have become English expressions?

2 Watch again and complete the summary.

Jonathan Swift was born in 1667. Although he was in poor health, he began writing **1)** .... , poetry, and political works. His book *Gulliver's Travels*, **2)** .... in 1726 under a **3)** .... , is regarded as a satire with elements of fantasy and parodies the **4)** .... known as "travellers' tales". The book is about Lemuel Gulliver's voyages to various locations, which include **5)** .... places such as Lilliput, but also real ones like England and Japan. The usage of the **6)** .... locations is for satirical purposes and political **7)** .... The novel's main theme is politics as well as the practical use of science, the limits of human understanding, how class and **8)** .... affect society, and the relationships between lies and the truth.

Writing

How does Gulliver's role develop and change in the course of *Gulliver's Travels*?

3 | Pride and Prejudice

Video Activities

VIDEO

1 Watch the video and mark the sentences *T* **(true) or** *F* **(false).**

1 Jane Austen was born in 1775. ....
2 She came from a small family. ....
3 Jane Austen was home-schooled by her mother. ....
4 *Pride and Prejudice* was far from Austen's world. ....
5 Elizabeth Bennet is the narrator of the story. ....
6 Mr. Darcy is self-important and antisocial throughout the story. ....
7 The protagonists will have a happy marriage by placing importance on love and self-knowledge. ....
8 *Pride and Prejudice* is one of the most popular works of English fiction today. ....

2 Watch again and choose the correct words to complete the summary.

Set in the early 1800s, the novel is about Elizabeth Bennet and her four **1) married/unmarried** sisters, who are courted by various eligible bachelors. The novel focuses on Elizabeth's prejudice and Mr. Darcy's **2) arrogance/pride**, which originally prevent them from finding love. Many of the novel's characters consider money and **3) education/status** vital and they also learn that their relationships in society and their potential for marriage are affected by their **4) wealth/families** and social standing. In the end Elizabeth overcomes her prejudices through her **5) work/friendships** and relationships with others, especially Mr. Darcy. The book's characters have inspired authors either to create their own stories or imagine new people encountering them. Other authors, however, have put a modern spin on the tale, mashed different genres for the sake of **6) fun/parody**, or made graphic novels based on the work.

Writing

The first line of *Pride and Prejudice* **is: "It is a truth universally acknowledged, that a single man in possession of a good fortune must be in want of a wife." Does the way the novel develops reflect this?**

4 | Frankenstein

Video Activities

1 Watch the video and answer the questions.

1 When was Mary Shelley born?
2 Who were her parents?
3 When did she write *Frankenstein*?
4 What is the full title of the book?
5 Where does *Frankenstein* take place?
6 Which poets was Mary Shelley influenced by?
7 Why does the monster become angry and kill Frankenstein's friend and wife?
8 Which is the most well-known adaptation of the book?

2 Watch again and complete the summary.

Mary Shelley was born in **1)** .... , England. She married the **2)** .... Percy Bysshe Shelley in her late teens. Despite her money problems and her children's deaths, she continued writing books and **3)** .... her late husband's work. The **4)** .... of *Frankenstein* was conceived when Mary and her husband were in Geneva with Lord Byron and John Polidori. Although *Frankenstein* is set in the **5)** .... century and influenced by the century's idea that organisms could be brought to life using electricity, the story was actually written in the **6)** .... The novel mainly focuses on the potential for destruction in one's **7)** .... for knowledge and how unnatural forces can lead to monstrous results. The **8)** .... issues regarding Frankenstein's act of giving life to a **9)** .... thing and whether we should be able to do it are also raised by the author. A **10)** .... in science fiction, *Frankenstein* also incorporates gothic and horror elements.

Writing

In what way is *Frankenstein* an example of a Man versus Nature conflict, and which of the two is the "winner" in the end?

5 | Wuthering Heights

Video Activities

1 Watch the video and mark the following *T* (true) or *F* (false).

1. Emily Brontë was born in 1717. ....
2. Emily had to go away to school after her mother died. ....
3. Emily Brontë wrote poems as well as a novel. ....
4. Emily Brontë's real name was Ellis Bell. ....
5. Heathcliff was given the second name of 'Earnshaw'. ....
6. *Wuthering Heights* became more popular in later years. ....
7. Emily Brontë referenced Stephenie Meyer and Albert Camus. ....
8. More than one film has been made of *Wuthering Heights*. ....

2 Watch again and complete the summary.

Published in **1)** .... , Emily Brontë's novel *Wuthering Heights* is one of the great novels in English literature – although originally it was deemed **2)** .... and earned mixed reviews upon initial publication. Coming from a family of novelists and poets, it was the **3)** .... novel Emily wrote before her early death. Its **4)** .... is dark and Gothic. It is set during **5)** .... , around two houses on the **6)** .... moors: peaceful Thrushcross Grange, and dark and **7)** .... Wuthering Heights. At first the author focuses on how society and **8)** .... affect people's relationships, but as the story **9)** .... , the novel's main themes are the effects of revenge, love, and betrayal in our lives. Thanks to its power and **10)** .... , *Wuthering Heights* has inspired many adaptations, including operas, graphic novels, and a role-playing game.

Writing

Although *Wuthering Heights* has a happy ending, the picture it paints of love is dark and full of tragedy. To what extent do you consider this a realistic depiction?

6 | *Moby Dick*

Video Activities

1 Watch the video and answer the questions.

1. When was Herman Melville born?
2. What did he do for a living before writing professionally?
3. Which events was *Moby Dick* inspired by?
4. When does the story take place?
5. What happens to the main characters of the book in the end?
6. Why does Ahab want to take revenge on the whale?
7. How many members does the crew of the Pequod consist of?
8. Which actor took roles in two different screen adaptations of the book?

2 Watch again and complete the summary.

Their father's failed businesses meant the Melville children grew up in **1)** .... However, Herman was able to study the **2)** .... After an inspirational **3)** .... voyage and influenced by real-world events, Melville wrote a novel about a ship called the Pequod, and its captain's quest for **4)** .... against a huge white whale called Moby Dick. The characters' personality **5)** .... allow us to explore their social classes and **6)** .... systems. But the novel is also about the **7)** .... between good and evil, man and nature, and the destruction of sanity. However, it wasn't until the **8)** .... that the novel became critically recognized. After that, it was adapted for film and television, and a coffee chain even took its name from Captain Ahab's first mate!

Writing

Describe the character of Captain Ahab and explain why his crew follow him so willingly on his hunt for revenge.

7 | *Great Expectations*

Video Activities

VIDEO

1 Watch the video and mark the sentences *T* (true) or *F* (false).

1 Charles Dickens was born in Portsmouth. ....
2 His first job was writing for journals. ....
3 *Great Expectations* was published as a whole in 1862. ....
4 *Great Expectations* is set exclusively in London. ....
5 It is written in an autobiographical style. ....
6 In the novel, Pip falls in love with Estella. ....
7 Abel Magwitch was the benefactor of Pip. ....
8 The 1946 *Great Expectations* film won three Oscars. ....

2 Watch again and complete the summary.

Born in **1)** .... in England, Charles Dickens was raised in a poor family and started publishing his own work in journals to make a living. *Great Expectations* is one of his most **2)** .... works. It is a **3)** .... novel set in London and Kent in the first half of the 19th century. Written in the **4)** .... person, it has many interesting **5)** .... Dickens describes life's **6)** .... and the characters' struggle to survive. Readers follow Pip's narration from his early childhood to adulthood. The novel deals with the themes of crime, social class, and **7)** .... , as well as the relationships between love, good, and **8)** .... through the forbidden love of Pip for Estella. The novel's memorable characters and dramatic plot have been used in many books, films, and musicals.

Writing

How does the relationship between Magwitch and Pip develop through the course of *Great Expectations*, and in what way does this mirror the moral message behind the novel?

8 | *Strange Case of Dr. Jekyll and Mr. Hyde*

Video Activities

VIDEO

1 Watch the video and answer the questions.

1. When was Robert Louis Stevenson born?
2. When did he publish his first story?
3. What was Utterson's profession?
4. How does Dr. Jekyll transform into Mr. Hyde?
5. What does Mr. Hyde look like?
6. How many copies did the novella sell within six months of its publication?

2 Watch again and complete the summary.

Robert Louis Stevenson was born in Edinburgh, Scotland, and was mostly educated at home, due to his regular childhood **1)** .... *Strange Case of Dr. Jekyll and Mr. Hyde* was written in the early 1880s. In the Victorian era, people had to **2)** .... their feelings and personalities in order to display a **3)** .... and proper appearance. The main theme of the **4)** .... is the inner **5)** .... between the good side and the evil side in humans. The unemotional, **6)** .... Utterson represents the perfect Victorian gentleman, in contrast to the **7)** .... Dr. Jekyll, who struggles to deal with his evil side. *Strange Case of Dr. Jekyll and Mr. Hyde* was a huge success and has **8)** .... pop culture worldwide.

Writing

Most people nowadays know the true identity of Mr. Hyde before they start reading *Strange Case of Dr. Jekyll and Mr. Hyde*. **Does this spoil the novel for the modern reader?**

9 | The Picture of Dorian Gray

Video Activities

1 Watch the video and mark the sentences *T* (true) or *F* (false).

1 Oscar Wilde was imprisoned for his political beliefs. ....
2 Oscar Wilde's sole published novel is *The Picture of Dorian Gray*. ....
3 *The Picture of Dorian Gray* was first published in 1880. ....
4 The novel is set in North London. ....
5 Basil Hallward paints Gray's portrait. ....
6 With every sin he commits, Dorian Gray physically ages. ....
7 Lord Henry Wotton corrupts Dorian Gray. ....
8 The novel was initially criticized for its lack of ethics. ....

2 Watch again and choose the correct words to complete the summary.

Oscar Wilde, born in **1) Dublin/Edinburgh** in 1854, was a well-educated writer of many poems and plays. His only published novel, *The Picture of Dorian Gray,* revolves around **2) aestheticism/immortality** and Gray's double life. In London's West End he is outgoing and reveling in life's **3) pain/pleasures,** whereas in London's East End he is dark, **4) elegant/seedy**, and associates with **5) lowlifes/gentlemen.** Readers witness Gray's **6) ascent/downfall** from a beautiful, young man to a selfish **7) criminal/artist.** Adopting Wotton's **8) immoral/moral** opinions, he **9) loses/sacrifices** his soul for eternal **10) youth/maturity** and beauty. *The Picture of Dorian Gray* has been adapted for ballets, books, operas, and the cinema.

Writing

In the original preface to *The Picture of Dorian Gray*, Oscar Wilde wrote "All art is quite useless." Is this the impression you received from reading the novel?

10 | The Time Machine

Video Activities

1 Watch the video and mark the sentences *T* (true) or *F* (false).

1 H. G. Wells started writing his own material at a young age. ....
2 Humankind is seen as having a negative future in *The Time Machine*. ....
3 The Time Traveller travels over 800,000 years into the future. ....
4 The Morlocks hunted during the day. ....
5 One of the themes in the book is the concept of community. ....
6 *The Time Machine* was published in 1890. ....

2 Watch again and choose the correct words to complete the summary.

H. G. Wells is best known as one of the Fathers of Science Fiction. He became interested in reading after he broke his **1) arm/leg,** and started writing in the 1880s. He was influenced by **2) biology/math** and this lead him to write the **3) novel/poem** *The Time Machine*. It is set during the nineteenth century and features a **4) scientist/writer** called the Time Traveller, who travels to the future and first meets the Eloi and the Morlocks. The Eloi appear as **5) ugly/beautiful** adults who act like children while the Morlocks are **6) hideous/affectionate.** The story was influenced by Wells' political views. He believed that progress should happen for the **7) upper/lower** classes of society. Since its publication, *The Time Machine* has captured the imaginations of many and has been adapted for radio, television, and the **8) theater/cinema.**

Writing

Many people say that, although science fiction is set in the future, it is a critique of the present. From your reading of *The Time Machine*, would you say that this is true?

11 | The Hound of the Baskervilles

Video Activities

1 Watch the video and answer the questions.

1 What did Arthur Conan Doyle study?

2 Where was *The Hound of the Baskervilles* set?

3 Who is the narrator of the novel?

4 Who was originally believed to be responsible for the Baskervilles' family curse?

5 In which novel was Sherlock Holmes first introduced?

6 When was *The Hound of the Baskervilles* first published?

2 Watch again and complete the summary.

Born in **1)** .... in Edinburgh, Scotland, Arthur Conan Doyle wrote short stories while he was practicing medicine. The main character in his stories is detective Sherlock Holmes. His intelligence, **2)** .... way of thinking, and his use of **3)** .... and deduction in his criminal investigations made Holmes very popular. In the **4)** .... fiction novel *The Hound of the Baskervilles,* Holmes tries to **5)** .... the mystery of Sir Charles Baskerville's death. Written in **6)** .... style, the novel's main theme is the exploration of good versus evil. Holmes and his assistant, Dr. Watson, represent the importance of **7)** .... Conan Doyle's biggest influence was Dr. Joseph Bell and the lecturer's **8)** .... methods of observation. Conan Doyle was knighted by the King and made crime fiction popular as a literary genre.

Writing

The Hound of the Baskervilles **has been described as Arthur Conan Doyle's most Gothic novel. What elements of Gothic fiction does he employ, and how effective are they?**

Drama

1 | Romeo and Juliet

Video Activities

1 Watch the video and decide if the following sentences are *T* (true) or *F* (false).

1 William Shakespeare was born in the 1500s.
2 Shakespeare came up with the story of *Romeo and Juliet* completely on his own. ....
3 The story of *Romeo and Juliet* takes place mostly in the city of Verona, Italy. ....
4 Romeo and Juliet's servants are the main speakers in the play. ....
5 Romeo kills Mercutio as revenge for the death of his friend. ....
6 *Romeo and Juliet* only became popular after Shakespeare's death. ....
7 One theme of *Romeo and Juliet* is that fate can bring two people together, even if their families hate each other. ....
8 The 1968 film version of *Romeo and Juliet* won an Oscar. ....

2 Watch again and complete the summary.

In the mid-16th century, William Shakespeare was born in Stratford-upon-Avon in England, and grew up to have great **1)** .... as a playwright, actor, and poet. One of his most famous plays is *Romeo and Juliet,* a **2)** .... that takes place in Italy during the **3)** .... The main characters are Romeo, Juliet, Romeo's friend Mercutio, and Juliet's **4)** .... Tybalt. Although Romeo and Juliet love each other, the conflict between their families and the choice they make to get married ultimately lead to their **5)** .... However, this tragedy teaches their families to put aside their **6)** .... in the interest of peace. Adapted in film, literature, music, opera, and **7)** .... , this incredible story is still able to fascinate and **8)** .... people today.

Writing

In what way is the play *Romeo and Juliet* a good example of Man versus Society conflict?

2 | *Hamlet*

Video Activities

1 Watch the video and mark the sentences *T* (true) or *F* (false).

1 Shakespeare was born in the mid-15th century. ....
2 Shakespeare was a poet and actor. ....
3 *Hamlet* is based on a true story. ....
4 *Hamlet* takes place in the Kingdom of Denmark. ....
5 Hamlet killed his father to become King. ....
6 The full title is *The Tragedy of Hamlet, Prince of Denmark*. ....
7 King Claudius is Prince Hamlet's uncle, and husband to his mother, Queen Gertrude. ....
8 Suicide and fear of death are not important themes in the play. ....
9 Charles Dickens has been inspired by *Hamlet*. ....
10 *Hamlet* is one of history's most filmed stories. ....

2 Watch again and complete the sentences.

1 William Shakespeare was married to Anne Hathaway at ....
2 He had his own playing company, who constructed their own ....
3 Shakespeare wrote *Hamlet* using dramatic speech, complex language, and blank ....
4 Hamlet discovers that his uncle had killed his father and seeks ....
5 His actions following his father's death and his anger towards his Uncle Claudius eventually lead to his downfall and ....
6 While remorseful for his crimes, Claudius doesn't want to give up his life or his throne, so he plans ....
7 Gertrude, Hamlet's mother, does care for her son but feels ....
8 Betrayal, revenge, and immorality eventually lead to maddening and ....
9 In the play's most famous speech, Hamlet touches on the topics of suicide and ....
10 A lot of authors have been inspired by Hamlet and created Hamlet-like ....

Writing

The theme of death is very important in *Hamlet*. Discuss some of the devices Shakespeare uses to keep it at the front of our minds.

3 | As You Like It

Video Activities

1 **Watch the video and choose the correct word to complete the sentences.**

1. Shakespeare went to a **public/grammar** school.
2. *As You Like It* is a **tragedy/comedy**.
3. It is set in **England/France**.
4. It follows the story of Rosalind, who falls in love with **Orlando/Duke Frederick**.
5. Orlando's brother is **Oliver/William**.
6. Celia falls in love with **Orlando/Oliver**.
7. *As You Like It* explores the **differences/similarities** between urban and country life.
8. *As You Like It* was first published in **1623/1632**.

2 **Watch again and complete the summary.**

As You Like It features both prose and **1)** .... It was written between **2)** .... and 1600 in London, England. The main action takes place in the **3)** .... of Arden, which contrasts with the Duke's court. This shows us that love can grow outside when you are **4)** .... Rosalind dresses up as a man, Ganymede, and goes to the forest with her **5)** .... Celia, who is dressed up as a poor woman. By the end, Rosalind, Orlando, and various characters all find love and **6)** .... , and Duke Frederick gives his brother back his **7)** .... Rosalind is beautiful, smart, and **8)** .... Orlando gets angry very easily but this changes when he falls in love with Rosalind and becomes **9)** .... and romantic. Compared to Rosalind, Celia is shy and **10)** .... She doesn't believe in love until she meets Oliver. The play's main theme is **11)** .... and how it can affect people's behavior and **12)** .... "Too much of a good **13)** ...." is a well-known expression first coined in the play. The play has been adapted for the **14)** ....

Writing

How does love affect the different characters in *As You Like It*, **and what does this tell us about Shakespeare's idea of love?**

4 | Doctor Faustus

Video Activities

1 Watch the video and replace the words in bold with the words in the list.

- a German legend • wealth • Lucifer • in Canterbury • the good angel
- sin • in Elizabethan theater • in Wittenberg

1. Christophe Marlowe was born **there**.
2. His first plays were successful **there**.
3. *Doctor Faustus* is based on **it**.
4. The most important action in the story happens **there**.
5. Faustus makes a bargain with **him**.
6. **He** wants the doctor to repent for his sins.
7. *Doctor Faustus* also touches upon **it**.
8. The character of Faust has become associated with individuals who sacrifice their morals in exchange for **it**.

2 Watch again and complete the summary.

Doctor Faustus is a **1)** .... with a few moments of comedy. It is written in **2)** .... verse and prose. There are two known **3)** .... of the play, but scholars usually refer to Text A from 1604 as the most definitive. *Doctor Faustus* is set in **4)** .... The play's only narration is provided by the **5)** .... Doctor Faustus becomes completely absorbed by his pursuit of **6)** .... After calling up a devil named Mephastophilis, Faustus makes a bargain with Lucifer. In exchange for his **7)** .... , Faustus will have Mephastophilis as his servant for the next twenty-four years. Though **8)** .... warn him against it, Faustus continues his quest for the world's knowledge. Faustus is very intelligent but he is slightly **9)** .... and thinks learning magic will help him become even more powerful. But his fate is the same as Mephastophilis': they both serve only Lucifer. One of the play's major themes is the fight between good and evil. Although the good angel tries to warn Faustus, the bad angel does what he can to keep him on the **10)** .... to evil. Other key themes include the risks involved with the quest for **11)** .... and the nature of fate versus free will. The legend of Faust has inspired a wide range of art, from opera, literature, **12)** .... , and theatrical works to video games, movies, films, and music.

Writing

The battle between good and evil is the main theme of *Doctor Faustus*. Discuss.

5 | The Importance of Being Earnest

Video Activities

VIDEO

1 **Watch the video and answer the questions.**

1. What is the play's full title?
2. Where was Oscar Wilde born?
3. What does the play parody?
4. What does the plot revolve around?
5. How does Jack differ from Algy?
6. What is Algernon more interested in?
7. What is Gwendolen like?
8. What is Cecily like?

2 **Watch again and choose the correct words to complete the summary.**

The Importance of Being Earnest was written in **1) Dublin/Worthing**, England, in 1894, and moves between London and Hertfordshire during the mid-1890s. Wilde uses these locations to mock late **2) Elizabethan/Victorian** high society.

The plot revolves around two friends, John and Algernon, who try to avoid their **3) social/work** obligations pretending to be a made-up person named Ernest. John-as-Ernest proposes to Gwendolen, and Algernon-as-Ernest proposes to Cecily. After several situations, the truth is revealed: the two men are **4) cousins/brothers** and John's birth name really is Ernest. This means the two couples can be together. John and Algernon are well-educated, wealthy men. They both try hard to secure their engagements, and deal with the problem of brother Ernest. Jack is very **5) protective/offensive** towards Algernon. Algernon is **6) vain/arrogant.** He takes few things seriously and is more interested in having fun. Gwendolen considers herself more cultured than country girl Cecily due to her **7) city/family** upbringing. The play discusses how lying to get out of your duties can get out of control and how truth and **8) honesty/honor** ultimately win out. It also explores how **9) success/reputation** and social class affect relationships and stresses the importance of being sincere and, of course, earnest.

With a **10) loose/tight** plot and a climax that unfolds near the end, *The Importance of Being Earnest* is a well-made play. It has been adapted for the radio, opera, and television.

Writing

Lying plays an important role in *The Importance of Being Earnest*, **though it is not always portrayed in an entirely negative way. Discuss.**

Poetry

Unit 1 – *Sonnet 18*

(p. 14)
thee (pron) = you
temperate (adj) = mild, not extreme; Shakespeare uses it to mean that his love is pleasant, like mild summer days
darling (adj) = much loved
buds (n pl) = blossoms, flowers
summer's ... date (phr) = summer does not last nearly long enough
eye of heaven (phr) = sun
his gold complexion dimm'd (phr) = often the sun is covered by clouds
every ... declines (phr) = everything fair (nice, beautiful) eventually becomes less fair
nature's ... course (phr) = the natural passing of time
untrimm'd (v) = removed of decorations, made beautiful no longer
thy (pron) = your
eternal summer (phr) = everlasting youth
fair (n) = beauty
thou ow'st (phr) = that you have
shall (modal v) = will
brag (v) = boast
thou wander'st (phr) = that you walk
lines to time (phr) = lines of poetry set to a meter (i.e. this poem)
grow'st (v) = grow

Unit 2 – *She Walks in Beauty*

(p. 24)
climes (n pl) = regions
aspect (n) = facial expression
mellowed (v) = calmed, made relaxed
tender (adj) = soft, gentle
gaudy (adj) = showy, flashy
raven (adj) = black
tress (n) = piece of hair
serenely (adv) = calmly
dear (adj) = precious, valuable
o'er (prep) = over
eloquent (adj) = expressive
tints (n pl) = flushes of color, as from blushing
all below (phr) = all people on the Earth

Unit 3 – *Ulysses*

(p. 34)
profits (n pl) = benefits
idle (adj) = inactive
hearth (n) = fireplace
barren (adj) = empty
crags (n pl) = cliffs
mete and dole (phr) = give out piece by piece
savage (adj) = uncivilized
hoard (v) = save up for the future
to the lees (phr) = to the last drop
thro' (prep) = through
scudding (v) = moving quickly and easily
drifts (n pl) = currents
the Hyades (n) = a constellation that supposedly signals bad weather
vext (v) = (past of vex) upset
roaming (v) = wandering
councils (n pl) = groups of people with various responsibilities
ringing (adj) = loud, noisy
wherethro' (conj) = through which
gleams (v) = shines
margin (n) = border
dull (adj) = boring; also, not shiny
unburnish'd (adj) = unpolished
eternal (adj) = everlasting
tho' (conj) = though
vile (adj) = disgusting, offensive
hoard (v) = shut away for future use
yearning (v) = desperately wanting
bound (n) = boundary, limit
sceptre (n) = scepter, a symbol of authority
discerning (v) = understanding
prudence (n) = wisdom
rugged (adj) = rough, uncultured
subdue (v) = tame, bring under control
centred (v) = most focused
sphere (n) = area
decent (adj) = adequate
offices (n pl) = obligations, roles
tenderness (n) = warmth, kindness
meet (adj) = proper
adoration (n) = worship
port (n) = place where ships dock
vessel (n) = ship
gloom (v) = become dark
mariners (n pl) = sailors
souls (n pl) = people
toil'd (v) = worked very hard
wrought (v) = worked
frolic (adj) = merry, happy
free hearts, free foreheads (phr) = free souls and minds
hath yet (phr) = still has
ere (prep) = before
work of noble note (phr) = noble act
unbecoming (adj) = unfitting, inappropriate
strove (adj) = (past of strive) struggled, fought
wanes (v) = comes to an end
deep (adj) = ocean, sea
'tis (contraction) = it is
seek (v) = look for
smite (v) = hit with force
sounding (adj) = making noise, loud
furrows (n pl) = deep, narrow grooves; here, it refers to track a boat makes in water
holds (v) = stays the same
baths/Of all the western stars (phr) = the oceans at the end of the world
gulfs (n pl) = abysses, deep canyons
the Happy Isles (n pl) = paradise, where heroes go after they die
Achilles (n) = a Greek hero who fought in the Trojan War
abides (v) = remains
equal temper (phr) = same thoughts and feelings
yield (v) = give in

Prose

Unit 1 – *Robinson Crusoe*

(p. 49)
exceedingly (adv) = very
thunderstruck (adj) = shocked
apparition (n) = spirit or ghost
a rising ground (phr) = a place that is higher than the surrounding area
fancy (n) = imagination
how...thither (phr) = how it got there
innumerable (adj) = many
fluttering (adj) = moving about very quickly without a pattern
fortification (n) = fortress, safe place
terrified to the last degree (phr) = extremely frightened
fancying (v) = imagining
affrighted (adj) = scared, frightened
whimsies (n pl) = silly ideas
as first contrived (phr) = like I first planned
apprehensions (n pl) = suspicions, ideas about bad things to come in the future
contrary (adj) = opposite
dismal (adj) = depressing
devour (v) = eat
perish (v) = die
want (n) = a lack (of something important, like food)

Glossary

Unit 2 – *Gulliver's Travels*

(p. 58)

academy (n) = a place where people study
growing waste (phr) = becoming run-down
warden (n) = a person in charge of an institution
projectors (n pl) = scientists, people involved in projects
meagre (adj) = meager, thin
aspect (n) = appearance, stature
singed (v) = burned
extracting (v) = removing, taking out by force
phials (n pl) = small bottles
hermetically sealed (phr) = closed in such a way so as to be airtight
raw (adj) = wet and cool
inclement (adj) = stormy
entreated (v) = begged
ingenuity (n) = intelligence, cleverness
dear (adj) = expensive
made (v) = gave
present (n) = gift
furnished me (phr) = given me
calcine (v) = change the chemical composition of something by heating it up, but remaining below the melting point
likewise (adv) = also
treatise (n) = academic paper
malleability (n) = ability to be molded or changed in shape
contrived (v) = developed
prudent (adj) = wise, practical

Unit 3 – *Pride and Prejudice*

(p. 68)

countenance (n) = facial expression
unaffected (adj) = not insincere
merely (adv) = simply
mien (n) = appearance
in general circulation (phr) = being talked about throughout the group
ten thousand a year (phr) = the amount of money (£10,000) that Darcy makes in a year, roughly equivalent to between $500,000 and $750,000 a year in today's terms after adjusting for inflation
pronounced (v) = said with authority
declared (v) = said with authority
disgust (n) = a feeling of great distaste
turned the tide of his popularity (phr) = changed the way people felt about him (i.e. people no longer liked him)
above his company (phr) = felt superior to the people around him
above being pleased (phr) = too proud to give into the good nature of the people around him
estate (n) = a large piece of property consisting of a building or buildings (usually a large home) and land
Derbyshire (n) = a region in central England
forbidding (adj) = unpleasant, unfriendly
made himself acquainted (phr) = met
principal (v) = important
unreserved (v) = not shy
amiable (v) = agreeable
occasionally (adv) = from time to time
violent (adj) = intense
slighted (v) = insulted by ignoring

Unit 4 – *Frankenstein*

(p. 78)

dreary (adj) = depressing, dark
beheld (v) = saw
toils (n pl) = work
amounted to (phr) = reached
agony (n) = extreme discomfort, pain
instruments of life (phr) = tools that Frankenstein will use to bring the creature to life
infuse (v) = put
a spark of being (phr) = an electric shock
pattered (v) = made a light tapping sound
dismally (adv) = in a depressing manner
panes (n pl) = windowpanes, pieces of glass
glimmer (n) = a faint light
convulsive (adj) = as if produced by convulsions or seizures, jerky, fitful
agitated (v) = moved
limbs (n pl) = arms and legs
catastrophe (n) = disaster
delineate (v) = describe accurately
wretch (n) = worthless person
infinite (adj) = everlasting
pains (n pl) = trouble
endeavoured (v) = tried, attempted
in proportion (phr) = the right size as compared to one another and the rest of the body
scarcely (adv) = barely
arteries (n pl) = tubes in the body through which blood moves
lustrous (adj) = shiny
luxuriances (n pl) = extravagances, nice but unnecessary things
horrid (adj) = causing horror, extremely awful
dun (adj) = gray-brown
shrivelled (adj) = wrinkled and dried up
complexion (n) = the color and appearance of a person's face
changeable (adj) = easily changed
inanimate (adj) = incapable of independent movement
deprived (adj) = denied, not allowed
ardour (n) = passion, enthusiasm
far exceeded moderation (phr) = was very excessive
vanished (v) = disappeared
endure (v) = put up with
aspect (n) = appearance
traversing (v) = walking around
compose (v) = calm
lassitude (n) = tiredness, fatigue
tumult (n) = excitement

Unit 5 – *Wuthering Heights*

(p. 88)

winsome (adj) = charming
indulge (v) = allow yourself something improper
sulkily (adv) = moodily, in an upset way
let it out (phr) = talk about it, admit it
consent (n) = agreement, acceptance
denial (n) = refusal
the old lady and gentleman (phr) = Edgar's parents
obstacle (n) = problem
striking (v) = hitting
breast (n) = chest
make it out (phr) = understand
mock at me (phr) = laugh at me, make fun of me
distinctly (adv) = clearly
the wicked man in there (phr) = her brother, Hindley
brought Heathcliff so low (phr) = made Heathcliff so uncivilized, treated Heathcliff so badly

degrade me (phr) = bring me down (socially, morally)
perished (v) = died, went away
annihilated (v) = completely destroyed
foliage (n) = leaves, greenery
resembles (v) = is the same as
eternal (adj) = everlasting

Unit 6 – *Moby Dick*

(p. 98)
eyeing (v) = looking at
superior (n) = boss
seemed struck with a thought (phr) = seemed to get an idea
thy (pron) = your
thee (pron) = you
aye (excl) = yes
my hearties (phr) = my good men, my sailors
dismasted (v) = literally, broke the mast (a tall pole on a ship) off; here Ahab uses it to mean the whale bit off his leg
sob (n) = a loud sharp breath taken while crying
heart-stricken (adj) = hit in the heart with a weapon
accursed (adj) = hateful
razeed (v) = literally, removed the top deck from a ship; here Ahab is again referring to his injury
pegging (adj) = walking on a peg leg
lubber (n) = a clumsy person
measureless (adj) = countless
imprecations (n) = curses
Good Hope (n) = one of the southern most points of Africa
The Horn (n) = Cape Horn, one of the southernmost points of South America
Norway's Maelstrom (n) = a strong current off the coast of Norway
perdition (n) = a doomed, terrible place where evil people go when they die
rolls fin out (phr) = dies
splice (v) = to join
harpooneers (n pl) = people who use weapons called harpoons to kill whales
seamen (n pl) = sailors
lance (n) = a weapon used to hunt whales
steward (n) = a person on a ship whose job it is to bring people food and drink
draw (v) = to pour
great measure (phr) = large amount
grog (n) = a kind of drink
long face (phr) = sad expression
wilt thou (phr) = will you
art not game for Moby Dick (phr) = aren't you eager to catch Moby Dick
vengeance (n) = revenge
how many barrels will thy vengeance yield thee even if thou gettest it (phr) = how many barrels of spermaceti will revenge earn you
it will not fetch thee much (phr) = you won't get much
Hoot (excl) = exclamation of amusement
thou requirest a little lower layer (phr) = you need a different explanation
if money's to be the measurer (phr) = if money is going to be the way we measure success
accountants (n pl) = people who keep track of money
computed (v) = calculated
girdling (v) = circling
guineas (n pl) = coins
three parts of an inch (phr) = third of an inch (about 0.8 cm)
fetch (v) = to get
premium (n) = price
smites (v) = hits
methinks (v) = I think
rings (v) = echoes
vast (adj) = very big in size
dumb (adj) = unable to speak or reason
brute (n) = animal
smote (v) = (past of smite) hit, struck, attacked
blindest instinct (phr) = most natural behavior
enraged with (adj) = full of anger for
blasphemous (adj) = disrespectful, going against the natural order of things

Unit 7 – *Great Expectations*

(p. 108)
concluded (v) = finished
I wish you ever well (phr) = I hope that you'll always be well
ever prospering to a greater and greater height (phr) = always succeeding and improving
all the "Sir" melted out (phr) = all the formality and stiffness left
chap (n) = man, boy
partings (n pl) = goodbyes
welded together (phr v) = joined by heat (usually used to refer to metals)
blacksmith (n) = a person who makes things out of iron or steel
whitesmith (n) = a person who makes things out of light metals, like tin
goldsmith (n) = a person who makes things out of gold
coppersmith (n) = a person who makes things out of copper (a kind of metal)
diwisions (n pl) = divisions, separations (the misspelling is meant to replicate Joe's working-class accent)
such (pron) = such people
figures (n pl) = people
what is private (phr) = in private places
beknown (v) = known
ain't (non-standard contraction) = is not
right (adj) = good, natural
wrong (adj) = unnatural
forge (n) = a blacksmith's workshop
meshes (n pl) = marshes, wetlands
forge dress (phr) = working clothes
supposing as (phr) = if
anvil (n) = a large block of iron on which blacksmiths work with hot metal pieces
dull (adj) = unintelligent
beat out (phr v) = figured out
nigh the rights (phr) = close to the truth
fancy (n) = idea, thought
dignity (n) = nobility, worth, respectability
dress (n) = clothing
recover myself sufficiently (phr) = calm myself down enough

Unit 8 – *Strange Case of Dr. Jekyll and Mr. Hyde*

(p. 118)
by theory (phr) = based on what I think
probable (adj) = likely
nature (n) = essential aspects of a person's character
stamping efficacy (phr) = overwhelming ability to be effective
robust (adj) = strong, healthy
deposed (v) = forcefully removed from power
virtue (n) = good behavior
slighter (adj) = thinner

countenance (n) = face, expression
broadly (adv) = widely
lethal (adj) = deadly
imprint (n) = mark, impression
deformity (n) = misshapenness
decay (n) = the state of decomposing or breaking down
idol (n) = something that looks like a god and that people worship
conscious (adj) = aware
repugnance (n) = disgust, horror
bore (v) = (past of bear) carried, had
livelier (adj) = more active
express (adj) = definite
single (adj) = having only one part
hitherto (adv) = up until this point
accustomed to call (phr) = used to calling
wore the semblance (phr) = looked like
misgiving (n) = feeling of uncertainty
flesh (n) = body
commingled (v) = blended
alone in the ranks of mankind (phr) = alone among all humans
lingered (v) = paused
conclusive (adj) = putting an end to any question
attempted (v) = tried
beyond redemption (phr) = without the hope of getting it back
flee (v) = run with the intention of escaping
dissolution (n) = the breaking apart into different fragments
stature (n) = way of holding the body

Unit 9 – *The Picture of Dorian Gray*

(p. 128)
conjecture (n) = guesses
fair (adj) = attractive
enamoured of (phr) = attracted to, in love with
corruption (n) = the process of becoming bad
minute (adj) = very thorough
hideous (adj) = shockingly disgusting
coarse (adj) = rough
bloated (adj) = swollen
mocked (v) = made fun of
sordid (adj) = dirty, filthy
ill-famed (adj) = having a bad reputation
assumed name (phr) = fake name used to keep people from discovering him
frequent (v) = visit often
poignant (adj) = strong, sadly touching
gratification (n) = satisfaction
ravenous (adj) = incredibly large

Unit 10 – *The Time Machine*

(p. 138)
hasty (adj) = overly quick
refrain (v) = stop
bitterly (adv) = resentfully, cynically
foliage (n) = leaves
fertile (adj) = supporting much life
gay (adj) = happy, pleasant
hither and thither (phr) = here and there
keen (adj) = very strongly felt
cupolas (n pl) = domed structures
steadfastly (adv) = unchangingly
watchword (n) = motto, creed
attained (v) = achieved
toiler (n) = worker
versatility (n) = the ability to do many things well
compensation (n) = payment
partake (v) = take part
feeble (adj) = weak
effected (v) = brought about
disjointed (adj) = out of order
retained (v) = kept
perforce (adv) = by necessity
initiative (n) = the ability and desire to do something
hitherto (adv) = up until this point
mortal wit (phr) = the human mind

Unit 11 – *The Hound of the Baskervilles*

(p. 148)
patter (n) = the sound of light quick steps
bank (adj) = a low long stretch of fog or cloud
fifty yards (phr) = about forty-five meters
glared (v) = stared intently
break from the heart of it (phr) = come out from the middle of it
exultant (adj) = happy because of a success
inert (adj) = not moving
paralyzed (adj) = not able to move
hound (n) = a kind of dog used for hunting
mortal (adj) = human
smouldering (adj) = smoldering, creating smoke but no flame
muzzle and hackles and dewlap (phr) = snout, hair, and neck
delirious (adj) = confused, disturbed
savage (adj) = uncontrolled, fierce
appalling (adj) = terrible, horrible
be conceived (v) = be thought of
bounds (n pl) = steps
track (n) = path, small road
following hard upon (phr) = following close behind
apparition (n) = thing that appears, usually supernatural
nerve (n) = courage, ability to act
vulnerable (adj) = able to be hurt
mortal (adj) = living
I am reckoned fleet of foot (phr) = people say that I am a fast runner
outpaced (v) = outran
the little professional (phr) = Lestrade, the police officer
spring (v) = jump
hurl (v) = violently throw
worry (v) = shake while held with the teeth
emptied five barrels of his revolver (phr) = shot his revolver five times
flank (n) = side of the body between the bottom of the ribs and the hip
shimmering (adj) = shining
insensible (adj) = not sensing anything, unconscious
brandy-flask (n) = bottle with brandy (a kind of liquor) in it

Drama

Unit 1 – *Romeo and Juliet*

(p. 160)
soft (exclamation) = wait, be quiet
yonder (adj) = that
breaks (v) = emerges
discourses (v) = talks
bold (adj) = brave, forward
fairest (adj) = most beautiful
entreat (v) = ask
spheres (n pl) = orbits
shame (v) = embarrass by outperforming
doth (v) = does
airy region (phr) = sky
stream (v) = shine
Ay me (phr) = oh my, oh dear
thou (pron) = you
art (v) = are
glorious (adj) = deserving of praise and honor
o'er (prep) = over
white-upturned (adj) = looking up so that the whites are showing

mortals (n pl) = human beings
lazy-pacing (adj) = slowly moving
bosom (n) = chest
wherefore (adv) = why
deny (v) = refuse to recognize
refuse (v) = do not accept
wilt (v) = will
sworn (v) = promised
thy (pron) = your
owes (v) = owns
doff (v) = remove
thee (pron) = you
baptized (v) = given an official name
henceforth (adv) = from here on
bescreen'd (v) = hidden, covered
stumblest (v) = stumble, come across
counsel (n) = private thoughts
saint (n) = good, virtuous person
Had I it written (phr) = If I had it written (down)
utterance (n) = speech
How camest thou hither (phr) = How did you get here
kinsmen (n pl) = relatives
o'er-perch (v) = fly over
Alack (exclamation) = Alas
peril (n) = danger
thine (pron) = your

Unit 2 – *Hamlet*

(p. 170)
slings (n pl) = attacks
outrageous (adj) = outside the bounds of normal decency
fortune (n) = fate
take arms (phr) = fight
that flesh is heir to (phr) = that we inherit just by being born human
consummation (n) = fulfillment
devoutly (adv) = seriously, sincerely
perchance (adv) = perhaps
rub (n) = catch, problem
shuffled off this mortal coil (phr) = cast off these worldly cares
give us pause (phr) = make us think
calamity (n) = disaster
contumely (n) = rude insults
pangs (n pl) = sudden, sharp pains
despised love (phr) = love felt for a person that is not returned
insolence (n) = rudeness
office (n) = official people, the authorities
spurns (n pl) = rejections
that patient merit of the unworthy takes (phr) = that a patient person gets/suffers from an unworthy person
quietus (n) = death
a bare bodkin (phr) = a naked or unsheathed dagger
fardels (n pl) = burdens, cares
weary (adj) = tiresome
dread (n) = fear
bourn (n) = boundary, border
ills (n pl) = problems
conscience (n) = consciousness, inner awareness
native hue (phr) = natural color
resolution (n) = determination
sicklied o'er (phr) = negatively influenced by
cast (n) = color
enterprises (n pl) = undertakings, actions
pith (n) = strength, courage
moment (n) = importance
awry (adv) = off course

(p. 175)
unfold (v) = show, reveal
shrewdly (adv) = sharply
mattocks (n pl) = tools for digging
'a (pron) = he

Unit 3 – *As You Like It*

(p. 180)
merely (adv) = just
players (n pl) = actors
parts (n pl) = roles (as in a play)
ages (n pl) = stages of development
mewling (v) = crying with soft noises, like a cat makes
puking (v) = throwing up, vomiting
satchel (n) = book bag
furnace (n) = a container in which heat is created by burning e.g. wood
woeful (adj) = sad
ballad (n) = song
mistress' (n) = lover's
bearded like the pard (phr) = having bristly facial hair, like a leopard's whiskers
jealous in honour (phr) = protective of his good name
quick in quarrel (phr) = quick to get angry
seeking the bubble reputation (phr) = willing to do strange/ silly things to look good
even in the cannon's mouth (phr) = even in the face of danger
justice (n) = a respected person, a judge
good capon lined (phr) = full of good chicken
severe (adj) = serious
formal (adj) = proper, serious
saws (n pl) = sayings
instances (n pl) = examples
lean (adj) = thin
slipper'd (adj) = wearing slippers
pantaloon (n) = an old man who never leaves the house
spectacles (n pl) = eye glasses
pouch (n) = a small bag used to carry money
hose (n) = tight pants
shrunk shank (phr) = shrunken (reduced in size) leg
treble (n) = higher notes in music
pipes (n pl) = musical instruments that make a high noise
history (n) = a play that tells about things in the past
oblivion (n) = a state of not being aware of anything
sans (prep) = without

Unit 4 – *Doctor Faustus*

(p. 190)
sound (v) = determine
thou (pron) = you (Faustus is talking to himself)
wilt (modal v) = will
profess (v) = claim, declare, say openly
commenced (v) = graduated
divine (n) = theologian, person who studies religion
in show (phr) = in appearance
level (v) = aim
art (n) = subject
Aristotle's (proper n) = Aristotle was a famous Greek philosopher
Analytics (proper n) = a book by Aristotle about logic
'tis (contraction) = it is
hast (v) = has
ravished (v) = had a powerful emotional effect on
Bene dissrere est finis logices (phr) = The purpose of logic is to create a good argument (Latin)
dispute (v) = argue
chiefest (adj) = most important
Affords this art (phr) = does this subject have
attained (v) = reached
end (n) = goal
fitteth (v) = fits
wit (n) = intelligence
on kai me on (phr) = Greek phrase meaning 'philosophy'
Galen (proper n) = an important ancient medical authority
ubi desinit philosophus, ibi incipit

medicus (phr) = where the philosopher leaves off, the doctor begins (Latin)
physician (n) = doctor
heap (n) = pile
eternized (v) = immortalized, remembered forever
Summum bonum medicinae sanitas (phr) = Latin, translated in the following line
end (n) = purpose
physic (n) = medicine, the medical field
Is not thy common talk found aphorisms? (phr) = Don't people take your everyday words as accepted wisdom?
bills (n pl) = prescriptions
whereby (conj) = through which, because of which
the plague (n) = a terrible disease from medieval times
desperate (adj) = without hope
maladies (n pl) = diseases
eased (v) = made easier to bear
but (adv) = just, simply, only
Couldst (modal v) = could
eternally (adv) = forever
esteemed (adj) = highly thought of
Justinian (proper n) = a Roman law authority
Si unaeademque res legatur duobus
***Alter rem, alter valorem rei,* etc.** (phr) = an inheritance law in Latin
petty (adj) = not important
paltry (adj) = unimportant, worthless
legacies (n pl) = things that people leave to others when they die
Exhereditare filium non potest pater nisi... (phr) = another Latin inheritance law
Institute (n) = principles of the law
mercenary (adj) = only motivated by money
drudge (n) = a person who does boring, meaningless work
external (adj) = outside of the mind
servile (adj) = suitable for a slave
illiberal (adj) = vulgar, in poor taste
divinity (n) = the study of religion
Jerome's Bible (phr) = a version of the Bible that was translated into Latin
sin (n) = disobedience, knowingly doing something wrong
Stipendium ... veritas (phr) = lines in Latin from the Bible; Faustus translates them in the following lines
deceive (v) = fool, trick
belike (adv) = probably
doctrine (n) = a specific set of beliefs
Che serà, serà (phr) = translated in the following line
adieu (excl) = goodbye
metaphysics (n) = ideas about the world that are not based on scientific observations
necromantic (adj) = having to do with black magic
heavenly (adv) = enchanting, interesting, delightful
Lines ... characters (phr) = special markings used in magic spells
omnipotence (n) = ultimate power
studious (adj) = studying a lot
artisan (n) = skilled worker
quiet (adj) = still, unmoving
poles (n pl) = the North Pole and the South Pole
at my command (phr) = under my authority
several (adj) = separate
provinces (n pl) = areas of authority
rend (v) = tear, split apart
dominion (n) = area of influence
stretcheth (v) = stretches
doth (v) = does
sound (adj) = in good condition
try (v) = test
deity (n) = the essential nature of being a god

Unit 5 – The Importance of Being Earnest

(p. 200)
purple (n) = royalty
commerce (n) = trade, buying and selling industries
Was he...? (phr) = Lady Bracknell is making a subtle joke. In the past, wealthy people were born into the purple (a color associated with royalty) of the aristocracy (the upper-upper class) or worked their way up through the means of trade or commerce. In the time of the play, however, wealth from commercial enterprises was becoming more widespread and it was more likely for a wealthy person to have been born into a commercial family than to have been born into an aristocratic one. Those who were members of the aristocracy often had to work to get there, usually by organizing advantageous marriages.
charitable (adj) = generous
disposition (n) = nature
seaside resort (n) = a vacation spot near the beach
hand-bag (n) = a small suitcase that is able to be easily carried
locality (n) = area, neighborhood
cloak-room (n) = a place where people may store their luggage for a short period of time
Victoria Station (prop n) = a busy railway station in London
Brighton line (prop n) = a part of the railway system that goes back and forth between London and Brighton (a town on the south coast of Britain)
is immaterial (phr) = doesn't matter
bewildered (adj) = confused, overwhelmed
contempt (n) = disrespect, hatred
decencies (n pl) = behaviors that are considered appropriate
that reminds...to? (phr) = During the French Revolution, many social institutions crumbled under pressure from political groups. The revolution was a very tumultuous period in French history and many people died. In addition, political unrest spread throughout Europe, leading to other conflicts.
indiscretion (n) = behavior that shows a lack of good judgment
season (n) = the social season, in which fashionable people spent time in London (as opposed to their country houses) and went to parties and balls. For many young women, it was the time during which they hoped to find an eligible husband.
alliance (n) = partnership
parcel (n) = a package